BRED FOR THE PURPLE

Bred for the Purple

Michael Seth-Smith

LESLIE FREWIN : LONDON

First published in 1969
by Leslie Frewin Publishers Limited,
One New Quebec Street, Marble Arch, London W1

Set in Scotch Roman
Printed by Anchor Press
and bound by William Brendon
both of Tiptree, Essex

World Rights Reserved
09 096220 6

Contents

□□□

Foreword

by His Grace the Duke of Norfolk, KG

☐☐☐

THE HISTORY of horse-racing is a treasure trove for all lovers of the sport, so aptly named 'The Sport of Kings'. In *Bred for the Purple* Michael Seth-Smith has written about the influence, hopes, ambitions, triumphs and disappointments of members of the Royal Family on the Turf. Against the background of their lives and the eras in which they lived, he has succeeded in showing the reasons for their interest in horse-racing. These reasons are highlighted by the use of letters in the Royal Archives at Windsor, which give a more personal insight into the pleasure that our kings, especially Edward VII and George V, found in following the careers of their race-horses. Royal horses have never been exempt from either the good luck or ill fortune which is constantly present in racing, and Michael Seth-Smith has colourfully described not only their victories and defeats but also the personalities of the trainers, jockeys and owners associated with them. No racing victory is more popular than that of a royal success and I am glad to say that we can read of many such moments in *Bred for the Purple*. Those people who are interested in the breeding and racing of the thoroughbred and who read this book will realise what a great part the Royal Family has played through hundreds of years in this enthralling occupation. As a nation we have been fortunate that this is so. In the coming years the interest shown by the Queen will always be an incentive to those who love the Turf.

Author's Introduction

☐☐

ON A COLD, wet January afternoon at Windsor races I mentioned to Sir Martin Gilliat, Private Secretary to Her Majesty the Queen Mother, that I had been invited to write a book about royal race-horses throughout the last three centuries. It was a suggestion which appealed to me, for our Kings and Queens have influenced racing in England ever since King James I first visited the village of Newmarket in 1605. I queried with Sir Martin Gilliat the possibility of there being any unpublished papers on this subject, and with his invariable kindness and understanding he offered his help. Days later I received a letter informing me that Her Majesty the Queen had given her gracious permission for me to see such relevant papers in the Royal Archives at Windsor Castle as might be available. I wish to acknowledge my gratitude to Her Majesty for allowing me the privilege of access to them.

During my visits to Windsor Castle I was given every possible assistance by the Librarian, Robert Mackworth-Young, and also by his staff headed by Miss Jane Langton. I wish to express my thanks not only for the efficient manner in which they answered my queries, but also for the skill with which they read letters and documents which I could not have comprehended without their expert and practised understanding of the handwriting of others.

It has been my intention throughout the book to describe the racing careers of the royal owners in relation to many events in their lives. It is my belief that this necessitates discussing their youth and their approach to racing. I must make it clear, however, that the views expressed are entirely my own, and are not derived from my researches in the Royal Archives, where I only saw material directly connected with racing.

Throughout the past ten months many people have generously helped me with information incorporated in this book, and I wish to thank them all. In particular Brigadier the Lord Tryon, Marcus Marsh, Gordon Fergusson a godson of Lord Wavertree, Miss Joyce Tomkinson, the Earl of Derby, Richard Shelley, and Mrs 'Bill' Rickaby; also Messrs Faber and Faber for permission to use an extract from *Memories of Racing and Hunting* by the Duke of Portland, Messrs Heinemann for an extract from the Greville Diaries and Messrs Cassell and Professor Aspinall for permission to quote the letters from Fox to Mrs Armistead.

Finally I wish to thank my wife, Mary, because without her help and encouragement I do not think that this book would ever have been written. I should owe her a great debt of gratitude if only for the innumerable hours she has spent typing the manuscript, but when I remember also her wise criticism and suggestions, and even more her forgiveness of my utter absorption and absentmindedness which on one occasion resulted in my posting a bar of chocolate instead of her letters, I realise to what an extent this book is also hers.

M S-S

Horsham, Sussex
March 1969

1

Early Days

□□

ATHELSTAN, GRANDSON of Alfred the Great, was the first
Saxon monarch to assume the title of King of England.
Crowned in AD 925 he possessed great ambition and ability,
and realised the importance of horses both in war and peace.
Before his death in AD 941 he attempted to improve horse-
breeding in his kingdom, and decreed that no horses should
be sent abroad except as royal presents – although he was
delighted to receive Germanic running horses as a gift from
Hugh Capet of France. His efforts were without avail and a
century later William the Conqueror made full use of the
superiority of his cavalry at the Battle of Hastings.

From this time successive kings, ever eager to possess the
finest horses in the land, were willing to accept horses
instead of money for the renewal of grants or the payment
of fines. Edward III spent one thousand marks on purchasing fifty Spanish horses and went to immense trouble to
ensure their safe conduct to England. When they arrived at
the Royal Stud it was estimated that each horse had cost
the King thirteen pounds, an enormous sum by the standards of the day. The prices asked by the dealers at Smithfield market for such horses, or those bred in Lombardy and
Italy, soared so high that in the reign of King Richard II a
proclamation was issued restricting the price at which
horses could be sold. This proclamation was ordered to be
published in the counties of Cambridge and Lincoln and the
East and North Ridings of Yorkshire, then the principal
breeding areas of England.

The Tudor Kings continued to encourage the breeding of

valuable horses. Henry VIII decreed that no stallion at stud should be less than fifteen hands, and that no stallion under fourteen and a half hands who was over the age of two years, should be allowed to run on forest, moor or common where there were mares. In 1514 Francesco Gonzaga, Marquis of Mantua, presented the King with some of his finest thoroughbreds which were sent to the Royal Stud at Hampton Court. Queen Elizabeth, recognising the knowledge of Neapolitans concerning the breeding of horses, commissioned Prospero d'Osma to report on the Royal Studs. There was no intention, however, of training the horses to race, even though the Queen attended a race-meeting at Salisbury only a few months before the Spanish Armada was sighted off Plymouth. Nearly four hundred years later Queen Elizabeth II won a race at Salisbury on 29th June 1967 with her horse Spanish Invader.

Salisbury races and those at Chester, Carlisle, Lanark and Stamford were unorganised in the days of 'Good Queen Bess', and the horses that competed were little more than slow, sturdy cavalry chargers who, although handsome and suitable for pageantry, had no pretensions to speed. The prizes for which they competed were usually bells adorned with flowers, and the races themselves only provided part of the day's sport.

Horse-racing began to make popular appeal during the reign of King James I. He loved the village of Newmarket and was content to establish his Court there whilst he spent his days hunting the hare and hawking in the vicinity. He was not especially interested in horse-racing, but was sufficiently shrewd to realise that the sport amused his courtiers. He was genuinely intrigued by the study of horse-breeding and was responsible for the purchase of the Markham Arabian. He died in March 1625, described as 'the wisest fool in Christendom'. Those of Puritanical thought were scandalised that he had ordered a pamphlet entitled *Book of Sport* to be read in churches on Sundays. The theme of the document was that, as their working week allowed men

12

no time for physical exercise, they should play games after church on the Sabbath. These games included archery, dancing and the 'sports of the maypole'.

Two years after King Charles I came to the throne, spring and autumn race-meetings were established at Newmarket. The races were invariably matches, with the horses ridden by gentlemen, whose grooms had been instructed to gallop the horses until they were fit enough to race. Pall Mall, a game recently introduced from France, tennis and cock-fighting also took up much of the Court's leisure hours whilst at Newmarket. Poaching in the vicinity was rife, and in 1636 the King commissioned Sir John Carleton, owner of Cheveley Park and a Deputy Lieutenant for the County of Cambridge, to preserve all game within a twelve-mile radius of Newmarket Palace – in reality a collection of buildings continually being added to by the Stuart Kings to provide accommodation for the Court. The preservation order was a difficult command to enforce, but nevertheless every innkeeper, common cook and alehouse keeper was bound in the sum of twenty pounds each year not to dress, buy or sell 'any venison, red or fallow, or any hare, pheasant, partridge or heath-poult'. The King, as a prisoner of the Parliamentary forces, paid his last visit to Newmarket in 1646. He remained only a few days, but the local squirearchy came to do him homage, he was cheered wherever he went, and flowers were strewn in his path.

Oliver Cromwell, although forbidding race-meetings for the reason that they might become a focal point of Royalist conspiracy, gave his approval to the breeding of horses and personally maintained a small stud, which included the famous White Turk and a mare subsequently known as the Coffin Mare, as she was discovered in a cellar at the time of the Restoration.

King Charles II had reigned for five years before he paid his first visit to Newmarket. A fine horseman, who loved to adjudicate in any sporting disputes, he frequently rode his own horse Old Rowley in matches, and his memory is perpetuated in the Rowley Mile. In 1665 he founded the Town Plate to be competed for on the second Thursday in October for ever, at a time when the people of England were still rejoicing at the overthrow of the Commonwealth. The exploits and escapades of the King and his noblemen and ladies of the Court were greeted with enthusiasm and John Evelyn wrote: 'I lodged this night at Newmarket where I found the jolly blades racing, dancing, feasting and revelling, more resembling a luxurious and abandoned rout than a Christian Court.' There was as much State business conducted from the Royal Palace at Newmarket as from Whitehall, and Pope claimed:

'Then Peers grew proud in horsemanship t'excell,
Newmarket's glory rose, as Britain's fell.'

King James II had little time to prove whether or not he might have patronised horse-racing, but King William III soon showed that he intended to support it whole-heartedly. He improved the Royal Stud at Hampton Court, ran horses at meetings throughout the land, and caused consternation by insisting that any horse valued in excess of five pounds owned by a Roman Catholic should be confiscated. In 1695 he appointed Tregonwell Frampton as Keeper of his Running Horses. For the next thirty years Frampton, professional gambler, trainer and match-maker, was the most influential figure at Newmarket and in legend has been described as 'The Father of the English Turf'. King William III died in March 1702, less than a month after he had fallen from his horse and broken his collar-bone whilst hunting with the Royal Staghounds near Hampton Court.

Queen Anne was thirty-seven years old when she succeeded to the throne. Her principal amusements were hunting in Windsor Forest, playing cards, and dancing as often as her gout would allow. She had been to Newmarket on several occasions before she became Queen and inherited

14

a stable there which was estimated to cost £13,260 per annum. In 1705 she announced her intention of returning to Newmarket and Sir Christopher Wren, as Surveyor General, was ordered to see that the Royal Palace, unoccupied since 1698, was made ready for Her Majesty's arrival. During her visit the Queen paid one thousand guineas for a running horse called Leedes and presented it to her Consort, Prince George of Denmark. Six years later she inaugurated Ascot races when she drove from Windsor Castle on Saturday 11th August 1711. Before her death in 1714 she had instituted 'Queen's Plates' at all the Ascot meetings and had encouraged race meetings at York, where she won races with her grey gelding Pepper and her bay horse Star. A spectator at Newmarket in the reign of Queen Anne described the scene:

> I had the opportunity to see the horse races, and a great concourse of the nobility and gentry, as well from London as from all parts of England, but they were all so intent, so eager, so busy upon the sharping part of the sport, their wagers and their bets, that to me they seemed just so many horse-coursers in Smithfield, descending, the greatest of them, from their high dignity and quality, to the picking one another's pockets, and biting one another as much as possible; and that with so much eagerness, as it might be said they acted without respect to faith, honor, or good manners. . . . You see no ladies at Newmarket, excepting a few of the neighbouring gentlemen's families, who come in their carriages to see a race, and then go home again.

Although neither King George I nor King George II took the slightest interest in racing, the fifty years following the death of Queen Anne saw the sport established as part of the national heritage of England. The famous stallion Flying Childers was foaled in 1715. Tregonwell Frampton died in 1727 at the age of eighty-six, and was buried at Newmarket after a lifetime spent as Keeper of Running Horses to five monarchs; in the same year the first Racing Calendar was published. Far more important was the first reference to

15

the newly formed Jockey Club which appeared in Mr John Pond's 1752 Calendar. The details concerned 'a contribution Free Plate to be run for at Newmarket in April by horses the property of the noblemen and gentlemen of the Jockey Club at the Star and Garter in Pall Mall'.

The first member of the Royal Family to be elected to the Jockey Club was William Augustus, Duke of Cumberland, second son of King George II. Born at Leicester House, London on 15th April 1721, it was his father's intention that he should enter the Navy. However within six months of his twenty-first birthday he was appointed to the rank of Major-General in the British Army. The next year he was badly wounded in the leg at the Battle of Dettingen, where 'he gave his orders with a great deal of calmness and seemed quite unwearied', according to a young ensign in the 12th Foot by the name of Wolfe, later to win immortality on the Heights of Abraham. Captain General of the British Army at the Battle of Fontenoy two years later the Duke fought heroically and Horace Walpole cynically wrote: 'Now he will be as popular with the lower class of men as he has been with the low women for the past three or four years. He will be the soldiers' great Sir as well as theirs.' In 1745 he commanded the army which routed and massacred the remnants of Bonnie Prince Charlie's Highland supporters at Culloden. In England, where he was considered a hero, he was given the Freedoms of York and London, and the sum of twenty-five thousand pounds a year was settled on him in addition to his Civil List income. Many public houses changed their name to 'The Duke's Head', Tyburn Gate was renamed Cumberland Gate and Handel wrote the oratorio 'Judas Maccabeus' in his honour. Only the jealousy of his elder brother the Prince of Wales, who surreptitiously fostered the news of Cumberland's cruel behaviour in Scotland by encouraging others to call him 'Butcher', marred his glory.

In the summer of 1745 he was appointed Ranger of Windsor Great Park and took up residence at Rangers (now Cumberland) Lodge. There were more than twelve hundred head of red deer in the Park, and in winter they were hunted every Tuesday and Saturday. The Hunt servants in their gold and scarlet livery, equipped with French horns, would single out from the herd the day's quarry. At the kill those who wished to run their horses for the King's Guineas at Ascot races had to apply to the huntsmen for tickets showing that they had qualified for entry by being present when the deer were pulled down by the hounds. The Duke loved hunting in the vast open heaths around Windsor where 'the broom and gorse and here and there impassable bogs and sheets of water dirty and deep' made it difficult country for the hounds and the horses. The Duke was not only addicted to hunting, but also was a Patron of the Prize Ring and was a great supporter of Jack Broughton, Champion of All England.

When in 1751 the Prince of Wales died and the question of a Regency was raised, the Duke was both indignant and mortified that he was not appointed as Regent. The reason was that he had influential and powerful enemies at Court, and the elder Pitt considered that he was too ambitious for self-aggrandisement. His antagonists were delighted when, after being recalled from virtual retirement to command the army defending Hanover, he was discredited by the signing of the peace treaty at Kloster Zevern in 1757. The King unfairly criticised him for failing in the campaign in which he had been surrounded by incompetent Hanoverian and Hessian officers with whom he was in continual disagreement. On his return to England he resigned from all his military appointments, and devoted the rest of his life to the breeding of race-horses, and as Ranger of the Great Park improving the royal property at Virginia Water, Ascot and Windsor. He was thirty-six years old, and described by Walpole as 'proud and unforgiving, fond of war for its own sake. He despised money, fame and politics, loved gaming, women and his own favourites, and yet had not one social virtue'.

Walpole's statement that Cumberland despised money was borne out by his generosity in giving his share of his father's estate to his two sisters. On a humbler scale was the occasion when he lost his pocket book containing hundreds of pounds at Newmarket races. When the book was returned to him by a half-pay officer, Cumberland insisted that the astonished soldier kept it, remarking: 'Keep it Sir, I am only glad that it has fallen into such good hands, for if I had not lost it as I did, its contents would now have been scattered among the blacklegs of Newmarket.' He had visited Newmarket for the first time in 1753. He would leave London early in the morning, and taking a route via Epping Forest and Bishop's Stortford would arrive at his destination some seven hours later.

During the year 1758 he made matches with his horse Spider, and also with the Rib colt, against horses owned by Lord Rockingham, the Duke of Bridgwater, the Duke of Devonshire and Lord Gowers. Most of these matches were for five hundred guineas a side and the records show that he lost more than he won. The following year he had thirty horses in training including five four-year-olds, six three-year-olds, and seven two-year-olds. In 1761 he bought a house in Upper Grosvenor Street from the Duke of Beaufort, gave away the bride at his nephew King George III's wedding, and later in the year stood as a sponsor at the christening of the Prince of Wales – subsequently King George IV. His love of racing made him a constant visitor both to Ascot and Newmarket where he had two fits in the autumn of 1763. He was enormously fat, had lost the use of one eye and was asthmatic. His old wound in his leg was giving him much pain and when an abscess formed on it he stoically braved the agony as the surgeon made the necessary incision. It was reported that he even held the candle during the operation. He died unmarried on 31st October 1765 at his Upper Grosvenor Street home. A

18

Cabinet meeting was about to take place in the House when he collapsed, suffering from a blood clot on the brain, into the arms of Lord Albemarle. He was buried with full military honours in Westminster Abbey.

Fifteen years earlier the Duke had been given Marske, a brown yearling colt, by John Hutton of Richmond, Yorkshire, in exchange for a chestnut Arabian. Marske gave the Duke's purple racing silks their first victory at Newmarket when he won the Jockey Club Plate in 1754. When Marske was retired to stud at Cranbourne Lodge he was not considered worthy to serve the Arab mares and at first was used only for farmers' mares at a fee of half a guinea and half a crown to the groom. Later he was allowed to serve the more valuable mares at the stud; including Spiletta, whom the Duke had bought from Sir Robert Eden in 1755. On All Fool's Day 1764 Spiletta gave birth to a common small colt foal. On the same day occurred the most total eclipse of the sun ever recorded. So little was thought of the foal that he was sold to a Mr Wildman, a Smithfield salesman, who on learning the circumstances of the birth of his new purchase decided on the obvious name of Eclipse. Horses were not seriously trained until they reached the age of four or five, and consequently Mr Wildman sent Eclipse to Epsom to be brought up until it was time for him to be raced. His breeder, the Duke of Cumberland, had been dead for nearly four years before Eclipse's first venture on Wednesday 3rd May 1769, when he competed for the Noblemen's and Gentlemen's Plate of fifty pounds, for horses that had never won thirty pounds, matches excepted, weight for age, four one-mile heats. There were four other contestants, one a five-year-old and the other three six-year-olds. Eclipse's training gallops had shown such promise that not only the touts but the entire sporting population of Epsom knew of his ability, and he started at very short odds. The first heat was little more than a procession and Eclipse, never out of a common canter, won easily ridden by John Whiting.

A curious incident, but one typical of the age, occurred before the second heat was run. It was obvious that Eclipse would win it, but there were doubts as to which of the other runners would be second. The notorious Captain O'Kelly, having judiciously discovered from Eclipse's jockey that he had every intention to win by as far as possible, loudly proclaimed that he would bet that he could place the remaining horses in the correct order. This prognostication, made by a man who had many enemies amongst the betting fraternity – chiefly because he usually managed to score off them – resulted in any number of wagers being accepted. Although it is almost certain that the owners of the other four runners agreed amongst themselves as to the outcome, they were outwitted completely by the astute Captain O'Kelly, who had remembered that the Jockey Club's Rules of Racing stated that if in a heat any horse was 'distanced' then officially he should be placed 'nowhere'. Eclipse won by so great a distance that the verdict 'Eclipse first and the rest nowhere', which was the Captain's forecast, proved correct and won him all his wagers.

Eclipse next ran in a fifty pounds Plate at Ascot which he won, before going to Winchester where he was successful in the King's 100 Guineas race. He ran on six more occasions during 1769 and won every time. His reputation was now established, but there were still some 'doubting Thomases' who claimed that he had never beaten a top class horse. However, in the spring of 1770, Mr Wildman matched Eclipse against Mr Wentworth's Bucephalus, the conditions being that the race was run over the Beacon course at Newmarket on 17th April, and Mr Wildman staking six hundred guineas to four hundred guineas, play or pay. Bucephalus was considered to be a champion, but he had no chance with Eclipse who trounced him.

Two days later Eclipse became the sole property of Captain O'Kelly, who the previous year had paid Mr Wildman four hundred and fifty guineas for a half share – no doubt out of his winnings when Eclipse distanced his rivals at Epsom. Mr Wildman insisted that his half share was now worth £1,500; but the incorrigible O'Kelly, always a gambler, but possibly one to whom 'loaded dice' were not unknown, suggested that the price should be either £1,000 or £2,000. He showed Mr Wildman three notes for £1,000 each, and put two of them in one of his coat pockets and the third in another pocket – inviting Mr Wildman to select one of the two pockets. The unfortunate vendor chose incorrectly and thus lost his share in Eclipse for a mere thousand pounds.

Within hours of Eclipse being bought outright by Captain O'Kelly the horse ran again at Newmarket, over a three and a half mile course. Once again he trounced his three opponents in the first heat, and in the second heat his owner again successfully wagered that the result would be 'Eclipse first, the rest nowhere'. During the rest of the season he ran on sixteen more occasions and was never seriously challenged by any of his rivals. There was no doubt in the minds of any who saw him race that he was a horse of exceptional ability, and was unbeatable.

Lord Grosvenor once offered O'Kelly the huge price of 11,000 guineas for Eclipse, but the offer was instantly refused. At a later date O'Kelly, when pressed to name his own price, suggested as the terms £20,000, an annuity of £500 a year for the rest of his life, and three brood mares. In fact he never seriously considered selling Eclipse, who won eleven King's Plates, was never touched by whip or spur, and became the most famous horse in the country. Once in a match he started at 70–1 on! The tragedy of Eclipse is that he was owned by Captain O'Kelly, who was never elected to any of the exclusive London clubs, and consequently was not able to enter Eclipse for the sweepstakes for which only horses owned by members of these clubs were eligible.

Eclipse was sixteen years old when the first Derby was run at Epsom, and the majority of modern thoroughbreds can be traced back in the male line to him. One of the immortal horses in Turf history he can justifiably claim to be the greatest horse ever bred. As a stallion he stood at Clay Hill, Epsom, where he died on the morning of 25th February 1789. Admittedly, the Duke of Cumberland was dead before Eclipse even raced, but nevertheless this great race-horse was 'bred for the purple'.

2

Florizel and Sam Chifney

□□□

ON 12TH AUGUST 1762 George Augustus Frederick,
first son of King George III, was born at St James's Palace.
His childhood, surrounded by nurses, tutors, governors and
clerics, and without the company of other children,
inevitably made him both spoilt and precocious. The
majority of his teachers were amply rewarded for their
services, and his Latin and Greek tutors became Archbishop of York and Dean of Christ Church. It must be
admitted that another of his instructors, Dr Dodd, was
hanged for forgery. As a boy the Prince once corrected Lord
Bruce for a mistake whilst quoting Greek. Offended by this
apparent humiliation Bruce resigned – only to be made an
Earl. Unlike his younger brothers, who were educated on
the Continent, the Prince of Wales remained in England,
cossetted, yet prevented by the Court's 'maddening hum-
drum, the stifling sobriety of its routine' from exercising
his high spirits. He believed that the Queen had brought
him up badly, and had taught him in all matters to equivo-
cate. His father, living more at Windsor and Kew than
London, constantly insulted him in front of his courtiers,
and jealously refused to accept him as more than a mere
child.

Against this background it is understandable that
Bishop Hurd gave as his opinion that the fifteen-year-old
Prince would become either the most polished gentleman
or the most accomplished blackguard in Europe – possibly
both. However, to the nation he was their Prince Charming,
born and bred in England. Tall, good looking and gracious,

his reckless escapades as a young man appealed and added to his popularity. Perdita Robinson, an actress and a beauty, and one of his first admirers, wrote of the 'irresistible sweetness of his smile, and the tenderness of his melodious yet manly voice', and showed him more affection than either of his parents.

In 1783, when the Prince attained his majority, the Whigs proposed that the King should give him one hundred thousand pounds a year from the Civil List. Outraged, the King did all in his power to prevent the independence of his son, and only with reluctance agreed to half this sum being provided whilst Parliament settled his outstanding debts. Installed in his own establishment of Carlton House the Prince chose as his friends such men as Burke, Sheridan and Lord Petersham, dandy and wit, under whose guidance he invented a new shoe buckle, an inch long and five inches wide. No one was more favoured by him than thirty-four-year-old Charles James Fox, who had inherited so many pleasure-loving characteristics from his ancestor King Charles II. Warm-hearted and a generous friend, Fox had made his political reputation by the brilliance of his oratory in a series of speeches on the American War. The King and Queen resented Fox's friendship with the Prince and accused him of leading their son to the three things they hated most – Wine, Women and Whigs. Also in royal disapproval was Georgiana, Duchess of Devonshire, who helped select the furniture and decorations for Carlton House, and who delighted to entertain the young Prince at Devonshire House, where he met not only politicians, but others willing to fawn upon their Florizel. He also met Mrs Fitzherbert.

It would seem, however, that the greatest influence was shown by his uncle, Henry Frederick, who had been created Duke of Cumberland a year after the death of the previous holder of that title, the 'Butcher of Culloden'. In 1771 the Duke had infuriated George III by marrying Mrs Horton, who had been born Ann Luttrell. Describing her, Horace

Walpole wrote: 'The new Princess of the Blood is a young widow of 24, extremely pretty, not handsome, very well made, with the most amorous eyes in the world, and eye-lashes a yard long. Coquette beyond measure, artful as Cleopatra and complete mistress of all her passions and projects.' No one was surprised that she enchanted her husband's nephew. Whether or not it was deliberately calculated to annoy the King, the dissipated Cumberland also set out not only to cultivate the friendship of the Prince of Wales, but to teach him the mysteries of the gambling card games Faro and Loo and Macao and Hazard. The Duke had succeeded his uncle 'Butcher' Cumberland as Ranger of Windsor Great Park and patron of Ascot races. His colt sired by Eclipse had run in the inaugural Derby in 1780, and he had entered horses which competed unsuc-cessfully in each of the two subsequent years. In September 1783 the Prince of Wales paid his first visit to Brighton to stay with his uncle, on whose recommendation he decided to enter into the ownership of race-horses.

In the winter of 1783/84 the Duke sold his nephew thirteen horses including a yearling, one of whose fore-bears was by the Sullaby Turk out of a mare owned by Oliver Cromwell. The race-horses were yet another extrava-gance he could ill afford, yet it appealed to his very nature, for 'all the pleasant devils were coaxing on poor Florizel, desire, and idleness and vanity, and drunkenness, all clashing their merry cymbals and bidding him come on'. Anvil, in 1784, gave him his first taste of victory on the Turf by winning a sixty-guinea stake at Newmarket. The following year his horses won sixteen races, principally at Newmarket and Ascot. Two of his horses ran unplaced in the Derby of 1786, won by Mr Panton's colt Noble. The first racing silks that he chose were 'crimson waistcoat with purple sleeves, black cap', but although they were altered at a later date, it was in these colours that the first royal victory in the Derby was achieved, when Sir Thomas won in 1788.

After winning his only race as a two-year-old, Sir Thomas was sold to the Prince who, on Derby day, drove from Carlton House in a carriage drawn by four horses with postilions preceded by outriders. Leaving London at eight o'clock the royal party arrived at Epsom just before the first race was run. The town was packed to capacity and it was virtually impossible to acquire accommodation. One gentleman who wished to hire a house for race week was told that he might have it if he would pay two years' rent. Sir Thomas, starting at odds-on, won from Lord Grosvenor's Aurelius, and nine others. This victory convinced His Royal Highness that his future and that of the Turf were inseparably linked – a view shared by the adventurers and blacklegs by whom he was almost submerged with flattery and adulation. They approved of his every action and applauded his every *bon mot*. At Lewes races the rain resulted in few spectators other than the royal party – which invoked 'I think I see a very handsome sprinkling of the nobility', surpassed by his remark on hearing that his father, whilst walking in fields near Windsor, had been pursued by one of the grazing oxen: 'I am sorry for it, but it is not the first time that my father has been in danger from a *lean ox*! – a caustic reference to George III's ardent passion for Lady Sarah Lennox.

In 1789 the Prince had innumerable horses in training, many of them under the care of Francis Neale. His reckless expenditure knew no bounds, and although the royal stable lads were paid only five shillings a week, the debts mounted ominously. Two colts by Dungannon were bought for five hundred pounds each and two mares covered by Dungannon cost the Prince forty-two pounds. The Derby on Thursday 28th May was won by Skyscraper, ridden by Sam Chifney, with two of the Prince's horses again unplaced. Undeterred by lack of success, he kept forty-one horses in training the following season, and few vendors who came to Carlton House with a prospective winner left without their pockets lined with gold. Aided

26

and abetted by men such as Sir John Lade and his wife Letty, once a 'Highwayman's moll', the Prince was leading an utterly profligate life. His debts were prodigious, but many of them the result of the skulduggery of those who dealt on his behalf.

His hopes of the Regency had been dashed by the improvement in his father's health in the spring of 1789, and his relationship with the Court jeopardised by the bitterness shown towards both himself and his brother the Duke of York by Queen Charlotte. This antagonism culminated in a duel between the Duke of York and Colonel Lennox. Lennox had fired first when the challengers met on Wimbledon Common, and the Duke's ear was grazed. To his credit he refused to return the fire, and Lennox's sister later requested the royal curl which had been singed. In the months that followed, the Prince of Wales was placed in an intolerable position. He thought that his mother deliberately attempted to discredit his every action in the eyes of the King, prevented him from partaking in the affairs of State, or serving his country in any purposeful manner. For four years, largely due to the influence of Mrs Fitzherbert, he had reformed his dissolute way of living and attempted to behave in a manner which would have made the Court approve and respect the Heir Apparent. His efforts were spurned, and he was compelled once again to dissipate his energies. His very nature demanded encouragement and appreciation and this was denied him. Small wonder, therefore, that his disappointment and anger led to a feeling of bitter resentment and impotence.

In his misery he turned to a life of riotous living at Brighton surrounded by the most unsuitable companions, typified by the notorious Lord Barrymore and his brothers. Amusing, eccentric and irresponsible they formed a buffer between the Prince and the world he wished to forget. The Barrymores, nicknamed 'Hellgate', 'Cripplegate', and 'Newgate' and their sister 'Billingsgate', like many others who became the closest associates of the Prince, were Irish.

These friends included Sheridan, Burke and Colonel George Hanger who, after serving with a Hessian regiment in the American Wars, was appointed an equerry to the Prince. He was constantly caricatured by Gillray, owing to his addiction to fanciful and elaborate dress, which resulted in his being described as an 'egregious coxcomb'. The summer was spent in a whirl of festivities, unsullied by the dreariness of the Court which had departed to Weymouth for the sake of the King's health. In addition to race-meetings and theatrical parties, there were cricket matches, dances and concerts. Tempers flared, debts grew, the future was uncared for, and money-lenders became increasingly prosperous. At Ascot in June the Prince's horse Escape finished second in the Oatlands Stakes, and two months later won at York, only a month after His Royal Highness had engaged Sam Chifney to ride his running horses at a salary of two hundred guineas a year. It was an appointment which was to lead to one of the most remarkable scandals in the history of racing.

Samuel Chifney was born in Norfolk in 1753, twenty-seven years before the inauguration of the Epsom Derby. Little is known of his childhood, but as a young man he worked at Newmarket in the stables of Fox before, at the age of eighteen, becoming attached to Richard Price, who was groom to Lord Foley. He had few difficulties with his weight, which throughout his riding career seldom exceeded eight stone, and his height of five feet five inches was ideal for his chosen career – that of a professional jockey.

There is no doubt that Samuel Chifney was born with a natural flair where horsemanship was concerned, and this ability allied to great determination, confidence which bordered on arrogance, and to a certain extent lack of skilled competitors led to his pre-eminence. He claimed that in 1773 when he was only twenty years old, he could ride horses in a more competent manner in a race than any other person. This was probably true just as was his assertion that 'in 1775 I could train horses for running better than any person I ever yet saw. Riding I learnt myself, and training I learned from Mr Richard Price, and where horses are trained by dolts that have been brought up under cobblers, there is much room for me to know more of the horses being fit or unfit for running, that they train, than they do themselves, if nothing unfair. I don't talk to grooms about horses: what I have to say about horses I say to noblemen and gentlemen. This has occasioned me to be very much hated and abused by those of this profession and their colleagues: noblemen and gentlemen, however, might soon stop those abuses. When their servants are represented to them that their conduct is scandalous they should make a strict inquiry into their conduct, and if the servant is at fault, he should be discharged.'

Chifney spent a great deal of time theorising about the art of riding. His theory on weight was that it should never be concentrated for too long in the same position. He was frequently heard declaiming his views on the subject of the distribution of a jockey's weight during a race, and would illustrate his argument by suggesting that if a heavy stone is carried for five minutes in one hand and then shifted to the other, the burden is greatly eased. It was his fortune to be born with 'good hands' – a gift which the gods so seldom bestow. His advice on how to ride a race, even though written nearly two hundred years ago, is still worth remembering:

The first fine part in riding a race is to command your horse to run light in his mouth; it keeps him the better together, his legs are the more under him, his sinews less extended, less exertion, his wind less locked; the horse running thus to order, feeling light for his rider's wants; his parts are more at ease and ready, and can run considerably faster when called upon, to what he can when that he has been running in the fretting, sprawling attitudes, with part of his rider's weight in his mouth.

29

And as the horse comes to his last extremity, finishing his race, he is better forced and kept straight with manner and fine touching to his mouth. In this situation the horse's mouth should be eased of the weight of his rein, if not, it stops him little or much. If a horse is a slug he should be forced with a manner up to this order of running, and particularly so if he has to make play, or he will run the slower, and jade the sooner for the want of it.

The phrase at Newmarket is that you should pull your horse to ease him in his running. When horses are in their great distress in running they cannot bear that visible manner of pulling as looked for by many of the sportsmen; he should be enticed to ease himself an inch a time as his situation will allow.

This should be done as if you had a silken rein as fine as a hair, and that you was afraid of breaking it.

Chifney won the Oaks four times – but managed to be victorious in the Derby only once, when in 1789 he rode Skyscraper owned by the twenty-five-year-old Duke of Bedford, who was to win the 'Blue Riband' on two other occasions before his death in 1802. An accomplished horseman, he can be given little credit for the match he made with Sir John Lade when, over the Beacon course at Newmarket, a distance of four miles, their horses were each set to carry fifteen stone, an utterly inhuman weight over so long a distance. As a boy at Westminster the Duke had been injured in an accident whilst playing cricket. Years later this necessitated an operation which proved fatal. He thought so highly of Chifney that if the famous jockey rode in a match against one of his horses, he insisted on his own challenger being given a weight allowance to compensate for Chifney's acknowledged mastery over his contemporary jockeys.

Chifney, who married the daughter of Smallman, a training groom, fathered six children. His love and enthusiasm for racing, and his belief that it was a way of life which his sons should adopt, gave him great hopes that they would follow in his footsteps. After William Chifney was born in 1784 and his brother Samuel two years later, their father never missed an opportunity to teach them every-thing that he himself knew about the art of race-riding. Instinctively he saw that the difference in character of his two sons – William, quick and intelligent, Sam, the more resolute and phlegmatic – meant that in the world of racing their careers would not clash. William was taught to train horses, whilst his younger brother was compelled to spend hours every day in the saddle, practising over and over again every conceivable ingredient of race-riding. His father would take him up Warren Hill and the two of them would ride race after race, with young Sam Chifney proudly being taught every trick of the profession, including how to 'wait in front' how to 'come from behind' and how to 'win by a short head'. As they returned into Newmarket in the cool of the evening, the boy's father would dream of the day when his son would carry on the Chifney tradition; and there seemed no reason why his dreams should not come true. His son showed ability, and the fact that His Royal Highness the Prince of Wales sometimes took young Samuel and his elder brother on his knee, and presented them with a shining guinea when he came to discuss his horses at their father's home, augured well for the future. Royal patronage was just what was needed.

On 14th July 1790, a year to the day after the Fall of the Bastille, His Royal Highness engaged Sam Chifney to ride his running horses. It seemed a wise choice, for the thirty-eight-year-old Chifney, at the height of his career, was the undisputed champion of the Newmarket jockeys. There was nothing that he did not understand about race-riding, or of the skulduggery associated with the making of matches. He knew the form and capabilities of virtually every horse that raced, and there were few with greater ability at assessing the outcome of each and every contest. Above all else, he was immensely ambitious for both himself and his sons, and the prospect and honour of riding for the Prince of Wales made tremendous appeal. Yet Chifney's

31

appointment was tragic and his total failure to co-operate with the others who managed the Prince of Wales' racing affairs resulted in disaster.

Shortly after Chifney had agreed to ride all the horses belonging to the Prince of Wales, his royal patron explained to him that he thought it best if before each race Chifney discussed his riding tactics with Mr Warwick Lake, the Prince's racing manager. It seemed sensible because the Prince himself could not be expected to know either the idiosyncrasies of each of his horses, nor the form of their rivals, matters with which both Lake and Chifney ought to be conversant.

But it was in this proposal, made by the Prince, that the root cause of the ultimate trouble lay. Chifney had complete contempt for Lake, and was convinced that he knew little or nothing about racing; whilst Lake considered Chifney to be merely out to make as much money as possible by gambling – which meant cheating with the horses he rode. Lake, born in 1745, was the younger brother of Colonel Gerald Lake who had fought with such distinction in the American War of Independence, later became first Lord Lake and was described as 'A brave, cool, collected man, extremely obliging and pleasant in the transaction of business, but without the resources adequate to the critical positions in which he is placed'. An inveterate gambler, he died a poor man. Admittedly there is no certain reason why his younger brother Warwick should have the same characteristics, but it is likely that they had much in common, in addition to being educated at Eton. Warwick Lake ultimately was appointed to be a Commissioner of Stamps and Gentleman of the Privy Chamber, and died unmarried on 31st January 1821.

At the time of Chifney's engagement by the Prince of Wales, Warwick Lake was forty-six years of age, seventeen years older than his royal master. One possible explanation of the antagonism between Lake and Chifney is that Lake realised that Chifney would not hesitate to inform the

32

Prince of Wales if he thought Lake's management of the royal horses was incompetent. There can be no question of Lake and Chifney agreeing to differ, and from the earliest days of their association it was obvious that they were at loggerheads. Both attempted to make trouble, and on countless occasions they blamed the failure of the Prince of Wales's horses as the responsibility of the other. When Chifney rode Scota for a Ladies Plate at Lewes in August, he disobeyed Lake's riding instructions, won, and then claimed that Lake had bet against the mare. Some time later, when Lake matched Magpie against Lord Barrymore's Seagull, Chifney disagreed with the conditions of the race, much to Lake's anger. Furious too was Frank Neale, training groom to the Prince of Wales. On more than one occasion Chifney complained that Neale produced the royal horses in a piteous state, totally unfit to run. Lake invariably sided with Neale, and this made the relationship of the three men insidious, especially as Chifney came to the conclusion that Lake was attempting to run the horses in a manner which would benefit his own betting transactions. The form of the royal horses became so inconsistent that Chifney hardly knew from day to day whether he was expected to win or lose. This infuriated him as it upset his own gambling plans!

Lake scored heavily over Chifney, in that being noble of birth and eloquent of speech, he could be more persuasive than the jockey who, however brilliant in the saddle, was lacking in erudition and grace compared with the Prince's racing manager. It is probable that until 1791 the Prince had little idea of the animosity between Lake and Chifney, principally because he was too preoccupied with matters of greater importance. It took the humiliating affair of 'Escape' to bring it to his attention.

Escape, sired by Highflyer, had been bred by the Prince of Wales, and purchased by a Mr Franco. One night, as an unnamed colt, he kicked through the boards of his stall and his leg became entangled. Miraculously no bones were broken and the horse escaped with only minor injuries. To commemorate the event, Mr Franco named him Escape. In the summer of 1789 Escape was resold to the Prince of Wales for fifteen hundred pounds. After he had been beaten at Newmarket in October, Chifney commented on how high an opinion he had of the colt, adding that he considered that the horse had been injudiciously ridden and that if he had ridden Escape the placings would have been reversed! In 1790 Escape, after winning a match at Newmarket, was defeated at Ascot in the Oatlands Stakes for which he started an even-money favourite. Two months later Chifney went to York to ride him for the first time. In his autobiography, published fourteen years later, he stated:

In the month of August, 1790, I was ordered to York to ride Escape, and directly after my return, Mr George Leigh, a person in His Royal Highness's household, told me, on Egham race-ground, that my conduct about Escape, at York, had been much canvassed and blamed by the company at Woburn, and by none so much as by the Duke of Queensberry. I shall therefore be particular in all that occurred on this occasion.
Before I set out for York I had been informed that His Royal Highness had taken three thousand to two thousand, in one bet, that Escape won both the Great Subscriptions; and immediately upon my arrival there I asked Casborne if Escape were well to run. He answered, 'Yes,' but upon my telling him my reasons why he was not so, Casborne came over to my opinion. I imputed no fault to Casborne, but thought he had not had Escape under his care a sufficient time to get him into running order. I charged Casborne, as he was most likely to see Mr W Lake first, in his way to York, to communicate these sentiments to him, which I should certainly do, the first time I should see him.
I no sooner saw Mr W Lake than I told him that Escape was not fit to run; yet I thought he might win, from his

being so superior a horse to those he had to run against, and I told Mr Lake that it was Neale's fault in not treating the horse in a proper manner before he left Newmarket, it being impossible for any man to get Escape well to run in the short time he had been under Casborne's care. Mr W Lake appeared very angry at my declaring that Escape had not been treated properly; and I further observed that Escape's unfitness to run was unpleasant to me, as His Royal Highness had much money depending upon his winning both days. However, as I had come such a great way to ride so good a horse, I would have a little bet upon him, and I took Mr W Lake thirty guineas to twenty-five that Escape wins both days. That was then the betting. I also betted five guineas the same way with a gentleman who lodged at Mr Knapton's coffee-house, and Mr Knapton kindly paid it for me. I had no other bet whatever on either of those two races in which I rode Escape at York, in 1790. After Escape had been beaten on the second day, Mr W Lake told me that he had hedged off all the Prince's money, but three hundred and fifty.

Escape was run very hard the first day by a horse that was publicly known to run but very moderately; but the next day Escape was beaten very easily.

Escape ran only once more in 1790 when at Newmarket in the autumn he was defeated by the Duke of Bedford's Skyscraper, the previous year's Derby winner. He wintered well, and as a six-year-old appeared for the first time on Tuesday 26th April, when he won at the Craven meeting, over the Duke's course, beating Lord Grosvenor's Skylark who started at 2–1 on. At Ascot Escape and Baronet were both due to run in the Oatlands Stakes, run over two miles, a valuable subscription race of 100 guineas each, worth over £3,000 to the winner, and in popular esteem just as important as the Epsom Derby, worth only £1,000.

A week before the race, Baronet and Escape, together with the seven-year-old Pegasus and four-year-old Smoker, also entered in the Oatlands Stakes, were given a trial at Epsom, each carrying the same weights as they were due to carry at Ascot. Much to his astonishment, Chifney was ordered to ride Pegasus by Lake, who presumably wished him also to ride Pegasus at Ascot. In the trial Escape beat Baronet a neck, but Chifney criticising the jockeyship of those ahead of him, thought that Escape ought to have won more easily if he had not been sent to the front too soon. After the trial, Lake and Chifney had an altercation about whether or not the touts would have taken note of the gallop, and if so, to what extent it would affect the betting at Tattersalls. Lake implied that any information seeping back to Tattersalls would have been imparted by Chifney who, justifiably indignant, pointed out that the blacksmiths who plated the horses and the stable boys who held them before the start could equally easily sell their information.

On the Sunday afternoon Chifney saw both Escape and Baronet in their stables at Ascot. Escape seemed listless, whilst Baronet appeared spritely and full of life. It is perfectly possible that amongst those who saw the Epsom trial there was someone who felt that Escape, having won the trial without the assistance of Chifney, would be a warm favourite for the Oatlands Stakes particularly if at the last moment Chifney decided to ride him, and, in order to safeguard the betting interest of others, nobbled him. However there is no proof for this accusation, although equally there seems little reason why Escape should have deteriorated so much in five days, unless there was some villainy afoot.

Once Chifney realised that Escape was not at his best, it is understandable that he was not prepared to ride him – particularly as he thought Baronet looked fit to run for his life. At face value the Epsom trial indicated that there was not a great deal to choose between the Prince's two horses, and one assumes that Chifney knew the strength of the opposition. However Baronet's form in public was not awe-inspiring. His only race in 1790 had been at Newmarket in the spring when he had been unplaced, and in 1791 he had not been on a race-course. The favourite for the Oatlands was a three-year-old owned by Lord Foley named Vermin. An unkind commentator of the day disparagingly wrote that at Newmarket the name Foley had lost all its original credit, and the blacklegs called for cash before the noble Lord could accomplish his bets. The witty George Selwyn, on learning that Lord Foley had crossed over to France to avoid his creditors, remarked: 'It is a pass over not at all to the liking of the Jews.' Vermin, after winning at Newmarket in the spring had run second in the Epsom Derby, and it was on this form that his favouritism for the Oatlands was based.

On Monday morning Chifney claimed that he backed Baronet to win him £500 at odds of 100–6, and later in the day took another £500–£17 at Tattersalls. The following morning he met His Royal Highness and Warwick Lake on the race-course and was immediately asked by the Prince as to whether he wished to ride Escape or Baronet. Chifney explained that he wished to ride Baronet, and a moment later the royal party rode off, but not before Chifney had heard the Prince order Lake to inform Bill Prince, a second training groom, to ride Escape.

At this stage the logical explanation seems to be that Lake, forgetting that Chifney was an expert race-reader from the saddle and not having heard that Chifney had backed Baronet to win over a thousand pounds, was under the impression that he would ride Escape, and had almost certainly told the Prince of Wales that this would be so. Therefore he must have been made to look extremely foolish when Chifney elected to ride the horse which had only finished second in the Epsom trial. To confirm this interpretation is the fact that an hour later His Royal Highness came back alone and said to Chifney, 'I thought you intended to ride Escape.' The Prince was naturally nonplussed by Chifney's explanation that Escape looked ill, for Lake had just told him that the horse was very well.

In the race Baronet, ridden by Chifney, won from Mr

Barton's Express and Lord Barrymore's Chanticleer, with Escape unplaced. As Baronet carried only eight stone four pounds and Escape nine stone ten pounds and both were six-year-olds, the weight itself must have been a great disadvantage to Escape, who significantly was not quoted in the betting. Afterwards Lake, in the presence of the Prince, told Chifney that Escape could have been second, thus almost confirming the Epsom trial form with Baronet, but that once Escape's jockey saw that Chifney had the race in safe-keeping he eased him up. This remark would appear to have been made to vindicate the running of Escape in the eyes of the Prince, who was not the most astute of race-readers.

During the summer the relationship of Chifney and Lake did not improve, and Lake bitterly resented the manner in which Chifney superimposed his opinions upon those of both himself and Neale. At York Chifney wrote to His Royal Highness:

> I think Traveller will be beat both tomorrow and Thursday. Creeper is well, and I shall back him against Walnut, and I shall take the liberty to tell Mr Lake to back him for your Highness to the losing of 200 gns that he win.[1]

In fact the running of Traveller was considered with the gravest suspicion.

Some time later Chifney wrote to the Prince telling him his opinion as to the value of some of His Royal Highness's horses. He valued eleven horses at a total of £7,950, of which total Escape was put in at £1,500. Baronet he only valued at £400, considerably less than Lance, St George and the Drone filly. For two unraced and untried horses he proposed a figure of £2,000 each.

Escape did not run again until the First October meeting at Newmarket when he defeated the Duke of Bedford's Grey Diomed over the four-mile Beacon Course. Even this

[1] *Royal Archives 25639/132*

38

match had the makings of a drama, because in a trial a few days previously Escape was trounced by some of his stable companions, one of whom, Don Quixote, was ridden by Chifney. Naturally enough Chifney was very depressed about Escape's chances against Grey Diomed, and told Lake that he thought the trial was very disappointing. On the way to the start of the match, Lake rode up to Chifney and begged him to back the Prince's horse, with such feigned insistence that Chifney reluctantly agreed to bet twenty guineas that Escape won. Why should Lake have been so persistent that Chifney backed Escape, when he knew that the jockey considered that the trial was unsatisfactory? There was so little love lost between them that no one could pretend that Lake wanted to help Chifney make money, even if he was certain Escape would win. One can only wonder whether it was a trap laid for Chifney in order to discredit him. Supposing before the race started that Lake could approach the Prince and tell him that Chifney refused to back Escape, who was 6–4 on in the betting, and then Escape lost! However Escape won by a narrow margin, so any trap, if there was one, misfired.

Two days later Escape and Grey Diomed ran again over the same course and distance, and Escape won comfortably, thus enhancing the form. A fortnight afterwards Escape was entered for a race over two miles against three others, Lord Grosvenor's Skylark, Lord Clermont's Pipator and Mr Dawson's Coriander. In *Genius Genuine* Chifney relates that His Royal Highness asked him if Escape would win:

> I now found myself under a peculiar embarrassment, for I very much wanted to tell His Royal Highness that I was doubtful of Escape being quite fit to run, and that this was my only reason for wishing His Royal Highness not to bet upon him; and yet I thought Escape might win without being quite well to run; therefore, if I made any complaint about Escape's condition, and he should afterwards win, I thought I should be represented by some as mischievous.

39

Those thoughts were what made me so slow in trying to break my opinion to His Royal Highness, that I was doubtful about Escape not being fit to run; under these impressions, I wished to be well timed in acquainting His Royal Highness with my doubts about Escape's fitness to run. Then His Royal Highness turned so very short upon me at the time I was going to make known my opinion; I became fearful that he was tired of hearing me; being conscious that I had been very often troublesome on the like occasions, that I immediately became so very much vexed that the strength of my limbs went from me in so extraordinary a manner, I never felt anything equal to it before. I thought it my duty to offer my opinion to the Prince, and I was trained to it from being questioned upon the same.

After the royal carriage departed, Chifney told Lake that the Prince had informed him that he was not likely to wager on Escape's chances, but had suggested to Chifney as to how he should ride the horse.

Escape was beaten, and the Prince, although he told Chifney that he had not lost money on the race, seemed displeased with his jockey for the unenterprising way in which the horse had been ridden. Chifney explained that for the past fortnight Escape had not had a sweat, or a strong gallop, and in his opinion was not completely fit. This must have infuriated Lake who was standing beside the Prince, as it seemed as though Chifney was once again discrediting him. Escape was also entered for a race the next afternoon, and Chifney pleaded with the Prince to allow the horse to run, claiming that he would run far better as that afternoon's race would have caused a good perspiration and made him considerably more fit.

The distance of the two races run on Thursday 20th October and Friday 21st October were different. In the first race, about two miles from the Ditch In, only the final two furlongs were run at a fast speed, and this did not suit Escape. It must not be overlooked, however, that Escape had proved himself an exceptionally good horse who, if you give Lake and Neale the benefit of the doubt, was difficult to train. Chifney thought that Thursday's race was just what Escape needed to bring him to peak condition, and said so without equivocation. Of the three horses who defeated Escape on Thursday 20th October, only Lord Grosvenor's Skylark ran again the next day, but the six runners also included Lord Barrymore's Chanticleer who had run in the Oatlands Stakes in June. At Ascot, Chanticleer, a four-year-old, carried seven stone ten pounds and Escape two stone more. At Newmarket Chanticleer carried seven stone seven pounds and Escape only a stone and five pounds more – so one could argue that Escape in the October race was nine pounds better off, but the difference in the distance of the race must also be taken into consideration.

Another factor not mentioned at the time is that the Second October Newmarket meeting had commenced on Monday 17th October in fine, dry and sunny weather, with the going on the firm side in consequence of there not having been any rain for over a fortnight. By the middle of the week the weather began to change, and on the evening of the 19th there were some scattered showers. On the 20th, the day that Escape ran and lost, there was a heavy thunderstorm in the late afternoon and torrential rain all evening. The following morning there were further heavy showers, which must have altered the going before Escape ran for the second time. Many horses act better on soft going, and Escape may have been one of them. In Friday's race, over four miles of the Beacon course, Escape was allowed to start at 5–1 against and won easily, carrying nine pounds more than the previous day. Within moments of Escape's victory bedlam broke loose, with Lake, tight-lipped and angry, greeting the Prince of Wales with the words, 'I give your Royal Highness joy, but I am sorry the horse has won.'

Lake's reaction was natural in the circumstance. Escape had won two matches early in the month, and then a

41

fortnight later had been greatly fancied by Lake and Neale to win again. Chifney had told them not to back the horse, but contrary to his advice, they had done so and lost heavily. Sheer obstinacy must have made them refuse to believe that the horse would improve sufficiently to win the next day, obstinacy blindly kindled with dislike of Chifney. It must have seemed to Lake that the jockey was sneering at him after Escape had won at 5–1 on the Friday, and Chifney's arrogant and unyielding attitude of 'I told you so' must have enraged him, both through his pocket and his pride.

When countless matches and races in the history of Newmarket have been the subject of nefarious practices, it is astonishing that this one particular one should be singled out for such far-reaching consequences. The explanation is that those of influence in the country saw in it an excuse to compel the Prince of Wales to curtail his extravagant gambling activities, especially with the lecherous debauched members of society who frequented Newmarket. *The Times* considered the episode to be an opportunity for a broadside, for it took the trouble to recount the incident in comparative detail on Wednesday 26th October:

> On Thursday last the Prince of Wales had a horse named Escape which ran with Lord Grosvenor's Skylark, Mr Dawson's Coriander and Lord Clermont's Pipator from the Ditch In (about 2 miles) and the odds were 2–1 on Escape but to the astonishment of all the Prince's horse was beaten by a considerable distance and DID NOT APPEAR DISTRESSED as beaten horses generally do.
> The next day Escape ran over the Beacon course (about 4 miles and a quarter) carrying a much heavier weight against Lord Barrymore's Chanticleer, Lord Clermont's Harpator, and Duke of Bedford's Grey Diomed, Lord Grosvenor's Skylark and Mr Dawson's Alderman. From the badness of Escape's running on Thursday the odds were 5–1 against him and high odds on Chanticleer, when to the equal astonishment of all, Escape beat them easily.
> A general murmur took place, and so loud as to reach the

Prince's ears. Colonel Lake rode up to the Prince saying, 'I wish your Highness joy, but am sorry your horse has won.' The Prince replied, 'I did not expect such a speech from you, Colonel Lake.' Colonel Lake answered, 'Your Highness must take it as it was meant.' Several more words took place and they parted in a PASSION. The Prince rode up to the Ring where the Duke of Grafton, Lord Grosvenor, Lord Clermont, Lord Barrymore, Lord Foley, Mr Fox and many others were, and DECLARED that if there was anything wrong IT WAS UNKNOWN TO HIM AND HIS RIDER should answer for it.

The business has been investigated and the rider declares that Escape on the first day lurched so much as to make him lose ground on the FLAT which he endeavoured to make good on the TURN of the Lands, but Escape tired so fast that he found it impossible to win the race and therefore he did not distress him to no purpose, and that he himself had lost money on the race. That the next day on the Prince asking him his opinion whether Escape would stand any chance he gave it that the distance being further he thought would suit Escape better, especially as he would be emptier, being a guttling horse and advised His Royal Highness to take the odds.

He declared that his orders both days were to win if he could and that he always acquainted the Prince before he rode what money he had on a race.

The trainer and most of the grooms in the Prince's stables were known to lose their money the 1st day and not seen to take the odds the second.

Colonel Lake lost a large sum the 1st day, and no person could suspect the Prince; therefore the business (if anything was unfair) lay either with those who had the management of the horse before running or with the rider. But those acquainted with racing make allowance knowing that horses run much better some days than others, and some horses run 4 miles better than they do 2 miles, a great deal does depend in the manner a race is run, and in the last Skylark made such strong play as tired himself and the others, therefore Escape being the strongest horse waited on them till he saw an opportunity to make his win. Large sums were lost on the race, and it is very natural for the losers to complain.

Those who won think Escape a good horse and make every allowance in his favour.

On Saturday 22nd October the Prince of Wales returned to Carlton House where he stayed the night before leaving for Brighton where, according to the Court Circular in *The Times* for Monday 24th October, he intended to reside for one month before returning to London for the Winter Season. It seems likely that as far as he was concerned the fact that Escape had been beaten on the previous Thursday and won on the Friday was forgotten.

He had other matters to concern him, not the least being that Mrs Martha Beaufroy, for many years his house-keeper at Newmarket, had died, and his chief postilion, John Pether, had cut his throat in so shocking a manner as to nearly sever his head from his body. It was assumed that his death was caused by worry over gambling debts, although there is no proof that the 'Escape' incident affected it.

At Newmarket episodes other than the 'Escape' incident were causing excitement, especially the case of Mr Ramsden and Mr William Clark, who went over to Bury St Edmunds to shoot pheasants between the two October Newmarket meetings. After the fatigues of the day they repaired to The Bell at Bury for supper. A dispute arose as to where the cheese was made. Words came to blows and Ramsden pulled out a knife from his pocket and stabbed Clark. The waiter tried to intervene and was threatened, whereupon he called out 'Murder!' Several people rushed in, including Sir Charles Bunbury, Senior Steward of the Jockey Club. In the general confusion Ramsden made his escape and was never seen again.

The members of the Jockey Club at Newmarket were far from satisfied with the running of Escape, and on Monday October 24th insisted that Chifney make two affidavits, copies of which were sent with a covering letter, by Sir Charles Bunbury to the Prince:

Sir,
I have the honour to transmit to your Royal Highness a copy of the affidavit made before Dr Frampton by Samuel

44

Chifney and which I have just received from Mr Weatherby.
I trust it will prove satisfactory.
Permit me to join my hopes that your Disorder is removed,
and that we shall have the pleasure of seeing your Royal
Highness in perfect Health and Spirits at the ensuing
Meeting.

> I am with highest Respect
> your R Highness most devoted servant
> Thos Charles Bunbury.[1]

The enclosed copy of Chifney's Affidavit stated:

Whereas several reports have been circulated tending to
injure the character of Samuel Chifney of Newmarket in
the county of Cambridge Riding Groom to His Royal
Highness the Prince of Wales who rode the bay horse
Escape for the sixty guineas Plate, Ditch In, at Newmarket
on Thursday in the Second October Meeting 1791 when he
was beaten by Coriander, Skylark and Pipator and likewise
the same horse for the Five guineas subscription on the
Friday following when he won beating Chanticleer, Skylark
etc and amongst other reports

That he the said Samuel Chifney wilfully lost the said race
on Thursday and

That he won Large Sums of Money on both the said
races

To clear himself from such unfounded Aspersions the
said Samuel Chifney came before me Thomas Frampton,
Doctor in Divinity, one of His Majesty's Justices of the
Peace, for the county of Cambridge and made oath

That he was equally solicitous to win the race on Thursday as on Friday and that he used his best endeavours to
accomplish it and

That he had no Interest or Concern whatsoever in any
bett made by any person on Thursday's race and only one
bett of Twenty Guineas on the Friday's race.

> Sam Chifney

Sworn this 24th day of October 1791

[1] *RA 25639/132*

Also a second affidavit:

> It having been reported that Samuel Chifney Riding
> Groom to HRH Prince of Wales was arrested at Ascot
> during the last Races there, for Three Hundred Guineas and
> that he the said Samuel Chifney was liberated by Thomas
> Clarke, sometimes called Vauxhall Clark, paying that sum
> for him, and such report tending to prejudice of the said
> Samuel Chifney
> That the said Samuel Chifney came before me Thomas
> Frampton, Doctor in Divinity One of His Majesty's
> Justices of the Peace for the County of Cambridge and
> made oath
> That he was not arrested at Ascot or at any other place,
> during the last Summer – neither did the same Thomas
> Clarke pay the before mentioned sum or any other Debt
> for him.
>   S Chifney
> Sworn this 24th day of October 1791.

Once these affidavits were signed they were returned to
Mr Weatherby, Clerk to the Jockey Club. Shortly afterwards
Chifney was ordered to appear before the Stewards of the
Jockey Club, Sir Charles Bunbury, Bart, Ralph Dutton, Esq,
and Thomas Panton, Esq.

3

The Sequel To Escape

☐☐☐

THOMAS PANTON was the brother-in-law of the third Duke of Ancaster, his father had at one time been 'Keeper of the King's Running Horses' at Newmarket, and his sister Mary, second wife of the Duke of Ancaster, became Mistress of the Robes to Queen Charlotte. In the scurrilous book *The Jockey Club or a Sketch of the Manners of the Age* is written:

> Tommy P—t—n is truly a well-bred, agreeable, good-humoured man, and though not endowed with any very brilliant accomplishments, yet he possesses that kind of abilities which is admirably calculated to conduct him pleasantly and successfully through life.
> We have already had occasion to remark, that no quality is more captivating than what is called good nature. It is no less happy for him who possesses it, than it is agreeable to those who fall within his society. Mr P—t—n always appears cheerful, and hence he is extremely popular amongst his acquaintance.

At the time of the 'Escape' episode, Panton was a man of seventy, whose horse, Noble, had won the Derby in 1786. He knew the Prince of Wales extremely well and two years earlier had ridden Hermit, a horse owned by the Prince in a match against Sir H Fetherston's Surprise, and been beaten. Within an hour professional jockeys were substituted and the race re-run. To Panton's anguish Hermit won easily. Nevertheless Panton, although not a great jockey, was one of the most knowledgeable of the Stewards, was known to be fair-minded and polite, and at one time Chifney had a retainer to ride all his horses.

Ralph Dutton, a younger brother of the First Lord Sherborne, was a great friend of the Duke of Bedford and Skyscraper, the Duke's 1789 Derby winner, was entered in his name. Sam Chifney had ridden Skyscraper when he triumphed at Epsom. Dutton appears to have been an easy-going man described as 'a good-humoured, social companion who plays an excellent game of whist and seems to follow up his own interest with as much zeal as any of his acquaintance'.

The last of the three who interviewed Chifney was Sir Charles Bunbury, who was by far the most important and influential. The Bunburys were originally a Norman family named St Pierre and derived the name of Bunbury from one of their manor houses. Sir Charles, born in 1740, became a member of the Jockey Club in 1768. His stud was famous, and there he bred Bellario, Sorcerer, Smolensko and Highflyer. He held decided views on every aspect of racing, one of the most meritorious in an age of brutality, being that he never allowed either his stable lads or his jockeys to touch his horses with a whip. It was his belief that such ill-treatment made horses vicious and restive, and even in matches he was unwilling to allow his jockeys to wear spurs. A contemporary wrote: 'Whatever might be the faults and peccadilloes of Sir Charles Bunbury – and who was there to throw the first stone at him – he was a man of naturally benign, compassionate and friendly disposition, and his plan for treating the race-horse, without suffering him to be abused by the whip and spur, which he laboured so long and steadfastly, though unsuccessfully, to make general on the turf, ought ever to be remembered to his honour.' He was vehemently opposed to the customary sweating gallops for his horses, and attempted to make the excessive four and six mile races unfashionable since he claimed that they were unnecessarily distressing for the horse.

In his early years he was advised and helped by Mr Croft, who lived in Norfolk and owned the famous horse Brilliant, who had the misfortune to be a contemporary of Eclipse. Even when lacking in experience Sir Charles conducted his racing affairs wisely, and avoided the profligate risks which seemed to enamour so many of his friends. Judicious in his ventures he made no secret of the fact that he bred race-horses entirely for profit. In 1777 he bought from Hon Richard Vernon at Newmarket a chestnut colt by Florizel, sired by Herod out of a Spectator mare, foaled in 1763 and bred by Mr Panton. This colt was named Diomed who on 4th May 1780 became immortal by winning the first Derby at Epsom. He started at 6–4 against and defeated eight rivals. In later races he won over £5,300 in stakes before being sent to stud, where he was not a success. At one time his stud fee was the modest one of two guineas, and even at its highest was only ten guineas. When the stallion reached the age of twenty Sir Charles Bunbury sold him for fifty guineas to go to America. After a rough crossing of the Atlantic Diomed was bought by Colonel John Hoomes of Virginia for a thousand guineas – a price which seemed excessive for so elderly a horse. Surprisingly Diomed found a new lease of life and for the next ten years he was a prolific sire, becoming, amongst other achievements, a direct ancestor of Lexington, one of the greatest horses in American race history.

Sir Charles Bunbury was educated at Westminster and Catherine Hall, Cambridge, and succeeded to his title and estates on the death of his father, Reverend Sir William Bunbury in 1764. Elected to the first Parliament in the reign of King George III, he represented Suffolk in nine consecutive sessions, with one exception, until 1784. When making his maiden speech in the House of Commons he spoke for only a few moments before hurriedly sitting down – and eliciting the pun from several humorists that perhaps an 'm' and not an 'n' in the name Bunbury would be more appropriate. In 1763 he was appointed secretary to the Embassy in Paris, and later became Chief Secretary for Ireland. At the funeral of Dr Johnson he attended as a pall bearer. One of his most notable characteristics was his kindness towards the poor, sick and friendless. He did much to help Mr Howard with his prison reform, and was appointed by Parliament to be a supervisor of penitentiary houses. His matrimonial affairs were tragic, for after marrying Lady Sarah Lennox, a great favourite of George III, he was compelled to divorce her in 1776. Years later she became the wife of Colonel Napier and the mother of the two redoubtable soldiers Sir Charles and Sir William Napier.

It is not too-far-fetched a theory that indirectly she was responsible for the attitude of Sir Charles Bunbury towards the Prince of Wales, over the 'Escape' incident. Born on St Valentine's Day 1744, the eleventh child of the Duke and Duchess of Richmond, she was still only five years old when she attracted the attention of King George II. Her father, a Lord of the Bedchamber, was not displeased that the King was enchanted by Lady Sarah, whom he had met for the first time when she was walking in Kew Gardens with her nursemaid. She was amusing and not in the least shy, and the elderly King was humoured by her childish charm.

The Duke of Richmond died in 1750, and for the next eight years Lady Sarah Lennox lived with her sister and her husband, the Earl of Kildare, in Leinster. On her return to England she was again presented to the aged King, who was once more enchanted by her. Another who was even more enchanted was the King's grandson, so soon to become King George III. At the age of twenty-two he was considered handsome, and moreover he was a bachelor. Small wonder, therefore, that Lady Sarah Lennox's relations did all in their power to encourage the further meetings between them. Early on the morning of 25th October 1760 King George II, having counted his money and drunk his chocolate, was found by his German valet on the floor of his closet, his right temple gashed by falling against a bureau. He died hours afterwards, and his young grandson became King, dominated by his mother and her adviser the Earl of Bute. It was tacitly agreed that there would be no coronation until the King had chosen his Queen. Court rumours persistently linked the name of Lady Sarah Lennox with his and, notwithstanding his supposed attachment for Hannah Lightfoot, it was fondly imagined by many that Lady Sarah would become his bride.

Horace Walpole, writing about the King's birthday, said :

> The birthday exceeded the splendour of Haroun Alraschid and the Arabian Nights when people had nothing to do but to scour a lantern and send a genie for a hamper of diamonds and rubies. Do you remember one of those stories, when a prince had eight statues of diamonds, which he overlooks because he fancies he wants a ninth, and to his great surprise the ninth proves to be pure flesh and blood, which he never thought of? Somehow or other Lady Sarah Lennox is the ninth statue and, you will allow, has better white and red than if she was made of pearls and rubies.

However Lady Sarah was not destined to become Queen, possibly because the King's mother, Augusta of Saxe-Gotha, not only was reluctant to allow her son to marry an English beauty, but also because she had never forgiven Henry Fox, Lady Sarah's brother-in-law, for opposing her Regency. It seems probable from the letters that George III wrote to Lord Bute, that he would have been very happy to make Sarah Lennox his Queen. What is not so certain is whether or not she wished to become his wife. When the news was announced that the King was to marry Princess Charlotte of Mecklenburg, she was understandably hurt, and in a letter showed her disappointment by commenting that the King had neither sense, good nature nor honesty. In the weeks prior to the royal wedding, at which she was a bridesmaid, Lady Sarah had the sense to remain silent. If

51

she considered she had been jilted, she did not comment upon it, and when her enemies and those of her family suggested cruelly that the King only wished her to become his mistress, she did not retaliate.

It is uncertain as to when Lady Sarah first met Mr Thomas Charles Bunbury, or to what extent her decision to marry him was influenced by the events of the previous year. It is probable that she was attracted by the thought that her country life at Barton would be similar to those years she had spent so happily at Carton in Ireland, but it seems unlikely that it was a true love match. They were married on 2nd June 1762 in the private Chapel at Holland House, when Sarah was eighteen and her bridegroom twenty-two. In the opinion of the bride's family, particularly Henry Fox, young Mr Bunbury was a 'chicken orator' whose fortune was too small and whose personal habits, particularly his nocturnal perambulations through the streets of London, left much to be desired. As a husband, Charles Bunbury was a failure; selfish and inconsiderate, he made no effort to enchant his bride. His unmarried sister managed Barton Hall whilst Lady Sarah adapted herself to the unsophisticated life of rural Suffolk. Her husband went off hunting without her, and in almost every respect treated her with a lack of love or affection. Because of her upbringing Lady Sarah bore her misery with fortitude and only her spirit and character prevented her from disclosing her unhappiness to her husband, although in letters to some of her friends she admitted her misery.

Two months after Lady Sarah's marriage, news arrived that Queen Charlotte had given birth to a son. It must have been news which emotionally stirred up memories of how different her own life might have been, and brought further anguish to her growing belief that her husband was impotent. A year later, with forced gaiety, she wrote: 'Pray now, who the devil would not be happy with a pretty place, a good house, good horses, greyhounds etc, for hunting, so near Newmarket, what company we please

52

in the house, and £2,000 a year to spend.' Yet even as she wrote these words she knew her misery and her plight. Her husband neglected her, and frequently made excuses to stay in London supposedly on Parliamentary business whilst she fretted at Barton. Inexorably she found herself craving for affection and solace which her husband was incapable of giving her. As the years passed by, her reputation became infamous, as society gossiped over her relationship with men such as the Duc de Lauzan and Lord William Gordon, by whom in December 1768 she had a daughter. A month later she left Barton, eloped with Gordon, and never returned to Sir Charles Bunbury.

Considering his dilatory nature her husband now acted with surprising speed in his efforts to divorce his wife. Divorce in the eighteenth century necessitated prolonged legal procedure which included preliminary hearings, and an application to Parliament. Hounded by society, as well as by Sir Charles Bunbury's legal advisers, Lord William Gordon and Lady Sarah Bunbury fled to Scotland. He resigned his army commission, but their idyll could not last, and eventually Lady Sarah returned to the haven offered her by her brother at Goodwood, whilst Lord William Gordon set out for Rome. The one redeeming feature of the incident is that Sir Charles Bunbury consented to the baby Louisa retaining his surname. Sadly, at the age of fifteen, Louisa Bunbury died, four years after her mother had married Colonel Napier, and five years after Sir Charles Bunbury's Diomed won the first Derby at Epsom.

Legal proceedings became so protracted that the divorce petition was not heard in the House of Lords until April 1776 – over seven years after she left her husband. Evidence was given by Sir Charles Bunbury's servants including Charles Brown, Margaret Frost, Roger Rush and Richard Javellaux. It was stated in evidence that Lord William Gordon and Lady Sarah had been seen 'in one bed' in a house at Redbridge near Southampton where they were staying as Mr and Mrs Gore.

If these facts are considered in connection with the 'Escape' incident the sentiments of Sir Charles Bunbury towards the Prince of Wales become clear. His wife had deserted him and proved his impotence. He knew, as well as everyone else, that there had once been a distinct possibility that Lady Sarah Lennox might have become the Queen of England, and thus the mother of the Prince of Wales. In his agony of mind, his indignation and venom made him find satisfaction in discrediting the man who might have been the child of the woman he married. He could not directly accuse the Prince of nefarious practice but by implication and by attempting to make Sam Chifney a scapegoat he might mollify his warped sense of deferred payment on the wrongs he had suffered.

Shortly after his arrival in Brighton, the Prince of Wales wrote to the Duke of Bedford:

> *Oct 27, 1791*
>
> I take the liberty of enclosing to you an article cut out of the Gazette of yesterday (which paper I only received this morning) as your name & mine appear in it together in a manner that must be very unpleasant to us both. Besides the total falsehood of the transaction having ever passed – yr Grace being absent from Newmarket at the period of time when it is so malevolently stated to have existed, the certainty I feel from the thorough knowledge I have of you, my dear Duke, of the impossibility of such a transaction ever happening between us under any circumstances makes me consider it as incumbent upon us both to contradict so atrocious a falsehood – I shall most heartily concur with you in persuing such measures as you may consider as most satisfactory & efficacious towards answering this purpose. I send this by my servant in order to avoid the delay of the post, & mean to be in London on Saturday.
>
> I remain, my dear Duke,
> Your very sincere friend,
> George.[1]

[1] *RA 41979*

54

To which the Duke of Bedford replied:

> I was out shooting when your Royal Highness's servant came. He has therefore been detained some time in waiting for this letter.
>
> It has always been my opinion, Sir, that when there is as little foundation for a malevolent paragraph as there is for the one your Royal Highness has sent me, the best way is to take no notice of it. However I only mention this as my private opinion, & if your Royal Highness thinks otherwise I shall very readily concur in anything you may think necessary to have done, as I should certainly be extremely hurt if any such report gained credit.
>
> I am at a loss to point out to your Royal Highness the most efficious way of doing it. You will perhaps see somebody in town who is conversant in these matters, I will therefore only repeat, Sir, that whatever is done if it meets with your Royal Highness's approbation, it will be perfectly satisfactory to me.
>
> I have the honour to be, Sir,
your Royal Highness's most
devoted & ever faithfull servant
Bedford.[1]

By Saturday 29th October the Prince was thoroughly disgruntled by the entire affair of Escape, but nevertheless he decided to return to Newmarket in the company of Sir John Lade. It seems astonishing that the Prince should have undertaken the long journey back to Newmarket, when it had been announced that he intended to stay at Brighton for a month. Admittedly he had horses running at the Newmarket meeting every day the following week, but if there were any members of the Jockey Club he wished to see, they could have been commanded to appear at Brighton.

On Saturday 29th October, *The Times* again took up the cudgels against the Prince and an editorial was published in

---

[1] *RA 38638*

the form of a conversation under the heading 'Polite Topic':

'Well, what do you think of it?'
'I do not know. It's a strange business. The Prince must be the soul of honour and therefore he's out of the question. But his rider, what do you say to that?'
'His rider. Let me consider. He says the horse increased his speed in proportion as the weight is heavier and the distance greater.'
'That's strange indeed, but this is the time for Revolutions in the systems of men and things and Revolution in horse racing of course.'
'Had O'Kelly been alive, he would have bet his own soul and the soul of St Patrick that the less weight a horse carried, the faster he would go, and the shorter the ground, the swifter in proportion would be the time.'
'Why is it not so now, the new jockeys must tell – but perhaps it is in horse-racing as it is in the new Constitution, making that which was incontrovertible justice 10 years ago, is downright injustice now. Things, Sir, are strangely altered of late.'
'But, in respect, to what the jockey says, what faith do you put in him?'
'What faith do you put in Tom Paine's book?'
'None, he builds his argument in a false foundation, and so down drops the structure.'
'Then until the rider can persuade me that ten stone are heavier than twelve, and that 2 miles are a greater distance than 4, ye and Tom Paine shall have the same degree of credit.'
'Do you think this business will open the Prince's eyes to objects more worthy of his attention, than Newmarket, and make him quit the black legged tribe for ever?'
'Born to rule over a mighty Empire, the wide field of politics should be his duty.'
'Horse racing, in its present state, is only for PROFESSED SHARPERS. A gentleman is soon ruined amongst them. It is a general and heartfelt wish in the bosom of the public that His Royal Highness should dispose of his stud and leave the group at Newmarket to prey upon each other.'

Also in *The Times* appeared a comment that the Escape at Newmarket, and the Escape from the Fleet Prison, are the only two public subjects of conversation of the day. They were both planned well, and proved successful, although it is evident that there was collusion somewhere. It was, however, the general census of opinion that the Prince was not a party to any conspiracy.

Charles Fox in two undated letters to Mrs Armitstead wrote:

I sincerely do not believe the Prince was concerned in the bad part of the business but people will suspect, as his conduct since has been very injudicious, as he does not seem displeased with his jockey & is very much so with Lake for telling him he was sorry he won, by which Lake only meant to say what I & all his friends would have said, that he was sorry a thing had happened, which would cause disagreeable conversation to the Prince.

and again:

Such a thing has been done by the Prince's people here as, in my opinion, amounts to an absolute cheat. Poor Lake, who is quite innocent of it, is quite unhappy. I hope the Prince himself was out of the secret, but those who are not partial to him will not believe it, and all to win about 800 sovs.

I was never more vexed in my Life & I consider it as putting an end to amusement here (at Newmarket) most completely because there are always people enough inclined to do wrong & an example of this sort is sure to encourage them.

It seems certain that the Prince spoke to both the Duke of Bedford and Sir Charles Bunbury when he returned to Newmarket. This was borne out by a short note he wrote to Sheridan from Newmarket on 2nd November:

I have only time to scribble a few lines just to say that Warwick (Lake) has made a very proper apology in presence of Fox, Dutton, Sir Willoughby etc and the Duke of Bedford explained to Dutton as well as personally to me

57

everything is proper, in consequence of which I am going with him together with the French to his shooting seat at Elden. I enclose you 5 lines. God bless you.
PS Pray meet me at the play.[1]

The affair was now nearly ended – except for the repercussions, which at the time no one could have anticipated. That they were far reaching is shown by the Prince's letter to Sir Charles Bunbury from Carlton House on his return from Newmarket.

6th Nov 1791

'Dear Bunbury,
I found on my arrival in London so many infamous and rascally lies fabricated relative to the affair that happened at Newmarket by republican scribblers and studiously circulated the country that I now find it absolutely necessary that these calumnies should be contradicted in the most authentic manner. After having consulted with many of my friends I leave what happened and the manner of contradiction to be discussed between you & my friend Sheridan who has been so good as to undertake the management of this matter.
If you think that any further enquiries are necessary respecting Chifney I only beg you will see such steps taken as you think most proper,

Very sincerely Sir,
GR[2]

Yet another editorial in *The Times* early in November stated:

If we have given wholesome advice to guard against the sharpers of Newmarket we are discharging our duty to society and we sincerely hope it will open the eyes of an Individual on whose conduct the hopes and fears of the British nation fix their attention with anxious and awful expectation.

[1] *RA 41980*
[2] *RA 25639/132*

The *Cambridge Chronicle* stated that there were reports that the Prince of Wales had for ever abandoned the sports of the Turf, and added that they hoped the reports were not unfounded.

There could be no doubt that the nation was thoroughly dissatisfied with the invidious position into which the Prince of Wales had been forced by the absurd attitude of both King George III and Queen Charlotte. Equally they were at last disenchanted at the life which the Heir Apparent was leading. The hideous state of affairs in France, with aristocratic, destitute and dispirited émigrées crossing the Channel, bringing with them stories of unbelievable atrocities, made Englishmen more determined than ever that their Monarchy should remain sacrosanct. It was understandable, therefore, that broadside after broadside appeared in newspapers against the manner in which the Prince of Wales was living. One heartfelt address pleaded 'to protect genius, to reward merit, to relieve distress, is what we look for from a munificent Prince, and when the nation is called upon to liquidate immense debts, without one single instance of this kind on record, to justify such a perversion of their money, it is perfidy to the public, and not a warranted liberality towards the Prince for Parliament to do so'.

Matters looked even worse as the debts of the Prince's younger brother, the Duke of York, had reached disastrous proportions by 1791, with cash and credit exhausted. The King was prepared to assist, but only on the condition that his son made a suitable marriage with a bride of his choosing. In consequence in September 1791, only three weeks before the incident of 'Escape', the Duke of York was married to the eldest daughter of the King of Prussia, Princess Fredrica. Tittle-tattle at Court was aroused by speculation and curiosity as to how the new Duchess would treat Mrs Fitzherbert. Strictly brought up in the Prussian Court, the Duchess of York was not prepared to acknowledge the Prince of Wales's relationship with her. This in itself was not

59

of vital importance, but it strained the friendship of the two royal brothers to the utmost, since the Heir Apparent thought that his younger brother ought to influence and persuade his bride to treat Mrs Fitzherbert with more cordiality. The Prince was now twenty-nine years of age, and beginning to tire of the incessant 'shifting sands' on which his life was built. His own debts were again mountainous, and the continual unpleasantness with creditors prevented any peace of mind.

Pressed on all sides to give up his lecherous associates, in addition to the pressure to settle his debts, the Prince might have felt that the Escape incident, trivial though it might be, would serve as an excuse to sever his connection with Newmarket. When Sir Charles Bunbury told him that no gentleman would match their horses against his if Samuel Chifney was engaged to ride, the Heir Apparent may have thought this a heaven-sent opportunity to regain his lost popularity. For popularity, above all else, was what he craved – other than the settlement of his debts.

A theory, which cannot be proved, is that behind the scenes the Prime Minister, William Pitt, saw in the 'Escape' affair the chance he had been seeking to woo the Prince from his undesirable friends. Pitt, patriot, statesman and in age only three years senior to the Prince of Wales, realised that everything possible should be done to redeem the tarnished reputation of he who would ultimately become King of England. One of Pitt's problems, however, was that if he asked Parliament for more money for the Prince he might seriously jeopardise his own reputation. It is not beyond the bounds of possibility that he brought pressure to bear upon Sir Charles Bunbury – formerly a Member of Parliament – in an effort to draw the Prince away from his racing interests. At all events, his debts, which by 1792 had risen to four hundred thousand pounds including an estimated annual loss on his race-horses of thirty thousand pounds a year, his lack of popularity, the steadying influence of Mrs Fitzherbert, his wish to renounce his former habits, and his determination to set an example to the Duke of York resulted in his decision to quit Newmarket. It took nearly a year before the truth of his actions became apparent to those most closely associated with the Turf, and not until he sold his horses at Tattersalls in December 1792 did the full realisation dawn that the Prince of Wales had severed his connection with racing, although he loyally continued to support Sam Chifney, to whom he generously awarded a pension.

Samuel Chifney continued to ride, train – particularly for Lord Sackville – and devote as much time as he could to teaching his sons William and Sam the art of his profession. But there is no doubt that the stigma of the 'Escape' affair never left him. At York in 1800 he was accused of deliberately stopping a horse, only a few weeks after a young member of the Jockey Club had been overheard at Brighton races to exclaim that he could not understand why 'that rogue Chifney' was still allowed to ride. The details of Chifney's career, admittedly autobiographical and excessively biased, are set out in a book which he published in January 1804. The title in itself is fascinating:

GENIUS GENUINE

by

Samuel Chifney
of Newmarket
A fine part in riding a race
known only to the author
Why there are so few good runners

or

Why the Turf horses degenerate

A GUIDE

To Recover them to their strength and speed
as well as
To Train horses for Running
and hunters and hacks for hard riding
To Preserve their strength
and their sinews from being so often destroyed

with

Reasons for horses changing in their running
likewise
A full account of the Prince's horse
Escape
Running at Newmarket
on the 20th and 21st days of October 1791
with other interesting particulars

*   *   *

sold for the author 232 Piccadilly
and nowhere else

*

Jan 9 1804

*

Chifney had written his book some time earlier, and
requested the permission of the Prince to allow its publication. This request was turned down in no uncertain terms;
in a letter, the authorship of which is uncertain, although it
may have been composed by Sir Benjamin Bloomfield –
the Prince's Private Secretary.

Aug 1800

I am commanded by the Prince of Wales to express the
singular astonishment with which HR Highness received
a pamphlet bearing your name, tending to explain and

elucidate certain transactions at Newmarket and elsewhere in the year 1791.

The Prince commands me distinctly to tell you that he can scarcely be brought to believe that any such publication could be authorised by you, because no servant in any capacity belonging to him ought to have presumed in any pretence whatever to bring forward HR Highness's name, without his previous knowledge and his positive permission. The Prince further observes that the circumstances which this pamphlet attempts to bring before the Public are of a nature so entirely out of all time and date, that it can only tend to the mischief of reviving a transaction which His Royal Highness has long since consigned to absolute oblivion and which has left no stain upon your professional character. And as HRH has no other connection with the Turf other than occasionally to run a horse at Brighton, Bibury, or some other such course for general amusement and for the object of promoting and entertaining so many, and so beneficial to the country, HRH cannot but feel vast indignation at so wanton and unseasonable a publication. In addition to this displeasure it naturally excites in HRH's mind the wonder that any conversation of his, whether correctly or falsely recited is immaterial, should have been treasured up in record since 1791 and only now brought forth to answer so ill judged and invidious a purpose.

Under those circumstances and with a feeling far removed from the first impression which this subject created, The Prince enjoins me to desire that you will decidedly suppress the publication of this pamphlet, and in order to prevent the Effect of those measures which otherwise HRH must unavoidably have recourse to in consequence of your having so improperly (not to use a harsher term) introduced his name, to recommend that you will without loss of time write such a satisfactory apology for your conduct on this occasion as may enable HRH to retain you in future in his service and thereby continue to your Family the benefit which he has extended to them for those 10 years past, and which it has been so much his desire to find no reason to recall.[1]

[1] *RA 25639/132*

To which Chifney replied:

22 *Aug 1800*
Samuel Chifney most respectfully entreats the Prince of
Wales to forgive the Liberty he has taken of sending his
Narrative, and humbly hopes nothing in it will cause any
displeasure to his Royal Highness.

The reference to retaining Chifney alludes to the pension
of two hundred pounds a year which HRH had given his
jockey every year since 1791. It was a typically generous
action of the Prince that, when he decided to sell his horses,
he should have agreed to pay money to Chifney, although
it was never absolutely clear as to whether or not the
payment was to be for the remainder of Chifney's life or
that of His Royal Highness.

In any event the story of Chifney's pension makes sad
reading. By the year 1800 he was badly in debt and sold
his pension, but before he could do so he had to obtain the
Prince of Wales's permission. This he did by approaching
Colonel Leigh. He found it difficult to get an interview, but
eventually saw Colonel Leigh, the Prince's Equerry, in his
dressing room at Carlton House, who told him that His
Royal Highness was pleased that if Chifney sold his pension
his debts would be settled – although, perhaps wisely, this
permission was never given in writing. The pension was sold
to Joseph Sparkes, of Brompton, for twelve hundred
guineas cash.

Little is known of Chifney after this, although he certainly
saw the Prince of Wales in Brighton in 1802 and told him
how much he was missed at Newmarket. Chifney claims
that the Prince replied: 'Sam Chifney, there's never been a
proper apology made: They used me and you very ill. They
are bad people – I'll not set foot on the ground more.' The
question of the publication of Chifney's book was also
discussed and permission granted. It was a miserable time
for the Chifney's, particularly as young William, after

assaulting Colonel Leigh whom he considered had defamed his father, was sent to prison for six months.

Colonel Leigh, who had been appointed manager of the royal race-horses in succession to Warwick Lake, had accused Sam Chifney of foul riding on one occasion. His son had never forgotten overhearing this incident and swore revenge, although he considered himself too young to challenge Colonel Leigh at the time. Brooding over the insult he learnt to box, for the sole purpose of landing a mighty blow on the unfortunate Colonel Leigh at a later date. This he duly did in Newmarket High Street in 1803 when he was eighteen years of age. Walking up to Colonel Leigh he told him that he intended to knock him down in defence of his father's honour. On his release from Cambridge prison he claimed that he would 'make door mats for a pony against any other inhabitant of Newmarket' for six months of hard labour had made him an expert at picking oakum. It is greatly to the credit of Colonel Leigh that he forgave the impetuous William Chifney and befriended him for the remainder of his life.

Old Sam Chifney, who had acquired additional notoriety by his boxing match against rival jockey Dick Goodison, the favourite of 'Old Q', on the 1st January 1799 before an aristocratic crowd in the Earl's Newmarket house, was arrested for debt and sent into the Fleet prison in 1805. Two and a half years later he died in misery, poverty and disgrace and was buried in St Sepulchres, Holborn, leaving a wife and six children.

There is a story that shortly before he died, a friend visited him and suggested that he should see a clergyman who would give him religious consolation as he faced his future state. Chifney thanked his visitor and requested time to review the situation. A little later his friend returned and said, 'Well, Sam, I have spoken to the parson of the parish, and he will come to see you whenever you please. What do you say to it?'

'Why, sir,' answered Chifney, 'I am obliged to you all the

same, but I have thought about it. I have made up my mind. I'll stand it all. I won't hedge.'

It took virtually the whole of the year 1792 for the sale of the royal horses to be completed. On 9th February the Duke of York wrote to the Prince of Wales from York House:

I should have sent you an account how I found everything at Newmarket the day before yesterday if I had not been obliged to wait for a letter from Dutton with the account of the arrangements we had taken for the Keep of your horses as long as they remain in training, and which we had not time while I stayed at Newmarket finally to settle.

I send you first of all enclosed a list of all the horses you have at Newmarket, with Dutton's remarks upon all the young ones, and shall now proceed to tell you in as few words as possible the arrangements we have taken, and to ask your directions accordingly.

Escape and Traveller are both engaged in the Great Stakes on Tuesday in the Craven Meeting, and as probably one of them must win it, it would be better not to sell them or turn them out of training till that engagement is over. As you are leaving the Turf and only running your horses for their engagements it would be better not to try them at all.

Creeper and Baronet have no engagements and therefore may either be sold or taken out of training directly.

Lance and the Highflyer out of an Engineer mare are engaged in the Oatlands, and must therefore remain in training till that is over, particularly as it is impossible to suppose that anybody will give any considerable price for them as they are not known. They had better likewise run without being tried. All the young horses are so deeply engaged that it would be totally impossible to sell any of them except Cannons and the Tandem filly who are both totally unfit to be trained, both having a violent roaring in their heads.

These young horses must be tried, as there are so many in the same Stakes.

As Serpent will be neccessary to try your horses with, it would be better that he remain at Newmarket.

Your present yearlings are likewise so deeply engaged that

it will be impossible to part with any of them, till after they are tried.

The colts and fillies now rising a year old have no engagements whatsoever except one, which is engaged with Lord Derby for two hundred guineas and therefore may be immediately parted with.

Thus far for the horses. I therefore wish to know whether you chuse that I should send for Baronet and Creeper, Cannons and the Tandem filly immediately. As for Serpent, as he must remain at Newmarket as long as you have any horses in training, have you any objections to give him to me for that time, by which means you will save the keep of him, and I shall return him to you when he has done running. With regard to riders, there being none in your stable fit to ride this Craven meeting for the different Great Stakes, Dutton is enquiring if there is one unengaged, and I will then acquaint you with it. Dutton has likewise arranged that Neale who is to remain with me, though by no means on the same terms as he lived with you, is to take your horses at livery, which is by far the cheapest way, if it meets with your approbation, and by Monday I am to know what he will do it for. I have told him that as you did not mean to come to Newmarket you did not chuse to clothe the boys any longer, and I have likewise ordered them to give up the house and stables that you have in the town. I have likewise to acquaint you that we have calculated the engagements you have at present, and allowing for the number of horses who will probably pay forfeit your engagements amount to eighteen thousand and twenty guineas.

I now wish to know as soon as you conveniently can inform me whether you approve of the arrangements we have taken, and whether I am to acquaint General Lake that he is to order your stud and such of your horses as I mentioned can be sold, to be advertised. I had forgot to say that if you still wish to sell Escape directly I will mention it to Tattersall and then pay forfeit for him in the Great Stakes.

There are two or three more things which I want to talk to you about, but I am at present in a hurry to dress for the Grenadier Club, but will mention them to you when we meet.

Adieu[1]

[1] *RA 44018/20*

Later from Newmarket, the Duke wrote again to the Prince:

9 April 1792

I am very sorry to be obliged to send you so bad an account of the running of your horses. Whisky, upon whom we had founded all our hopes, for the Great Stakes, was beat very easily indeed. Grosvenor's Fortitude out of Zantippe won in a manner in a canter. We were such favourites till the moment of starting that I was not able to bett a halfpenny for you, which so far was lucky enough. As soon as the horses came out to start, there was a general cry for Grosvenor. Little Whisky did all he could but he was obliged to yield to superior powers. He was likewise beat by Wentworth's horse. This gives us but a very bad prospect, at least till October. We tried Lance on Saturday evening, who beat Serpent about half a length even weight. This will make him very forward in the Oatlands but alas I am affraid that there is very little chance of him winning. I hope to be able to sell Escape today for five and twenty hundred guineas. I wish we could sell almost every horse in your stable. I shall, however, write to you again at the latter end of the week, and will then tell you exactly what I think must be parted with.[1]

and three days later:

In consequence of the discretionary power you gave me when I saw you last Friday to sell the worst of your horses without their engagements, Dutton and I drafted six of them which were in no form whatsoever as racehorses and at the same time were perfectly unfit for you to ride, and we sold them today at the hammer, and everyone says that they went astonishingly high. As for those which are engaged we considered that it would be only an expence to you to put them up to publick auction without any chance of getting rid of any one of them. We therefore made Tattersal declare publickly that they were to be sold by private contract, and at the same time I sold Escape to Tattersal for five and twenty hundred guineas. He had said that it might be pounds and not guineas. I

[1] *RA 44022*

told him he might write to you about it, but that I could only consent to guineas. Bunbury wants very much to have Amelia for the five hundred guineas, but at the same time he wants to strike the sum off the debt you owe him. I told him that I would acquaint you with it, but that as I only acted as your commissioner I could not consent to deliver the mare up without having the money down upon the board, and that if any person offered me the money before I had your answer I should certainly sell the mare. Let me know as soon as you can whether you chuse to let Bunbury have the mare upon those conditions or not. I hope you are pleased with the different arrangements we have taken for you. I mean with the money I received to pay as far as I can what you owe here, and to meet the arrangements with Neale for your horses, as long as you have any, to stand at livery with him. Dutton has desired me to ask you if you would not allow him to provide a plain brown or blue coat for the boys who remain with your horses, as they have no wages, and otherwise would be discontented. As for your livery we think you had better not give it them. I sold Lavrestina at your sale as I found he was good for nothing.[1]

The Prince was still smarting about the 'Escape' incident and the money he owed Bunbury and in an effort to divert him it was arranged that he should review the 10th Light Dragoons at Brighton.

Three months later the Duke once more wrote to his brother from Newmarket:

11 July 1792

Before I left London last Thursday I desired General Lake to mention to you the absolute necessity of your young horses coming up directly to Newmarket to be put into training. You are allready two months later than any other person, as almost every person's two year olds are brought here to be trained about the second Spring Meeting, and the General and I agreed that they should arrive here yesterday, but I now understand from him that you now wished them to be again stopped till you have seen them. I think it right to represent to you the great detriment you

[1] *RA 44023*

are likely to do your horses by this, as it will now be very difficult to get them ready by the end of October, and should the winter prove a hard one, we shall be obliged to force the horses in order to get them in order for spring, which may do them a great deal of mischief. I think therefore that unless you can see them in the course of this week, you had better order them to be sent here directly.

Mother Bunch to our great surprize won yesterday the Filly Stakes. The Saltram filly out of Flora ought to have won it but Grosvenor's mare ran against her and knock'd her quite out of the course and she never would face the other horses again. As yet we have been very successfull, and Ralph is of opinion that there are one or two more things we must win this week.[1]

This letter was followed up by one from Woburn:

16 July 1792

As I understand that you have left London and therefore am not sure whether I shall see you before Brighthelmstone Races or not, I think you will be glad to hear that I yesterday sold Serpent to O'Kelly for two hundred and fifty guineas. I hope you will approve of this as he certainly never could have made you a riding horse and as his last running with Skylark was so excessively bad that he could be of no more use in the stable. Cinderella was lame, and after a great deal of disputing with Bunbury we agreed to let him have her at one hundred and fifty guineas. The Sa[l]tram filly out of Vestal was so very bad that it was not worth while keeping her in training, and as she appears to be likely to make some time or other a saddle horse I have sent her up to Carleton House with the Volunteer horse out of Miss Kitty, who will not stand training but yet may be of use to you hereafter to ride, when she has been fired and turned out. We have in general been very successfull but Mad Doctor, who from his first trial appeared the best of our young horses, when he came to run in publick would not run at all. He is however so deeply engaged that we must still keep him in training and run him the next time without trying him. The Flora filly ought to have won the July Stakes but Grosvenor's filly

[1] *RA 44027*

70

run against her very soon after they started, and she never would face the other horses again. I have received in stakes for you within a very few pounds of what is sufficient to pay the bills, and have now no more money of yours in hand; on the contrary, you owe me something.

I understand that Brighthelmstone Races are fixed for the 31st. I shall therefore come down to you on the 30th and Ralph Dutton has promised to come with me. I have sent Whisky and the Anvil horse out of Mrs Siddons to Brighthelmstone, who I trust will both arrive safe, and both win. Adieu. I have not time to add more.[1]

Several of His Royal Highness's horses ran at the October Newmarket meetings, chiefly against his usual rivals, the Duke of Bedford, Lord Grosvenor, Sir Charles Bunbury and Mr Panton. His brother wrote :

20 Oct 1792

You will see by the enclosed list that I have won a race with my Drone Filly. I had so little idea of it that I had sent a Commissioner to hedge my stake but luckily he could not do it, Volanti won very easy; the odds were two to one against her. As you are so great a winner by these meetings I mean tomorrow to settle your account thus far with Weatherby, and leave in hands about a thousand pounds in order to pay the stakes next Meeting and the different quarterly bills here, after which I shall take out what remains and after paying Hulse the money he sent me, deliver the overplus into his hands for you. Adieu.[2]

The entire saga of the sale of the Prince's horses can be learnt from the letters from his brother, who in mid-November wrote yet again:

I lose no time in acknowledging the receipt of your letter, which I have just this moment found at my return from shooting. Many thanks for your goodness in trying to settle Jeffreys' business, but I am affraid he does not now stick to what he at first said. However, if it were possible

[1] *RA 44028*
[2] *RA 44040*

to obtain a short delay I think some fresh mode may still be struck out to satisfy him. I shall take care to give the necessary orders tomorrow at Newmarket for every horse to be ready to come up at the shortest notice to London. Dutton will himself go over to settle everything. As, however, it would certainly be more advantageous, for the sale to let it be known for some days beforehand, I cannot help recommending to you to have the horses advertised immediately and not to have the sale before Thursday sennight, or rather Monday fortnight at earliest. As it is not worth while keeping mine, alone, what are not sold by private contract before, I shall send up and dispose of them at your sale.[1]

I send you two lines to acquaint you that I have this day sent the list of your horses at Newmarket and their engagements to General Lake. I could not send them sooner as I only received the list of the horses from Newmarket on Sunday evening and it took me near four hours to make out the engagements. The horses will not be ready to travel till the middle of next week as most of them were in physic. I am affraid therefore that it will be impossible to have the sale before Thursday fortnight at earliest. Stepney told me you was very anxious to have Glaucus, but I am very sorry to tell you that Paget had already bought him.[2]

The sale of the royal horses took place at Tattersalls on Monday 10th December 1792.

The stallions Anvil and Saltram were sold for seven hundred guineas each, eleven brood mares fetched 1,728 guineas, and fourteen horses in training with their engagements fetched 2,671 guineas. The Duke of York's stud, sold at the same time, produced 1,218 guineas. It was the end of an era.

[1] *RA 44041*
[2] *RA 44042*

4

The Colours Change

□□

THE NEW YEAR opened with events of such importance across the English Channel that the fact that His Royal Highness had disposed of his race-horses caused little comment. At the end of January Louis XVI was guillotined, and the Reign of Terror began. Horrific stories of atrocities in Paris were told by the terrified aristocrats lucky enough to escape to the sanctity of England. For the next twenty-two years England waged war against an erstwhile Corsican corporal who proudly brought France back to her senses and made her once again the most powerful nation on the continent of Europe. The battles of the Peninsular War, the military victories of the Emperor Napoleon and his brilliant generals Ney, Murat and Soult, and the illustrious names of men such as Lord Horatio Nelson, Sir John Moore and the Duke of Wellington gave Europe some of the greatest moments in her history. Waterloo and the defeat of Napoleon ended an era which for gallantry has never been surpassed.

Life continued to bring troubles for the Prince of Wales, even though he had sold his race-horses. His debts were still mounting, and events beyond his control were straining his relationship with Mrs Fitzherbert, for his younger brother Prince Augustus Frederick had secretly married Lady Augusta Murray in Rome in 1793. When the King learned of this alliance, he invoked the Royal Marriage Act of 1772 and had the marriage annulled. It placed the Prince and Mrs Fitzherbert in an utterly invidious position.

Desperately worried by his debts he attempted to raise

money at exorbitant rates of interest on the King's life. This produced only thirty thousand pounds and even offers of Irish peerages failed to tempt the money-lenders. The only recourse was to plead for mercy to his father – who now found himself very much in the seat of power where his son was concerned. The events in France and the British successes abroad were greatly increasing his popularity, and steadily reducing the influence of the Whig party. His son had no influential friends in either House of Parliament, and the King felt justified in recommending that the Government opposed any question of settling the Prince's debts unless he accepted his father's terms. In his heart the Prince knew that these terms would include the renunciation of Mrs Fitzherbert and his marriage to someone of his father's choosing, almost certainly a German Princess. From his viewpoint there was only one saving grace. The decision to annul his brother's marriage had been taken by the highest legal authorities in the realm, and in consequence he resigned himself to forsaking Mrs Fitzherbert with the excuse that circumstances beyond his control were forcing him to do so. In any event he now found attraction in the company of Frances, Countess of Jersey, wife of the Lord Chamberlain who had been Master of the Buckhounds from March 1782 until May 1783. The Countess, already a grandmother, realised that her influence over the Prince would bring handsome rewards. If she could persuade him to acquiesce to his parents' demands it would inevitably advance her reputation in the eyes of the King, and also, although this was sheer speculation, enable her to retain her relationship with the Prince, who was almost bound to dislike his chosen bride. It has been suggested that there were two suitable candidates – the Queen's niece, Princess Louise of Mecklenburg, and Caroline, Princess of Brunswick, niece of George III. Louise – ultimately Queen of Prussia – had the advantage in beauty and ability, but the fact that she was a relation of his mother damned her in the Prince's estimation, and in any event in December 1793 she married Frederick William, Crown Prince of Prussia. Consequently Caroline of Brunswick was the only choice. From Lady Jersey's point of view Caroline of Brunswick was infinitely preferable, for it was almost beyond the bounds of possibility that the Prince would fall in love with his future wife, whom he felt compelled to marry in order to settle his debts. The marriage took place in the Chapel Royal on the evening of 8th April 1795, less than a month after the Prince had sent his favourite 10th Hussar officer – Beau Brummell – to escort her from Dover to London. It was apparent in the months that followed that the marriage was a failure. The Prince's debts were debated in Parliament, and to his consternation his belief that they would be discharged in full was thrust aside, as alternative suggestions were put forward. In vain did he complain that he was being unfairly treated. Pitt proposed that his income should be increased to £125,000 a year and £20,000 be allowed towards the cost of Carlton House, but also that £73,000 per year should be deducted by the Treasury each year towards settlement of his debts which had reached almost £400,000. His fury was still unabated nine months later when his daughter Princess Charlotte was born.

It was always with Mrs Fitzherbert that the Prince found most happiness and the first years of the new century brought them both great contentment. Poverty is comparative, but the Prince's finances were now at a very low ebb. In 1800 he had begun to race his horses again, winning King's Plates at Guildford, Winchester, Lewes and Lichfield. Occasionally he ran a horse at Newmarket, but his interest in the Newmarket races was desultory. His pleasure grounds were Brighton and Lewes. Tom Raikes, a diarist and commentator of the age, describing the scene wrote:

> In those days, the Prince made Brighton and Lewes Races the gayest scene of the year in England. The Pavilion was full of guests; the Steyne was crowded with all the rank

and fashion from London during that week; the best horses were brought from Newmarket and the North, to run at these races, on which immense sums were depending; and the course was graced by the handsomest equipages. The 'legs' and betters, who had arrived in shoals, used all to assemble on the Steyne at an early hour to commence their operations on the first day and the buzz was tremendous, till Lord Foley and Mellish, the two great confederates of that day, would approach the ring; and then a sudden silence ensued, to await the opening of their betting books. They would come on perhaps smiling, but mysterious without making any demonstration; at last Mr Jerry Cloves would say, 'Come, Mr Mellish, will you light the candle, and set us a-going?' Then, if the Master of Buckle would say, 'I'll take three to one about "Sir Solomon",' the whole pack opened, and the air resounded with every shade of odds and betting. About half an hour before the signal of departure for the hill, the Prince himself would make his appearance in the crowd – I think I see him now, in a green jacket, a white hat, and tight nankeen pantaloons and shoes, distinguished by his high-bred manner and handsome person; he was generally accompanied by the late Duke of Bedford, Lord Jersey, Charles Wyndham, Shelley, Brummell, M Day, Churchill, and, oh, extraordinary anomaly! the little Jew, Travis, who, like the dwarf of old, followed in the train of royalty.

The Downs were soon covered with every species of conveyance, and the Prince's German waggon and six bay horses [so were barouches called when first introduced at that time] – the coachman on the box being replaced by Sir John Lade – issued out of the gates of the Pavilion, and, gliding up the green ascent, was stationed close to the great stand, where it remained the centre of attraction for the day. At dinner-time, the Pavilion was resplendent with lights, and a sumptuous banquet was served to a large party; while those who were not included in that invitation found a dinner with every luxury at the clubhouse on the Steyne, kept by Raggett, during the season, for the different members of White's and Brookes's who chose to frequent it, and where the cards and dice from St James's Street were not forgotten.

The Pavilion was constantly being enlarged or altered, until it took the form of an Oriental palace whose architect had run riot. The Prince spent more and more time at Brighton surrounded by his friends – and by Mrs Fitzherbert. Not until 1811 did the final break in their alliance become apparent. In November 1810 the death of Princess Amelia left the King mortified and permanently insane, and the Prince, despite opposition from the Queen and Perceval, the Prime Minister, became Regent on 5th February 1811, and King nine years later.

During these years, with Napoleon exiled to St Helena, Nelson dead, and the Duke of Wellington the most respected man in Europe, the Prince Regent did not race at all, even though he fastidiously changed his racing colours five times. In 1790 he altered them from 'crimson waistcoat with purple sleeves and black cap' to 'purple, white striped waistcoat, with scarlet and white striped sleeves, black cap'. Two years later they were changed to 'purple waistcoat, scarlet sleeves trimmed with gold, black cap'. In 1801 they were again altered to 'crimson waistcoat, purple sleeves, black cap' and remained as these until he became King, when they were once more altered to 'crimson body, gold lace, purple sleeves, black cap'. The Jockey Club, in 1805, had sent him a letter requesting his attendance at Newmarket:

Sir Thomas Charles Bunbury and Lord Darlington to
       the Prince of Wales.
Sir
We humbly beg leave to represent to Your Royal Highness that we are deputed in our official Situations as Stewards of Newmarket to convey to you the unanimous wish of all Gentlemen of the Turf now present at Brighton, which we respectfully submit for your consideration.
From various Misconceptions or Differences of Opinion which arose formerly relative to a race, in which Your Royal Highness was concerned, we greatly regret, that we have never been honoured with Your Presence there since that Period, but experiencing as we constantly do, the singular Marks of your Condescension and Favour, and

considering the essential benefit not only that the Turf will generally derive, but also the great satisfaction that we must all individually feel from the Honor of Your Presence. We humbly request that Your Royal Highness will bury in oblivion any past unfortunate Occurences at Newmarket and that You will again be pleased to honor us there with Your Countenance and Support.

We have the Honor to be Sir
Your Royal Highness's
very dutiful and obedient servants.
Thos Charles Bunbury

Brighton July 30 1805   Darlington.[1]

It was to no avail. Either from indifference or pique, the Prince found no further necessity to race at Newmarket or for that matter on any other race-course from 1807 until 1827.

The death of his brother the Duke of York in 1827 persuaded him to re-kindle his love for racing. During the Duke's life he was able to take an interest in his racing activities, and almost certainly was a partner in some of the Duke's horses. He was now a man of sixty-four who had been King for nearly seven years. When the Duke of York's sale was held at Tattersalls on Monday 5th February three lots were bought on his behalf. He paid 560 guineas for a three-year-old by Whalebone, 230 guineas for the dam of the stallion Moses and 320 guineas for a brood mare. In total the sale produced 8,804 guineas, of which the highest price was the 1,100 guineas given by the Duke of Richmond for Moses, who had won the Derby in 1822. An eye-witness commented on the scene:

It was with sad regret that I lately saw poor Moses taken from his box at Hampton Court, and conveyed with the rest of his Royal owner's stud to the hammer at Tattersall's. I met him on the road – a thousand melancholy recollections rushed into my mind – England had lost one of her fondest and best beloved Princes, whose benign countenance and fascinating manner shed a cheering and

[1] RA 40449

brilliant lustre around every circle in which he moved, and whose playful mind delighted in making and in seeing others happy, himself content to be simply a sharer with them – the cause, too, unknown often but to the heart from which the secret orders flowed, and which asked no other return, but the sacred pleasure – the knowledge of having done good. In him the manly sports of England, and the Turf in particular, have lost one of their keenest followers, their best friend, and their most distinguished supporter: and here were the animals that had been his delight and pleasure, being dragged to a public sale, to become the property of any one whose purse was the heaviest, and who chose to open its strings the widest.

So much, thought I, for human greatness! and such, I suppose, will be the wind-up of us all, whether we have studs, or any thing else. No sooner dead than comes the undertaker – then the heir, or creditor – then the auctioneer; and it is ten to one, if within a few weeks is left the semblance or a trace of the being that is gone. However, to moralise over-much is neither my present purpose, nor my inclination at any time. The digression I must leave to plead for itself. But to return to our subject, and to Moses. He is a right bred one certainly, by Whalebone,* out of a Gohanna mare, but he could not run on, therefore he is none of mine; and why? – for the least complex of reasons – his fore-legs and feet could not carry him. Whalebone is too apt to get them so. Moses, however, is otherwise a lovely horse – the sweetest head imaginable, and great depth in his hind quarter. His fore-legs, too, though terribly deficient in substance below the knee, are not, like the Smolenskos, long in the cannon bone; and they are otherwise fine sinewy limbs, and the hind ones uncommonly good. From sound well-limbed mares, I am inclined to think his stock will be good.

He is a great loss to the London neighbourhood, and will, I should think, be no acquisition where he is gone – into Lord Egremont's country. The North would have been the place for him; but, from the circumstances of his career being so short, and the cause of its being so, I doubt much they would have sent their mares to him.

*This fact is undeniable; and, but for its being too tedious, I would demonstrate it upon incontrovertible evidence.

79

In 1821, only a few weeks before the death of Sir Charles Bunbury, the twenty-seven-year-old Charles Greville had been appointed to manage the Duke of York's horses. A grandson of the third Duke of Portland, he was educated at Eton and Christ Church, Oxford, but left the University after a short term as an undergraduate when he was appointed private secretary to the Earl of Bathurst. Whether or not he proved his worth as the Duke's racing adviser, he unquestionably bequeathed posterity an insight – though possibly biased – into the lives of many of the personalities of the era. In his Diary he wrote on 12th February 1827:

The Duke of York was no sooner dead than the public press began to attack him, and while those private virtues were not denied him for which he had always been conspicuous, they enlarged in a strain of severe invective against his careless and expensive habits, his addiction to gambling; and above all they raked up the old story of Mrs Clark and the investigation of 1809, and published many of his letters and all the disgusting details of that unfortunate affair, and that in a manner calculated to throw discredit on his character. The newspapers, however, soon found they had made a mistake, that this course was not congenial to public feeling, and from that moment their columns have been filled with panegyrics upon his public services and his private virtues. The King ordered that the funeral should be public and magnificent; all the details of the ceremonial were arranged by himself. He showed great feeling about his brother and exceeding kindness in providing for his servants, whom the Duke was himself unable to provide for. He gave 6,000l to pay immediate expenses and took many of the old servants into his own service. There appeared a few days after the Duke's death an infamous forgery, purporting to be a letter or declaration written by him a short time before his death (principally upon the subject of the Catholic question), which, however, was disavowed by Taylor, but not till after many thousand copies had been sold. I dare say many people believe still that he was the author of this pamphlet. All his effects either have been or will be sold by auction. The funeral

80

(Below) King Edward VII (right) with his horse, Minoru, winner of the
1909 Derby, with H Jones up. Lord Marcus Beresford, the King's Racing
Manager, is on the King's right, with Richard Marsh, the King's Trainer,
centre (Radio Times Hulton Picture Library). Persimmon (above left),
J Watts up, won the 1896 Derby for the King when he was Prince of Wales,
while Diamond Jubilee (above right) won the Triple Crown for him in 1900
(Photos by W W Rouch)

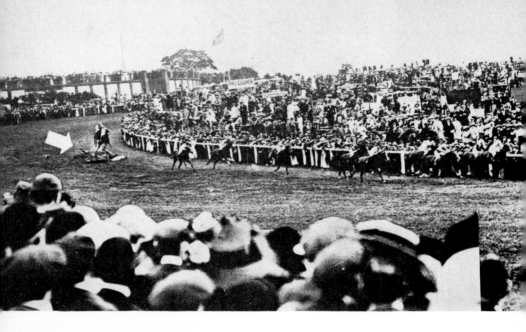

(Above) The historic occasion at Tattenham Corner in 1913 when the suffragette, Emily Davison, threw herself under King George V's horse, Anmer (The Mansell Collection). Ten years later (below) King George V (left) rides in Windsor Park with his four sons – the future King Edward VIII and King George VI nearest him (Radio Times Hulton Picture Library)

took place a fortnight after his death. Nothing could be managed worse than it was, and except the appearance of the soldiers in the chapel, which was extremely fine, the spectacle was by no means imposing; the cold was intense, and it is only marvellous that more persons did not suffer from it. As it is the Bishop of Lincoln has died of the effects of it; Canning has been dangerously ill, and is still very unwell; and the Dukes of Wellington and Montrose were both very seriously unwell for some days after. The King was very angry when he heard how miserably the ceremony had been performed.

There can be no question as to the misdeeds or the debts of the King's younger brother. Amongst those owed money by the Duke of York was Ralph Dutton whose widow accepted an annuity of £606 in lieu of the debt of £6,060 which remained unpaid at the time of his death in 1804. He was jealous of the Duke of Wellington, would gamble all night and all day, was pleasure-loving and indolent. He was pilloried unmercifully in the scurrilous pamphlet 'The Jockey Club or a sketch of the manners of the age' and it was claimed that Monsieur de Mirabeau wrote: 'Le D D'Y puissant chasseur, puissant buveur, rieur, infatigable, sans grace, sans contenance, sans politesse, ressent une espèce de passion pour une Femme Mariee a un Mari jaloux qui le tourmente et le detourne d'un établissement.' Yet he was a brave man, an entertaining companion and popular with the British public.

He died at a time when London was in a fever of gambling madness, and clubs were mushrooming up overnight. In *The Sporting Magazine* of April 1827 there appeared an editorial against these hells:

> Hark'ee, Sir – these are not the words of a fool – there will be, before the summer ends, such smashing, crashing, and ruin in this fine abode as is dreadful to contemplate. Many young sprigs of fashion will be nipt in the bud, as hundreds have already been. But this is only half the mischief. Many a fond husband will be sent home to his

still fonder wife, if not pennyless, what is worse – heartless: all social circles in high life will feel the baneful influence of this enchanting mansion – this splendid Hell; for 'tis now said, that not to be a member is next to not being in the world.

Others, too, crusaded against gambling, especially from the pulpit. Typical of the sermons to which the sporting fraternity listened was: 'Why waste your life thinking so much of what you call "flimsies"? These Bible leaves are God's "flimsies", and when you carry them to heaven he will cash them on sight.'

Very few of the gambling houses were honestly run and all employed nefarious characters to assist the house profits. At some of the 'Hells' the proprietor kept a man whose sole duty was to swallow the dice if there was a raid by the authorities. William Crockford opened his famous club in St James's Street at the end of 1827, after a career which had already carried him from the poverty of a Temple Bar fishmonger to the wealth which enabled him to spend over £90,000 on the decorations of his new club, pay his cook, Ude, a salary of £1,200 a year, and put up a bank of £5,000 every night whilst Parliament was sitting. The owner of several race-horses, he is reputed to have benefited considerably from the defeat of Mameluke owned by his rival John Gully in the 1827 St Leger. Mameluke had been bought as a yearling from Mr Elwes by Lord Jersey, son of George IV's close friend, Frances, Countess of Jersey. In the Derby Mameluke and Glenartney, also owned by Lord Jersey, finished first and second, with Glenartney starting favourite. After the race rumours sped fast and far that Edwards, the jockey on Glenartney, had backed Mameluke and that Lord Jersey and his associates had won a fortune. Proof that there was a certain amount of sharp practice attached to the race came when Lord Jersey sold Mameluke to John Gully for £4,000, a thousand less than a bid which had been made for Glenartney and refused.

Gully stood to win £40,000 if Mameluke won the St Leger, but it was significant that no matter how much money was gambled on the horse, his odds remained at 4–1. Torrential rain soaked the course on the morning of the race, and the starter Mr Lockwood was later dismissed for the manner in which he deliberately allowed false start after false start until Mameluke was utterly distressed. Eventually Mameluke was hopelessly left at the post, and in the circumstances proved himself to be an unlucky loser by managing to make up the lost ground to such an extent that he finished second to Matilda. A sidelight of the expense of staying in Doncaster for the St Leger is given by a foreign visitor who said:

> I veel tell you de Yorkshiremen are de damned rascal nothing without de guinea. I am arrived here on de Monday; and go to de Angel for a bed. They recommend me a logement, and I have de miserable chambre, and a dirty salon with my friend, for which dey charge ten guinea though I stop two days only. We dine at de ordinary of de hotel; and have a dinner execrable, for which we pay a guinea chaque. We went to go to de rooms to hear de bets as we were told, prix d'entree encore une guinea. When we go to de stand to see de race, encore une guinea; and now that we go dey charge a guinea for de stand of a carriage at de inn, et pour le lit de mon domestique, encore une guinea. Oh, foutre! Noding without de guinea!

Mameluke was ridden in the St Leger by Sam Chifney, son of the author of *Genius Genuine*. He had first ridden for the Prince of Wales at Stockbridge in 1802 when he was a mere stripling of sixteen summers. The Prince had engaged his mother's brother, Smallman, who had previously been private trainer to the Earl of Oxford, to train a few horses for him at Albury Grange near Winchester, and young Chifney was sent to ride out for his uncle. The royal horses remained at Winchester for only a short time before being stabled in the Old Pavilion yard at Brighton, and Chifney returned to Newmarket. He won his first

Oaks in 1807, the year after his famous father's death, and in the course of the next fifteen years rode four more winners of the fillies Epsom Classic. He rode his first Derby winner in 1818, when England was still rejoicing at Napoleon's downfall, on Mr Thornhill's Sam – named after himself. Two years later he again won the Derby on Sailor, also owned by Mr Thornhill, a popular member of the Jockey Club, and the Squire of Riddlesworth in Norfolk. For the next decade the Chifney brothers were on the crest of the wave, living at Newmarket in princely style. Mr Thornhill and Lord Darlington gave them all their horses to train, and their success was phenomenal. When King George IV decided to once more enter into ownership, Chifney rode many of his horses. In 1827 Dervise, in the royal colours, but in the name of Delmé Radcliffe, won at Southampton, Mortgage won at Winchester, Salisbury and Warwick and Maria at Ascot. The racing public were delighted that their King was reviving his interest in racing, and *The Sporting Magazine* editorial stated:

It is to the presence of Royalty alone that Ascot undoubtedly ranks first amongst all our provincial and now that His Majesty has again taken to the Turf, the public seem more anxious than ever, by their attendance at the Meeting, to evince their entire approval of his noble conduct in so spiritedly coming forward to support this our grandest and most beneficial of all British sports. Truly gratifying was the sight to behold so large a portion of the Nobility and wealth of England assembled to testify their regard for the sovereign so universally and deservedly beloved throughout his dominions. The Turf has not a more powerful supporter than His Majesty and I am sure it must have been a matter of great regret to him when the Royal Stud, formerly at Hampton Court was given up. At the time I expressed my objections to such paltry excuses as were made for committing so gross an outrage upon the personal feelings of His Majesty: but he cheerfully submitted to the advice of those whom he had condescended to consult on State affairs and at once gave up what I believe through life has been to him his greatest source of amusement and gratification. The very limited stud which His Majesty now possesses is supported entirely at his own private expense, and is placed under the superintendence of Delmé Radcliffe Esq, who has recently received a formal official appointment as Gentleman of the Horse.

The Derby of 1828 had resulted in a dead-heat between the Duke of Rutland's Cadland and Mr Petre's The Colonel. Zinganee, owned by the Chifney brothers, was greatly fancied for the race, but ran disappointingly. Bred by the Marquis of Exeter he had been bought by the Chifneys after he won his only race as a two-year-old, at Stamford. At Newmarket in the spring of 1828 he had won the Newmarket Stakes, before his abortive effort at Epsom only a month before George IV gave his Jockey Club dinner, described by Charles Greville:

June 29, 1828: I dined yesterday with the King [*George IV*] at St James's – his Jockey Club dinner. There were about thirty people, several not being invited whom he did not fancy. The Duke of Leeds told me a much greater list had been made out, but he had scratched several out of it. We assembled in the Throne Room, and found him already there, looking very well and walking about; he soon, however, sat down, and desired everybody else to do so. Nobody spoke, and he laughed and said, 'This is more like a Quaker than a Jockey Club meeting.' We soon went to dinner, which was in the Great Supper Room and very magnificent. He sat in the middle with the Dukes of Richmond and Grafton on each side of him. I sat opposite to him, and he was particularly gracious to me, talking to me across the table and recommending all the good things; he made me (after eating a quantity of turtle) eat a dish of crawfish soup until I thought I should have burst. After dinner the Duke of Leeds, who sat at the head of the table, gave 'The King'. We all stood up, when his Majesty thanked us, and said he hoped this would be the first of annual meetings of the sort to take place there or elsewhere under his roof. He then ordered paper, pens etc, and they began matches and stakes; the most perfect ease was established, just as much as if we had been dining with the

Duke of York, and he seemed delighted. He made one or two little speeches, one recommending that a stop should be put to the exportation of horses. He twice gave 'The Turf', and at the end the Duke of Richmond asked his leave to give a toast, and again gave 'The King.' He thanked all the gentlemen, and said that there was no man who had the interests of the turf more at heart than himself, that he was delighted at having this party, and that the oftener they met the better, and he only wanted to have it pointed out to him how he could promote the pleasure and amusement of the turf, and he was ready to do anything in his power. He got up at half-past twelve and wished us good night.

In the autumn The Colonel won the St Leger by three lengths. Amongst those whom he defeated was Colonel King's filly Bessy Bedlam, who at the York Spring Meeting had won two races on the same afternoon. Prior to the race *The Sporting Magazine* reported that, 'Mr Delmé Radcliffe, by command of the King has written to Colonel King to purchase Bessy Bedlam. The Colonel, with that honourable feeling for which he is so pre-eminently distinguished, stated in reply that he had pledged his word and honour to the public that she should run for the Leger and the mare having two other engagements namely for the Fillys Stakes at Doncaster, and the cup at Lincoln, he also considered himself pledged that she should, if fit, start for those stakes, but those engagements over, she should be at His Majesty's service.'

In fact the proposed sale for a figure of £3,000 did not materialise as His Majesty decided to buy Fleur de Lis instead. The prices he paid were high, and for Fleur de Lis he gave 1,500 guineas, with a contingency of the same amount again if she won the St Leger. For The Colonel he paid 4,000 guineas, transferred to the account of Mr Petre at Coutts Bank, in the hope that this Classic winner would win the 1829 Oatlands for him. Delmé Radcliffe wrote on 18th January 1829 to Sir William Knighton (Privy Purse):

I am indeed well aware of the care required in the expenditure of another person's money, & I am fully sensible of the high honour of the trust confided to me.

I have always examined the Bills & enquired into every charge. I can safely assert upon my honour that to my knowledge there is not an exhorbitant or improper charge. Some purchases have certainly occurred at enormous prices. I did not recommend such a sum to be given for The Colonel, but when His Majesty commands me positively to buy a horse, I must obey.

At Newmarket nine horses including young ones are now in training. One head lad under Edwards and a boy nearly to each is required in a racing establishment.

At Hampton Court there are eighteen brood mares, nine foals rising one year old, two colts rising 2. Two stallions and one more soon expected.[1]

The Oatlands was one of the greatest races ever witnessed at Ascot, for in addition to The Colonel, Zinganee and Mameluke were also competing, so that the field included two Derby winners, a St Leger winner, an Oaks winner and the winner of the Cup the previous year.

A few days before the race William Chifney wrote to the Earl of Darlington:

My Lord, I lose no time in answering your lordship's note, desiring me to remit my opinion of the horses in the Ascot Cup.

Cadland and Mameluke are good horses; the latter, at times, shows temper, and will require the most skilfull management to make him run his best form amongst a field of horses, and the slightest mistake in this respect will be fatal to him for the race. The Colonel is badly shaped: his ribs and quarters are much too large and heavily formed, and will cause him to tire and to run a jade; independent of this defect, the course, of all others, is especially ill suited to him, and will cause him to fall an easy victim. Still his party are so exceedingly fond of him as to think no horse can defeat him, and they have backed him for an immense sum. In the face of all this, I entertain

[1] *RA 25639/131*

the most contemptible opinion, for the distance of ground, and I fear nothing whatever from him. Lamplighter is not sufficiently good to cope with the company he will have to meet; and neither Green Mantle nor Varna, although good mares, can have a chance with the old horses over this strong course.

I have the best horse in England at this moment in Zinganee; and if the race is desperately run, which I hope and anticipate it will be, and my brother sends him out the last three-quarters of a mile, to keep the pace severe, I shall be very much surprised and greatly disappointed if I do not see him with the Cup on Thursday without the slightest degree of trouble, notwithstanding the powerful field of horses he has to contend against.

I am, your Lordship's most obedient servant,
William Chifney.

A contemporary account of the day stated:

Thursday was considered by all as the grandest day ever seen at Ascot, both as to number of people, elegance of dress, and rank in life and what they came to see was never equalled in the memory of the oldest man, nor recorded in history, apt as old men are to fancy what wonderful things were done in their younger day. The value of the horses for the Gold Cup on the morning of the race was considered by good judges, and men moderate in their calculations, to be worth the enormous sum of forty-five thousand pounds. This will be less surprising when it is considered that amongst them are two winners of the Derby, a winner of the great Doncaster St Leger, a winner of the Oaks, one of this Cup last year, besides the winner of the Craven Stakes, and Claret at Newmarket, with others of equal value and character, which I merely mention here as the great attraction.

The King arrived a little before 2 o'clock, when the best arrangements were made that could be made, with the ten times told tens of thousands (countless as the sand upon the sea shore) the nature of the ground, and the present system of rails and ropes (which I have no hesitation in saying is very bad) would allow but a good King I have no doubt and have long known, goes a long way towards preserving order and regularity in a multitude.

On the bell ringing to saddle, Lord Maryborough canters down the course to see that all is fair and other things. Then he canters back to show the King how well a man of 70 years of age can ride. All this galloping about, however, does a great deal of good, saving many no doubt from dangers and death, and keeping many in their places who are very apt to get out of them.

. . . Now for the Cup, which, had it been as large as the Devil's Punch bowl and full of nectar, could not have made a greater noise or excitement. It was not, however, on account of its size, its beauty, its value or its contents, but the contention for it, and the honour of obtaining it, as well as consigning more than the wealth of some States into the hands of certain adventurers, and at once deciding who really had in his possession the best race-horse in England. The Cup itself is worth 100 sovs, the stakes worth 340 sovs after the second horse has withdrawn his stakes. On the morning of this eventful day it transpired that Mr Chifney had sold his horse, Zinganee, the first favourite, to Lord Chesterfield for 2,500 guineas, to be delivered after the race, and should he win, his lordship to have the cup and Chifney the stakes of 340 sovs.

There were nine at the position for starting, which had previously paraded before His Majesty, and afterwards down the immense lines of carriages, stands, booths and people on foot, and though the horses passed them three times, once in a walk and twice in running, there were many thousands who never saw anything but a carriage or two on each side, and the same before and behind. The carriages were packed without horses as close as soldiers in a solid square, twenty deep at least, parallel with the course, extending all the way to the turn, and part of the way on the London side. Therefore, those in the middle saw, as the blind Irishman saw pictures, by report, and but from having to say that they were at Ascot races, they might just as well have remained in their own drawing room. Amongst those who got the best places were some who had sent their carriages previous to the day, and arrived at the course by other means, leaving it again at night in the care of watchmen, of which there were great numbers.

At the end of three false starts, eight out of the nine came well away, leaving the brother to Lapdog with his head the wrong way. In passing us the first time, Oppidan was taking the lead with strong running, making play for Cadland. . . . Opposite to the Betting Stand Chifney and Wheatley, as if by signal, called upon their horses, and at once shewed their superiority – Zinganee as much before Mameluke, as Mameluke before the rest, proving Zinganee the best horse in England. Mameluke second – the rest holding those elevated situations to which their former grand exploits to just entitled them.

Chifney, who rode Zinganee, was now past his prime, yet still the greatest jockey in England. In most of his races he liked to drop his horse out until he was almost last, and then with a judgement of pace, which astonished many of his contemporaries, he would overhaul his rivals and finish with his famous rush which brought him to the front just before the winning post was reached. His elegance in the saddle was consummate, and like his father his appreciation and understanding of race tactics were unequalled. Unlike some of the jockeys of the era he never won a race through sheer brute force, and if he had a fault it was his reluctance to ride a front-running horse as he disliked the thought of pounding hooves behind him. His greatest triumph came when he and his brother bought an unbroken yearling from Sir John Shelley for one thousand guineas in 1828. Named Priam this colt, who did not run as a two-year-old, was described by Lord Chesterfield as the only faultless blood horse he had ever seen. In the spring of 1830 he won at Newmarket before competing in the Epsom Derby for which he started favourite. He was a brilliant horse, and won readily. The Chifney brothers collected a small fortune on the race, and later sold Priam to Lord Chesterfield, who won two Goodwood Cups with him before he was sold to America. John Kent wrote of him: 'I have seen all the best horses that have flourished and had their day for more than sixty years past, and I now repeat my well-considered opinion that Priam was the most perfect race-horse I ever saw. His constitution was magnificently sound; his temperament and nervous system beautifully attuned; his shape, make and action were faultless. No weight known to the Racing Calendar could crush his spirit. All courses came alike to him.'

Priam's Derby victory not only brought the Chifneys a fortune and made them the spoilt darlings of the racing world, but it indirectly sealed their fate for, like so many others, they went to the well once too often. In 1834 they thought that in Shillelagh they had another Priam and backed him to win more money than ever before. He was beaten by Plenipotentiary, and the Chifneys returned to Newmarket dispirited and considerably poorer. In future, of necessity, their lavish standards were severely curtailed, and once again they were compelled to act the role of servant and not master.

Much to the fury of Admiral Rous they were still befriended by the aristocracy, but like their father they could not maintain their position. Sam Chifney became progressively more and more lazy, declining to ride other than for his masters such as Lord Darlington and Mr Thornton, and making no financial provision for his old age. He was content to breed 'Vauxhall Clark' game birds – named after his father's betting confederate – and play with his pet foxes at his home at the end of the Bury Hill gallop, Newmarket. His indolence became such that even when playing cricket, a game he loved, he refused to field and would lie half asleep until it was his turn to bat. Eventually he left Newmarket and went to Hove where he died unmourned in 1854, aged sixty-eight. It is a disheartening commentary that searches of local Brighton newspapers of the day have found no comment on the death of such a man, who paid his last visit to Epsom to see his nephew Frank Butler ride West Australian to win the Derby the year before his death. Three years later William Chifney died, equally poor and equally forgotten, a feeble old man wrapped in a blue cloak, his broad-brimmed hat secured by a coloured bandana kerchief.

In the year 1829, although King George IV failed to win the Oatlands with The Colonel, his colours were successful at Goodwood, Epsom, Lincoln, Ascot and Northampton. At his dinner to the Jockey Club, he seemed morose, and talked on subjects other than horse-racing, although he did proclaim his distress that so many blood horses were being exported from England. His attention had, no doubt, been drawn to an article which had recently appeared stating that 'the mania for horse-racing in France seems to have subsided a little, but great attention is still paid to the breed of horses for hunting and the better kind of carriage horses. The exportation of horses from France from 1823–1827 inclusive, was 16,000 of which nearly one-third were sent to Spain, and about one-sixth to England. The importation during the same period was 109,500, of which one-twentieth came from England.'

By the New Year of 1830 the King was seriously ill. He still maintained his love of horse-racing, although from time to time he imagined he was not only the owner of winning horses, but also their jockey. In his delusions he also led the charge of the Dragoons at Salamanca. Suffering from dropsy, he spent most of each day in his room, little knowing of the bickering amongst the Court over his relationship with Lady Conyngham.

Death came to him at three o'clock in the morning of 26th June 1830. His physicians had told him that they could do no more on his behalf, and he had sent for the Bishop of Chichester from whom he received the Last Sacrament. The Duke of Wellington, now Prime Minister, commented, 'I always said he would die like a man', after hearing of the fortitude with which the King faced his last hours. Around the neck of the dead King was a black ribbon with a locket containing a miniature of Mrs Fitzherbert, surrounded by diamonds. Before his death the King had commanded the Duke of Wellington, whom he had appointed his executor, to ensure that nothing should be removed from his body after death. The Duke strictly adhered to this injunction. A sidelight on his duties as executor is shown by a receipt given on 15th December 1831.

> Received the 15th day of December 1831 of His Grace the Duke of Wellington and Sir William Knighton Bart, executors of his late Majesty King George Fourth deceased, the sum of one hundred pounds on account of services performed in furnishing early racing Intelligence, being in full of all demands.
>
> Ruff.[1]

[1] *RA 25639/131*

5

William and Victoria

ENGLAND HAD paid scant attention to Prince William, Duke of Clarence, third son of King George III, until the death of the Duke of York in 1827 made him Heir Presumptive to the throne. At the age of thirteen he had entered the navy as a midshipman, and was formally promoted through successive ranks until in 1801 he became Admiral of the Fleet, even though he had been living ashore with Mrs Jordan for many years. Notwithstanding the fact that she bore him five sons and five daughters, he married Princess Adelaide, eldest daughter of the Duke of Saxe-Meiningen in 1818. Twelve years later he cast aside the obscurity which had dominated his life and became known to his loyal subjects as King William IV.

Unsophisticated, yet shrewd, the sixty-four-year-old King had little love for those who had fawned upon his brother, and made it perfectly clear from the outset of his reign that he intended to be guided on all matters of importance by the good sense of the Duke of Wellington, in whom he had implicit faith. A practical man, he showed that he was not to be overshadowed by his new responsibilities by commenting, as he signed the declaration of Accession, 'This is a damned bad pen you have given me.' Affable, kind and considerate, he behaved as a country squire. Pomp, luxury and ceremony did not appeal to him, and although his supposed eccentricities, such as his irrelevant speeches and his refusal to put his servants into mourning for his brother, alarmed the Court, they were harmless. A devoted father, he found sinecures for most of his children, dismissed those at Court whom he believed to be antagonistic to him, placed his friends in positions of authority and spoke kindly of Mrs Fitzherbert. His daughter Elizabeth's husband, the Earl of Errol, was made Master of the Horse.

The new King had not shown great interest in horse-racing during the reign of George IV, but instinctively felt that the Turf should be supported, even to the extent of settling the outstanding debts of the late Duke of York at Newmarket. In total these debts amounted to about three hundred pounds, the jockey Goodison being the principal creditor.

Within six weeks of his Accession, William IV scored a notable triumph when the horses which he had inherited from his brother finished first, second and third in the Goodwood Gold Cup. Fleur de Lis was the winner, Zinganee was second and The Colonel third. Amongst the competitors which the royal horses defeated were Green Mantle, who had won the Oaks in 1829, Glenartney, second in the Derby to Mameluke, and Tranby, who won the next year was to be one of the twenty-nine horses ridden by Squire Osbaldeston in his famous match against time at New-market when he covered two hundred miles in seven hours nineteen minutes. For the match, which was run in heats of four miles, the Squire wore a purple silk jacket, black velvet cap, doeskin breeches and top boots.

The Colonel broke down whilst running in the Oatlands in 1831 and never raced again. The King attended the Ascot races on the first day of the meeting, but apparently bored by the sport did not go on the subsequent day when the afternoon ended with a match between Camillus and Apuntado, ridden by Mr Bouverie and Squire Osbaldeston. This race caused 'Gentleman Riders' to be rebuked in *The Sporting Magazine*:

'You see nothing but waving arms and yellow leather breeches in convulsions! . . . If gentlemen will, in silk

jackets, mount Racers, there really ought to be an Act of
Parliament passed to put them down.

The next afternoon, Gold Cup day, the King and Queen
were again present and like other racegoers realised the
futility of the Gold Cup conditions, which restricted entries
to horses owned by members of the Jockey Club, or of
certain London clubs. The reason for this farcical condition
was an attempt to prevent John Gully, the ex-pugilist and
rival of Crockford, from winning the prize with his horse
Mameluke. In consequence only two moderate horses
competed for the 1831 Gold Cup, which was won by Cetus,
owned by Sir Mark Wood.

At Ascot, William IV promised to give one hundred
guineas for a three-year-old race at Hampton where Lord
Errol was a Steward. He also promised to attend the races,
but failed to do so, much to the disappointment of the
crowds who flocked to the meeting, which they found
easier to reach from London than Ascot. In the booths set
up alongside the Thames one could see 'The Yorkshire
gigantic fat boy', 'The Tragedy of the Oddingley Murders'
or 'The African Boa Constrictor'. In other tents the game
of mechanical horse-racing was in progress whilst villainous
scoundrels dressed as jockeys tempted the crowds with
the cry, 'walk in, gentlemen, walk in: a few thousands is
nothing to us'. The crowds felt safe as the newly formed
police were also present, listening to the glib talk of the
'swell mob'.

The King was expected to stay with the Duke of Richmond for Goodwood races, but the visit did not materialise.
It was hoped that Fleur de Lis would win the Goodwood
Cup for the third successive year, but although she ran
creditably, she was defeated by Priam one of the best
horses of the century. This was Fleur de Lis's final race, as
at the King's instigation she was retired to stud where
she was mated with The Colonel.

At Brighton a week later His Majesty's Gold Cup was

Two of King George V's most
successful horses, both ridden by
Childs – Scuttle (*above*) and
Joe Limelight (*right*). HRH Prince
of Wales (*below*), the future King
Edward VIII, mounted on Little
Favourite (Photos by W W Rouch)

Two winners for Her Majesty: *(above)* Aureole, Eph Smith up, after the 1954 Coronation Cup (Radio Times Hulton Picture Library), and Carrozza *(below)*, ridden by Lester Piggott, who won the 1957 Oaks (Central Press)

won by the favourite Mahmoud. To their consternation the stewards discovered that, inadvertently, two Gold Cups had been given by the King. Consequently another race was hastily improvised to provide additional sport, and save the trouble of returning the second cup.

In the spring of 1832, when Parliament was in the throes of passing the Reform Bill, the King decided to sell his horses in training and concentrate upon the Royal Stud, keeping about twenty-five mares whose progeny would be sold annually at Tattersalls. In consequence of this decision, five colts were sold at Newmarket for 845 guineas and three fillies for 410 guineas; and at a later dispersal sale a batch of horses in training fetched 2,437 guineas.

Royal Studs at Hampton Court, Tutbury and Malmesbury had been established during the reign of King Henry VIII, but the puritanical minds of the Commonwealth Leaders led to their dispersal in 1650. Nearly one hundred years elapsed before the revival of the Hampton Court Stud. By 1834 the stud, divided into forty-three paddocks of three to five acres each, consisted of twenty-three mares and the stallions The Colonel, Waterloo, Tranby and Helenus. The Colonel was advertised to serve thirty mares a year at twenty sovereigns and one sovereign the groom, Helenus and Waterloo at only five sovereigns and Tranby at ten sovereigns. Tranby had been a stallion at Hampton Court for three years before being sold to America. He arrived at City Point aboard SS Hackaway (Captain R Fisher) in February 1835 and was praised by the New York Press as 'a nine-year-old, and a beautiful rich dapple bay, without white, except a small ring around the coronet of his near hind foot'. To replace Tranby, the stud bought Actaeon from Viscount Kelbourne for one thousand guineas.

It was the policy of the stud, under the care of Mr Waley, who had worked for the Royal Family all his life and had been stud groom to the Duke of York, not to enter any of the foals for stake races prior to their sale. A visitor to the stud at this time, after praising all he saw, could not resist adding the conundrum, 'When was Lord Albemarle not Master of the Horse?' To which the frivolous answer was, 'when his nag spilt him!'

The young stock at the stud were fed on the finest oats, which in 1834 cost twenty-seven shillings a quarter – considered a very high price. The King would frequently visit the stud, and no doubt his youthful training on the quarter-deck caused one of the eight stud grooms to comment, 'The King has a terribly quick eye to anything wrong. If there is a rail or a pale out of place in a fence, he is sure to see it.'

The King had generously donated a hundred guineas to the Liverpool Aintree meeting, and followed up this gift by one of even greater value when at the Derby dinner he presented the Jockey Club with the hoof of Eclipse set in gold to be competed for annually at Ascot by horses, the property of members of the Jockey Club.

It was to be a sweepstake of a hundred guineas each to which His Majesty added a further two hundred sovereigns. The first race for this trophy was won by Lord Chesterfield's Priam.

At Ascot an elderly ruffian dressed as a sailor threw a stone at His Majesty, who was hit on the forehead; luckily the force of the missile was deadened by the 'good stout beaver' that the King was wearing.

The following year, as the King was returning to Windsor after the first day's racing at Ascot, one of his grooms fell from his horse and was killed. A week earlier His Majesty gave his Jockey Club dinner. Amongst those present were the Dukes of Cleveland, Richmond, Dorset, Grafton and Rutland; Marquesses of Westminster, Conyngham, Chester-field, Albemarle, Jersey and Lichfield; Viscount Lowther, Lord Robert Manners and General Grosvenor, Mr Thornhill and Mr Berkley Craven. It was a representative body of the hierarchy of English racing. The Duke of Cleveland's Shillelagh, ridden by Chifney, had recently finished second to Plenipotentiary in the Derby with Lord Jersey's Glencoe

third. Two years later Bay Middleton was to give Lord
Jersey his third and final Derby victory, whilst on the
evening of the Epsom race Mr Berkley Craven, a loser who
felt he could not settle his debts, shot himself.

The Jockey Club, in existence for about seventy years,
was beginning to exercise its undoubted authority over
the affairs of all race-courses. In 1832 they had recom-
mended in a notice in the Calendar that their Rules and
Orders, although applicable to Newmarket only, should be
adopted elsewhere. One of the reasons which encouraged
them to increase their influence was the support of the
King. During the seven years of his reign he conscientiously
patronised horse-racing even though the sport did not
attract him. He felt that the English people found enjoyment in their racing, and this was sufficient reason for him
to give his approval. Although he had no wish to keep
horses in training, and in the first year of his reign was
reputed at Goodwood to have answered his racing advisers'
enquiry as to which horses should compete with 'start the
whole damned fleet', he saw the wisdom of improving the
Hampton Court Stud. He also was responsible for suggesting
many of the new schemes for Ascot, which were carried
out by his daughter's husband, the Earl of Errol. At his
Jockey Club dinner on 8th June 1836, he proposed that the
fundamental problem which was causing Ascot races to
decline in popularity was that too much responsibility was
in the hands of the Master of the Buckhounds. As a result
of the discussions begun at this dinner a new Clerk of the
Course, Mr William Hibburd, was appointed under whose
competent guidance Ascot's glories revived.

King William died on 21st June 1837. If he had lived
for another decade, the Hampton Court Stud might have
become the finest in the country; yet tragically within six
months of his death the entire stock was sold. It was a
senseless action – possibly affected by the Dowager Queen
Adelaide's possession of the paddocks as Ranger of Bushey
Park, and also by the disagreement between her, Lord

Errol and the young Queen. In an effort to avert the sale members of the Jockey Club petitioned the Government:

> We the undersigned have heard with great concern of the probability of the dissolution of the Royal Stud at Hampton Court. We think that the great and permanent attraction of the annual stud sale, by producing competition, enhances the value of thoroughbred horses, and thus promotes the improvement of the breed throughout the kingdom. We trust therefore that Her Majesty's Government may be induced to advise the Queen to retain the establishment; and we have the less scruple in expressing this hope because we are persuaded that, under judicious management, the proceeds of the sale would be found, upon an average, to cover all the expenses of maintaining the stud.

Amongst those who signed were the Dukes of Beaufort and Richmond, Lord George Bentinck, Lord Chesterfield and Mr Greville; but although the proposed sale was discussed in Parliament it took place on 25th October 1837. The prices were high, with both the French and Prussian Government agents bidding. Fleur de Lis was bought by Monsieur Lupin for 550 guineas, The Colonel for 1,550 guineas and Actaeon for 920 guineas. In total the sale produced 15,692 guineas, which was a larger amount than anticipated – but nevertheless inadequate compensation for the tragic dispersal of the stud.

The news of the death of William IV was brought to Kensington Palace by the Archbishop of Canterbury and Lord Conyngham, the Lord Chamberlain, in the early hours of the morning of 21st July. Miraculously the King had lived for almost two months after the eighteenth birthday of his niece had been celebrated, and the risk of a Regency was averted. The young Queen, whose father had died before she was a year old, wisely preferred the friendship of Melbourne and Baroness Lehzen to that of her mother and her secretary Sir John Conroy, and from the outset of her reign asserted her independence. Conroy anticipated and schemed for high office, but his hopes were quickly dashed and even his expectations for the Order of the Bath and an Irish Peerage were not fulfilled.

As a young girl the Queen had been taken to Worcester Races by her mother, co-incidentally on the same day as Fleur de Lis won the Goodwood Cup for the second time. She had gone to Epsom on Derby Day 1831, when the King's colt Mustachio had run without distinction, and in 1835 she saw Queen of Trumps win the St Leger at Doncaster. However, although she had ridden since her childhood, she had little interest in horse-racing, and any form of gambling was anathema to her. This anathema is understandable as her father, the Duke of Kent, had accumulated a mass of debts, and after the Battle of Waterloo sought asylum in Brussels to escape his creditors. Only the imminent birth of his child, who might have had a remote chance of becoming Heir to the Throne, made him return to England where the Prince Regent allotted him rooms in the south-east wing of Kensington Palace. Here the future Queen was born and a month later baptised Alexandrina Victoria.

On 20th January 1820 her father died of inflammation of the lungs, and six days later, on the death of her grand-father King George III, her uncle the Prince Regent was proclaimed King. The nation became aware of the import-ance of the little girl, less than a year old, who was living with her mother on a comparatively small annuity of six thousand pounds a year at Kensington Palace. As an only child 'Drina' had as her companions Prince Charles and Princess Feodora of Leiningen, the son and daughter of her mother by her first marriage. These two children were devoted to their half-sister, as was her governess Louise Lehzen, daughter of a Lutheran clergyman in Hanover. In her youth 'Drina' spoke German and English, and her tutors, under the direction of Rev George Davys, were pleased with the progress she made in studying French

101

and Italian. It was not considered necessary for her to read novels, or to play more lively games than battledore and shuttlecock. Her mother's brother, Prince Leopold, took an interest in her welfare, but he was by nature cautious and far-sighted and in personality far removed from George IV and his brothers.

In 1826 'Drina' was invited with her mother to stay with King George IV at Windsor. Even at the age of seven she was tactful, and won the King's affection when, asked by him to choose a tune for the band to play, she suggested *God Save the King*. A month later she met the Duke of York, who thoughtfully organised a Punch and Judy show for his niece. Everyone approved of the serious-minded little girl although, when the Duke of Clarence became William IV, it was evident that there would be serious altercations between the Duchess of Kent and the King over the propriety of the Princess Victoria's associating with the King's children by Mrs Jordan. She did not attend his Coronation and the knowledge of the disputes between her mother and her uncle, who for reasons best known to himself resented her, did nothing to further her regard for the King's children. On her fourteenth birthday the King, in an effort to overcome the family quarrels, gave a dance for young people at Kensington Palace – still separated from London by fields and lanes. Two years later Princess Victoria paid her first visit to Royal Ascot, driving up the course with the King, who had refused to give an Ascot dinner, on the grounds that he would have had to invite his Ministers, and he would rather see the Devil than any of them in his house. At the time of her next visit to Royal Ascot she was Queen of England.

In her journal for 13th June 1838 she wrote:

> . . . Lord Melbourne said he had not been to Ascot Races since he left Eton, 42 years ago! The Eton boys are now not allowed to go to Ascot, but in Lord Melbourne's days they were much less severe than they are now. . . .

and on the following day:

> ... Precisely at a quarter past twelve we set off for Ascot. ...
> It was very bright and fine when we got there, and such
> myriads of people there – more than ever were there, they
> say. Lord Melbourne found Ascot much changed of course
> since he was there. He never left the stand, and stood
> near me near the window in the beginning. I was <u>so</u> happy
> that he should be seen with me, in such Public Occasions.
> He does not care the least about the Races, but yet was
> amused and pleased. I stayed five races. The first race, the
> Windsor Town Plate, was won by Fulvar Craven's
> Doncaster; the 2nd by Lord Jersey's Ilderim; the 3rd (the
> St James Palace Stakes), a most interesting race, by the
> Duke of Portland's Beotian; the 4th (for the Cup), also very
> interesting, by Lord George Bentinck's Grey Momus, and
> the 5th by Lord Exeter's Mecca. Between the 2nd & 3rd
> race we took luncheon. I sat between Lord Anglesey &
> Lord Melbourne. Unfortunately it came on to rain after the
> 2nd race, and went on raining. ... We came home at a
> quarter past five. I was much amused. Wrote my journal.
> At half past seven we dined. ... I sat between Lord
> Anglesey & Lord Melbourne. I asked Lord Melbourne if
> he was tired. He said not. Spoke of the races, and of betting.
> I said I had not betted this day as it bored me. He replied,
> 'It's much better not', for that spoilt the grandeur of the
> race. He admired the races & was amused with them, he
> said. I said I feared he had been rather bored part of the
> time. He said not: 'I was rather tired, I slept for half an
> hour when I came home.' ... I then asked him if he thought
> it would be well, if, on occasions like the Races I should
> wear my Star & Ribbon; he said yes. ... Lord Anglesey
> said that he had felt the draft in the stand in the morning,
> upon which Lord Melbourne said, 'You should have asked
> Her Majesty's leave to put on your hat', which is quite
> true, but Lord Anglesey would not allow.

It was at this meeting that the Earl of Lichfield introduced
to Her Majesty Bell, a diminutive young apprentice
jockey who had won the Ascot Stakes. After presenting
him with a ten-pound note, the Queen asked him how much
he weighed and was amused at his reply, 'Please, Ma'am,
master says as how I must never tell my weight.'

103

The Queen married in February 1840, and she and her husband, Prince Albert of Saxe-Coburg-Gotha, went to Epsom for the Derby on 3rd June. The Grandstand Association enthusiastically spent two hundred pounds on new fixtures and fittings in honour of her visit, and as the paddock was converted into a promenade for the Queen, the horses were saddled near Langley Bottom. The crowds did not greet Her Majesty with as much patriotic fervour as might have been expected and, although she appeared to enjoy the gloriously hot summer afternoon, the visit was never repeated. At Ascot later in the month racegoers gave both the Queen and the Prince Consort a much greater welcome when they appeared on the first day of the royal meeting. Great improvements were being made at Ascot, and not only was the new Grandstand now completed, but in an effort to help the public the Judge hoisted the number of the winner into a large black board erected at the side of his box at the end of every race, thus ending the constant disputes as to which horse had won. Another innovation was the shrubbery laid out behind the Grandstand.

Three years later the Queen and the Prince Consort drove over from Claremont to Mickleham, near Leatherhead, to see Cotherstone, the Derby favourite, at exercise; but the visit did nothing to increase the Queen's interest in racing. She attended Royal Ascot only as a social occasion each year, and after the death of the Prince Consort in 1861 she never again visited any race-course, and it was left to the Prince of Wales to give royal patronage to race-meetings.

In 1851 the Prince Consort suggested that the Royal Stud should be re-formed. For some years after the dispersal sale in 1837 the paddocks were leased to Mr Charles Greville and General Peel, younger brother of Sir Robert Peel, whose Orlando had been runner-up to Running Rein in the scandalous 1844 Derby, after which the winner was disqualified on the grounds that he was a four-year-old. In 1850 General Peel gave up his share of the tenancy and it seemed a suitable moment to re-establish the stud. Very little success was achieved in the next two decades, and it was not until Springfield, sold to Mr J H Houldsworth in 1874, won the Gimcrack Stakes as a two-year-old, each of the nine races in which he ran as a three-year-old, and as a four-year-old beat Silvia the Derby winner in the Champion Stakes, that a Hampton Court bred horse proved outstandingly successful. In 1888 at the annual sale, held on the Saturday of the week after Royal Ascot, John Porter and Sir Robert Jardine bought for five hundred guineas a chestnut colt by Springfield named Sainfoin. A few weeks before the Derby he was re-sold to Sir James Miller, a rich young officer in the 14th Hussars, for six thousand pounds plus half the Derby stake should he win. A torrential downpour at Epsom marred the day for most spectators, but not for the supporters of the Kingsclere stable, for Sainfoin won by three-quarters of a length, ridden by J Watts. It was a wonderful week for the Hampton Court Stud, for Memoir, who had been sold at the same sale as Sainfoin, won the Oaks for the Duke of Portland, and subsequently won the St Leger. During the 1880s, when the stallions Springfield, Melton and Zealot stood at the stud, brood mares owned by Lord Falmouth, Lord Zetland and the Duke of Portland visited Hampton Court annually. One of the best sales took place three weeks after Sainfoin and Memoir's notable Epsom victories, when twelve fillies and eight colts were sold for fourteen thousand guineas. This total included the five thousand five hundred guineas paid by Baron Hirsch for the yearling sister to Memoir, named La Flèche.

Although the Prince of Wales had established his own stud at Sandringham in 1886, the complete dispersal of the Hampton Court Stud in June 1894 was regrettable. The Duke of Portland as Master of the Horse, and Colonel Maude who managed it so ably, were both bitterly disappointed, but their requests for the continuance of the stud were overruled. One hundred and ten lots were sold, and the stud was not revived until 1929.

6

'It is a Prince Your Grace'

□□

THE PRINCE OF WALES was born on 9th November 1841 at Buckingham Palace. The aged Duke of Wellington, who was in the Palace at the time, is reputed to have asked the nurse, Mrs Lily, 'Is it a boy?' 'It is a Prince, Your Grace,' she answered indignantly. Within a month of the birth of her eldest son the Queen wrote to her uncle Leopold I, King of the Belgians: 'I wonder very much who my little boy will be like. You will understand how fervent are my prayers, and I am sure everybody's must be, to see him resemble his father in every respect, both in body and mind.' There can be no doubt that the Prince Consort had decided views as to the upbringing of his son, with little or no emphasis being placed upon sporting activities. It is not surprising, therefore, that until the Prince of Wales went to the University, his interest in field sports lay dormant. As a small boy, much of his training was directed by his governess, Lady Lyttleton, whose son George married a sister of Mrs Gladstone.

Like all children he was fascinated by conjurers, and after Anderson, known as 'The Wizard of the North', had performed at Balmoral, the Prince told the geologist Sir Charles Lyell: 'he cut to pieces Mamma's pocket handkerchief, then darned it and ironed it so that it was entire as ever, he then fired a pistol, and caused five or six watches to go through Gibbs head, but Papa knows how all these things are done, and had the watches really gone through Gibbs head he could hardly have looked so well, though he was confounded.' Gibbs was a footman.

Before the Prince's seventh birthday, his parents had taken advice from many of their relations and the leading authorities in England as to how their son ought to be educated. Obviously his future was of vital importance to the nation, and many pamphlets and newspaper articles propounded theories on the subject of the education of the Heir Apparent. Baron Stockman contributed a lengthy memorandum which virtually coincided with the opinions of both the Bishop of Oxford, and Sir James Clark, the court physician. Eventually the Prince Consort invited Mr Henry Birch to become Albert Edward's tutor, at a salary of eight hundred pounds per annum. Birch had been educated at Eton, where he had been captain of the school, before going to Kings College Cambridge, and then returning to Eton as an assistant master. He supervised the daily routine of the Prince's education for three years before being succeeded by Frederick Gibbs – no relation of the footman!

Gibbs, a Fellow of Trinity College, Cambridge, who had also been called to the Bar, was heartily disliked by Albert Edward. This dislike was not based on the fact that the Prince was made to work long hours six days a week, but because Gibbs was humourless, dedicated and unyielding. On one score, however, Gibbs seems to have pleased his royal pupil, for he strongly advocated that the Prince should be given the opportunity of meeting other children of his own age and, even though this suggestion met with slight opposition from the Queen, boys from Eton were encouraged to meet the Prince. As he became older his father, tireless in his exertions to introduce his son to every aspect of English life, insisted that he attended ceremonies and public occasions. He saw his mother hold the first investiture of the Victoria Cross in Hyde Park, he saw troops departing for the Crimea, toured the Great Exhibition and watched the funeral of the Duke of Wellington. He was also taken to Ascot races, but for no other reason than that it was considered part of his education, just as a visit to a museum or an art gallery might have been thought advantageous.

The first signs of independence for the sixteen-year-old Prince came in the spring of 1858 when it was agreed that he should take up residence at White Lodge, Richmond. Gibbs and the Reverend Charles Tarver, his personal chaplain, went with him, and so, too, did three young men – all in their twenties – who were appointed as his companions. One was Lord Valletort, eldest son of the Earl of Mount Edgecumbe, and the other two were Major Christopher Teesdale and Major Lindsay of the Scots Fusiliers, both of whom had won the Victoria Cross for outstanding bravery in the Crimean War. Even to a young man who realised the importance of his own future life, the glamour of being in the company of two Victoria Cross winners must have been considerable, but it is doubtful if any of the three companions were particularly interested in either racing or gambling. It should also be pointed out that within six months of his appointment Lindsay married an heiress, Sarah Harriet, only daughter of Baron Overstone, an influential figure in the banking world, so it is likely that during the few months that he was with the Prince he had other matters on his mind. Charles Kingsley, at the Queen's command, went to White Lodge to deliver a series of historical lectures to the Prince. The author of *Westward Ho!* became a lifelong friend who in later years was frequently a guest at both Sandringham and Marlborough House.

In October 1859, a month before his eighteenth birthday, the Prince went to Christ Church, Oxford. Much to his regret, during the previous three months when he had been in Edinburgh undergoing intensive cramming, he had been forbidden to accept invitations to join local shooting parties. It still seemed the policy of his parents, and those advisers to whom they paid most attention, that he be kept as far as possible in 'splendid isolation'. Even at Oxford he was not allowed to live in college, and an establishment, Frewin

Hall, off Cornmarket Street, was rented for him and his staff. On his first night at Oxford he went quietly back to Frewin Hall having signed his University entrance papers, unlike a former Prince of Wales – later George IV – who, on a visit to Christ Church, attended a banquet in the Great Hall of the College, where the majority of the diners were in a complete state of intoxication. However, although it appeared that his parents wished him to entertain only dons and professors, his undergraduate contemporaries had other ideas and did all within their power to see that he lived as one of them. He became a member of the Bullingdon Club, where his friends included Sir Frederick Johnson and Mr Henry Chaplin. In the summer he played cricket, whilst in the winter when the cold froze the surrounding lakes he joined skating parties, sometimes in the moonlight; and hunted with the Earl of Macclesfield's hounds. The news that he was risking his neck by careering across Oxfordshire on a full-blooded hunter brought an immediate warning from the Queen to which he replied:

15th March 1860

My dear Mama,

Many thanks for your letter of the 10th which I received a few days ago, and for your kind injunctions that I should be careful when I go out hunting. I am generally very careful, because I know that there is always a certain risk, though not so much really as some people think. Last Tuesday I went out with Lord Macclesfield's hounds, and I am glad to say I had no fall, though there were a great many during that day. Gen Bruce hurt his knee rather, as somebody did not hold a gate, which in closing, hit his knee.

Yesterday the undergraduates of Christ Church had some games or athletic sports which I went to see, and I send you a programme thinking it might amuse you. I am so glad that you and Papa are enjoying your stay at Osborne, which I can imagine after London. I hear you return next Tuesday. . . .[1]

[1] *RA Add Mss A/3/10*

On another occasion, an irate Oxfordshire farmer demanded twenty shillings a head compensation for damages to his land after certain members of the hunt had ridden across his farm. It was explained to him that the Prince of Wales was amongst the party, but this did not dissuade him one farthing, and every 'trespasser' was compelled to pay up!

In July 1860 the Prince visited Canada and America, on a tour which can be considered the beginning of his official duties. One sidelight of the tour is that it became virtually the first occasion on which great use was made of press telegrams by the crowd of reporters who followed the royal party. One enterprising reporter used to send long chapters from the Gospel according to St Matthew and the Book of Revelations to his editor to monopolise the telegraph wires whilst he wrote his daily copy on the day's events. Other sidelights of the tour included seeing Blondin crossing Niagara Falls on a rope walking on stilts and carrying a man on his back. On being presented to the Prince of Wales, Blondin offered to take him across the Falls, but the offer was declined.

The Prince was fêted throughout America, although from time to time there were 'incidents'. At a dance in New York he wore white kid gloves that were many sizes too big – they had been sent by a lady who alleged that she was young and pretty and that she was going to the ball, and that if she saw he was not wearing the gloves she would come up close to him and shoot herself!

Early the following year the Prince of Wales became an undergraduate at Trinity College Cambridge, although, as at Oxford, it was decided that he should not live in college, but in the village of Madingley some three miles away. There is no evidence that he was affected by the close proximity of Newmarket.

During the summer, when he went to Ireland, he incurred his parents' displeasure by becoming too friendly with a young actress introduced to him by officers stationed on The Curragh. His father, wishing to discuss this and other matters with his son, stayed at Madingley Hall on the night of 25th November 1861. He was distressed by the death of his cousin King Pedro V of Portugal and the 'Curragh incident' involving his son, which had been exaggerated out of all proportion in his mind. He became seriously ill early in December and died during the night of 14th December. Tragically Queen Victoria chose to believe that her husband's death had been caused by anxiety over their eldest son's conduct, which was both unfair and untrue, for the Prince Consort had died of typhoid. It was evident, however, that the Queen was displeased with her son.

With the hope that absence would make the heart grow fonder, the Prince was sent on a tour of the Middle East which included, after a stay with the Emperor Franz Joseph in Vienna, Venice, Albania, Cairo, Jerusalem, Jericho, Bethlehem, Damascus, Constantinople and Athens. It was an exhausting trip, but an enjoyable one, on which there were countless opportunites for shooting, and the bag of quail, partridge and other game was prodigious. However there seemed little interest in horses, and very great interest in Princess Alexandra of Denmark whom he met for the first time in the Cathedral of Worms towards the end of the tour.

On 10th March 1863, the marriage of His Royal Highness the Prince of Wales and the Princess took place in St George's Chapel at Windsor. At this time the Prince's finances seemed adequate, although they were modest by comparison to the vast wealth of men such as the Dukes of Westminster, Portland, Buccleuch and Sutherland. He received about £50,000 a year from the Duchy of Cornwall and possessed a capital sum – less than the annual income of some landowners – out of which £220,000 had been spent early in 1861 in buying Sandringham. Previously owned by Mr Spencer Cowper, the seven-thousand-acre Norfolk estate was purchased on the recommendation of Lord Palmerston, who was Cowper's step-father. There can be no

111

doubt that Sandringham was an immensely happy choice for the Prince's country home. Too much importance need not be attached to the fact that geographically it was far removed from Windsor. This was purely coincidental, for at one time other estates which were considered were Newstead Abbey, Eynsham in Oxfordshire, owned by Lord Macclesfield, Hatherop in Gloucestershire and Elveden in Suffolk. Although the house at Sandringham was dilapidated and inadequate in size much of the early married life of the Prince of Wales and his bride was spent there, for their house-warming party at Marlborough House was not given until the end of June 1863. When in 1869 a new house was built for the Prince, Her Royal Highness, who liked her boudoir so much in the original house, requested that it be copied exactly in the new Sandringham mansion.

The years 1863–1877 could be described from the Prince of Wales's viewpoint as the 'Years of Wilderness'. His mother was reluctant to allow him to participate in affairs of State, whilst at the same time he was expected to fulfil his part in diplomatic and ceremonial occasions. He had a substantial income, but an even larger expenditure, and the question of increasing his allowance was frequently discussed. Disraeli was understanding, but disinclined to propose that Parliament voted him more money, even though about twenty thousand pounds a year was overdrawn. He gambled moderately at cards, particularly whist, and he bet on horses only in comparatively small amounts.

In July 1867 Queen Victoria complained that he attended Goodwood Races, and in his reply he explained that he would be the last to encourage gambling or betting by his presence at race-meetings or anywhere else.[1] Two years later he again wrote in similar vein to his mother, and added his belief in the importance of members of the Royal Family being present at Ascot races as 'it is an opportunity for the Royal Family to show themselves in public – wh. I

[1] *RA H1/132*

112

am sure you must desire – & after all Racing with all its faults still remains, I may say, a National Institution of the Country'.[1] Frequently he warned his friends against the follies of gambling – at a time when the exploits of Lord Hastings were common knowledge – and when Lord Marcus Beresford wanted to match his horse Caramel against Sir Beaumont Dixie's Kismet for one thousand pounds, the Prince, who was present when the wager was made, insisted that it should be reduced to five hundred.

The Prince's real love was shooting and his energy and enterprise made Sandringham one of the finest shooting estates in the country. Obviously, however, as 'First Gentleman of Europe', he led the social set, and legion were those who attempted to make his acquaintance. At his instigation the Marlborough Club was founded, after he quarrelled with the committee of Whites, and his closest friends became members. He himself was elected a member of the Jockey Club in 1864 and enjoyed the days he spent at Newmarket. However, there was no question of his owning race-horses. His financial resources would not stand it, and also he was not as yet sufficiently interested in racing. No exact date can be given as to when thoughts of ownership first entered his mind, but it must be realised that Queen Victoria would have objected strongly to the royal colours appearing on a race-course. It seems certain, therefore that any possibility of the Prince owning horses would necessitate them either being in partnership, or else secretly competing in the name of another owner.

In 1863 the Prince of Wales had become Regimental Colonel of the 10th Hussars. The Hussars were stationed at Hounslow in 1871 and decided to hold their annual steeplechase at Down Barn near Southall. There were five races and the three judges were Prince Edward of Saxe-Weimar, Lord William Beresford and Lord Rosebery. Other than regimental supporters there were few spectators, as the races were held in semi-secret. The entries for the

[1] *RA Add Mss A/3/137*

Challenge Cup for bona fide hunters, distance three miles, were:

HRH The Prince of Wales'	Champion—	
		Captain Rivers Bulkeley
Lord Valentia's	Wellington—	Captain Wood
Hon P W Fitzwilliam's	Punkah	—Owner
Lord Valentia's	Vent Piece	—Mr Woods
Mr Smith Dorrien's	Marquis,	—Owner
Major St Quinten's	Crusader	—Owner

Everyone hoped for a royal victory, but unfortunately Champion fell at the brook, and although remounted, could only finish second to Wellington who won handsomely by ten lengths. Amongst those present were Lord Carrington, Lord Aylesford, Colonel and Mrs Owen Williams and a host of the Prince's sporting friends.

Although the Prince began to consider seriously the prospect of owning horses, there is every likelihood that the final decision to enter horses in his own name resulted from his visit to India in 1875. Included on his staff, in addition to Lord Aylesford and Lord Carrington, who went as his personal guests, were Colonel Owen Williams as an equerry and Lord Charles Beresford as an ADC. The Princess of Wales did not accompany her husband on the trip, which proved to be an outstanding success from everyone's point of view, whether Queen Victoria's, Disraeli's or the Indian Princes. Two days after his arrival in Bombay, the Prince celebrated his thirty-fourth birthday, and for the next seventeen weeks banquets, ceremonial receptions where the Indian Princes and Rajahs paid their respects to their future sovereign, big game hunts and visits to Poona, Madras, Calcutta, Benares and Lucknow followed in non-stop succession. Throughout the tour the native Princes generously presented the Prince of Wales with costly gifts – which were supposed to be strictly limited to a value not exceeding two thousand pounds, but often the presents, some of which had been bought in London, were far more

114

valuable and were, by right, the Prince's personal property. Each day was so strenuous for the Prince that, although he enjoyed every moment of his journey, it was essential that he was surrounded by those with whom he could relax completely in his few leisure hours. Hence the very great care with which his retinue had been selected. Two of them were to have life-long associations with him. Dighton Probyn, his equerry, was forty-two years old at the time of the tour, but knew India and her problems better than most men. Joining the Bengal Cavalry in 1849 he had fought gallantly throughout the Indian Mutiny, being present at the Siege of Delhi, the Battle of Cawnpore and the Relief of Lucknow. He was mentioned in Dispatches seven times and his Victoria Cross was gazetted in June 1858. In 1870 he had become a Major-General after serving both in the China campaign and the Umbeyla expedition.

The second of the Prince's staff with whom a strong friendship was formed during the Indian trip was Lord Charles Beresford, his ADC. The Beresfords of Curraghmore were an enchanting family whose ancestral home near Waterford was one of the best loved homes in Ireland. In the winter months over one hundred horses were kept in the stables, and the innumerable house guests hunted six days a week. Lord Charles Beresford, second son of the fourth Marquis of Waterford, was born in 1846 and joined *Britannia* as a naval cadet at the age of twelve. During the next decade he voyaged to Honolulu and Vancouver, China, Japan and Australia as well as spending eight months in the royal yacht *Victoria and Albert*. He rode in his first race in Corfu and won it, although he lost his cap in the process, and his horse ran three times round the course before he could pull him up. One of his favourite dictums was 'horses are like Irishmen – easily managed if one knows how to handle them'. In 1874 he had been returned as Conservative member of Parliament for Waterford. The election organised in typical Irish fashion was not without its amusing side. On the eve of the poll

Lord Charles found one of his opponent's supporters sticking up bills outside a public house. After a fight and a drink the rival left without his bills, which were promptly taken back to Curraghmore. Stealthily Lord Charles crept into the bedroom of one of his sleeping brothers and plastered not only the walls and ceiling with the offending bills, but also his brother's clothes, his towels, and even the floor. At breakfast the infuriated brother cried out, 'Charlie, there are some bold men amongst the enemy, one of them got into my room last night!'

Lord Charles Beresford was also responsible on at least one occasion for assisting His Royal Highness on the spur of the moment. Shortly after the Prince went to live at Marlborough House he invited Queen Victoria to inspect his new home. Amongst the downstairs rooms was one which the Prince had furnished as a very comfortable smoking-room – completely overlooking the fact that his mother abhorred smoking, and would not tolerate it. She was already in the house when her son realised the problem of preventing her from seeing this smoking-room. He explained his predicament to Lord Charles, who promised to solve it. This he did by putting a notice 'WC Under Repair' on the door, which satisfied Her Majesty, without closer scrutiny.

There were five Beresford brothers, who at one time were described as 'gallant and high-spirited officers', 'adventurous heroes' and 'princes of good fellowship'. The eldest John Henry, had married Lady Blanche Somerset, only daughter of the Duke of Beaufort, and hunted an area of seven hundred and twenty-five square miles, four days a week. The third brother Lord William, educated at Eton, in 1867 joined the 9th Lancers who were stationed in Dublin. Amongst his brother officers were Captains Hugh McCalmont, 'Roddy' Owen, 'Bay' Middleton and 'Sugar' Candy, all of whom spent much of their leave at Curraghmore. When Lord William Beresford came into his share of the family money he considered it 'so inadequate to my needs that I decided to use my capital as income so long as it would last, and re-arrange my life again when it came to an end. I started a coach, a stud of hunters, some race-horses and laid myself out for a real good time. I managed to hold on until just before the regiment were ordered to India. Then as the fateful day drew near I thought I would have one final flutter at the Raleigh Club. A turn up of three cards at £1,000 a card. I won the lot, was able to pay up all I owed and clear out to India, cleared out but a free man as to debt.'

At the time of the royal visit to India, Lord William Beresford was on the staff of the Viceroy Lord Northbrook. Naturally he was delighted to see his brother Charles and reminisce with him over the famous sweepstake at Williamstown in which they and their younger brother Lord Marcus Beresford had competed the previous August. Lord Marcus was at this time a young subaltern in the 7th Hussars, little dreaming that in the years ahead he would be appointed Master of the Horse to the Prince of Wales, and be largely responsible for the great success that his royal master enjoyed on the Turf

Born on Christmas Day 1848 he was sent to school at Harrow. Harrow races were 'out of bounds' but nevertheless he frequently attended, sometimes disguised as an unrecognisable ragged Irish lad. Once a Harrow master gave him a 'tanner' to hold his horse, a 'tanner' promptly invested with a local bookmaker and turned into half-a-crown. Sent to India in 1867 with the 7th Hussars he bought several ponies which he raced with considerable success. Nine years later he returned to Ireland as ADC to the Governor, the Duke of Abercorn, and took part in the Williamstown race which his brother William won on Woodlark. Previously, when his regiment had been stationed at York, he rode the winner of the Subalterns Challenge Cup. His first important victory as a gentleman rider was on his own horse Chimney Sweep, when he won the Grand Military Chase at Croydon in November 1872. Chimney Sweep was

117

a top-class steeplechaser who finished second to Reugny in the 1874 Grand National, and subsequently was fourth in both 1876 and 1877, before gaining a deserved victory over the Aintree course, when he won the 1878 Grand Sefton.

Much of Lord Marcus's skill in the saddle was learned from Mr Fothergill Rowlands who trained his horses at Pitt Place, Epsom. In the 1860s Rowlands had done a great deal to revive the flagging sport of steeplechasing, and had ridden his own horse Medora in the 1863 National, the same horse carrying him to victory in the Grand Steeplechase at Baden Baden. His head lad John Jones, who used to ride Chimney Sweep in the majority of his races, was the father of Herbert Jones, who was later to become famous as the Prince of Wales's jockey.

Many of the aristocratic 'bloods' kept their horses with Rowlands, but their determination to gamble on anything and everything constantly led to disagreement. It was an era when highspirited and dashing subalterns found daytime excitement in steeplechasing, and the names of 'Bay' Middleton, Prince Kinsky, 'Tip' Herbert, 'Roddy' Owen and a score of others were synonymous with gallantry.

In 1876 four of 'Fogo' Rowlands' owners, Lord Duppling, Mr Fitzroy, Mr Paget and Lord Marcus Beresford, removed their horses from Pitt Place and set up their own training establishment near Banstead. Perhaps selfishly they persuaded Jones to leave Rowlands and take out the licence to train their horses, although it was not he who had the final word as to the management of the stable! Lord Marcus rode his own horses whenever possible, and scored his greatest triumph as a jockey at Bogside in 1876 when he won the National Hunt Chase, at a time when his brothers were in the company of the Prince of Wales in India. Like them he was a brilliant raconteur, a great practical joker, the possessor of immense charm, whose wit was described as 'both subtle and scathing, daring or saucy'. When asked in his Club by an officious and elderly member, 'Whose tobacco do you smoke, Lord Marcus?' he replied, 'My own, of course.' He had a zest for living that enabled him to find 'good in everything' and he was beloved by all who came into contact with him. He lived in an era when 'gentleman riders' included some of the most exalted names in the country, and feats of horsemanship brought prestige and bonds of friendship which lasted a lifetime. It is no small wonder therefore that on his return from India the Prince should turn to him for advice on the question of buying a steeplechaser.

What in all probability occurred is that the Prince, throughout his Indian tour, found himself constantly listening in his off-duty moments to racing talk amongst his staff, which frequently was exaggerated until a Mullingar selling plater ridden by a Beresford became a Derby or a Grand National winner, upon whom the owner had invested hundreds of pounds at generous odds. Naturally these dreams of the Turf impressed him, and he began to consider the financial costs of ownership and the possibility of being able to afford to race on a small scale.

There was no suggestion that any of the gifts received during his Indian tour were sold – in fact many of them were displayed at Marlborough House on his return – but they gave an assurance of additional wealth. In his memoirs, Lord Suffield, who accompanied the Prince of Wales on the tour, wrote :

> The Indian princes themselves expressed much annoyance that any comparison should have been made between their gift's and the Prince's . . . As a matter of fact we took with us £40,000 worth of presents, and besides being valuable they were beautiful and quite remarkably well chosen. But so generous were the Rajahs that it was with no little difficulty they were persuaded to limit the value of their gifts. One indeed, the Maharajah of Cashmere, proposed to make presents to the value of £50,000, and was not at all pleased at having to cut them down to £5,000. . . . The Maharajah did present the Prince with a sword that was studded with gems from hilt to point, and worth at least £10,000. . . . At Indore, when the Maharajah Holkar

presented his numerous and beautiful gifts to the Prince, we were all rather touched to find that a very pretty necklace for the Princess was among them. . . . Of material things we took a cargo worth a king's ransom. The gifts made to the Prince were quite beyond valuation.

Although it is recorded that the Prince of Wales's colours were first worn at Newmarket at the July meeting of 1877, when his Arab pony Alep was matched against another horse of the same breed owned by Field Marshal Lord Strathnairn, and was beaten by thirty lengths, this race does not in reality constitute the début of the Prince into ownership. There is a likelihood that, earlier than this date, he had an interest in some form or another in a few race-horses, especially those that ran in the name of Lord Aylesford. It is also recorded that Leonidas won the Military Hunt Steeplechase at Aldershot on 14th April 1870 in the colours of the Prince of Wales, ridden by Mr 'Wenty' Hope Johnstone. However the Prince's true début on the Turf came with the purchase of the two steeple-chasers Congress and Jackal. Lord Marcus Beresford had ridden Jackal to win the 1878 Craven Steeplechase at the Liverpool autumn meeting. There were only two runners, both of whom refused, but Jackal eventually completed the course and was judged the winner, even though the race had taken about twenty minutes instead of the usual five or six! Nevertheless it seemed to Lord Marcus that Jackal, who had at one time been labelled a 'dreadful thief', would be an ideal horse for the Prince. His previous career was extraordinary. Owned by Forbes Bentley, he ran disappointingly in the Stewards Cup at Goodwood when gambled on, and was eventually acquired by Richard Marsh, who was training at Banstead Manor, near Epsom. To his astonishment Jackal proved a fluent jumper, and brought off a coup for the stable when he won a maiden hurdle race at Croydon ridden by his trainer, who gambled not only all his available cash, but also his watch, which he valued at fifteen pounds, upon the supposed certainty who obliged at 5–1. Jackal was then taken to France where he won a valuable hurdle race at Auteuil, and was sold to Mr Baltazzi for two thousand pounds. Richard Marsh rode him in the Grand Nationals of 1875 and 1876 for his new owner, whilst in the 1878 race he finished fourth in the colours of Captain Machell. The Prince of Wales saw this National, staying at Croxteth with the Earl of Sefton. Prior to the day's racing, straw which had been laid below the balcony from which the Prince was to watch the National caught fire, but the flames were put out before any damage was done. Lord Marcus Beresford had been trying to buy Jackal for some time and succeeded in the autumn of 1878. He also bought Congress, and passed both steeplechasers on to the Prince of Wales for two thousand pounds.

It was the intention to run both horses in the National, for which Congress had been given twelve stone seven pounds. He was a fine stamp of steeplechaser who previously had run in five Nationals and had twice been second. Sadly, a few days before the 1879 race, he broke down in training and never ran again, much to the disgust of Lord Marcus who was riding him in his final gallop when the disaster occurred. Royal hopes were now pinned upon Jackal who ran in the 'light blue, black cap' colours of Lord Marcus. Jackal ran with credit to finish second, but had no chance with the winner, The Liberator, who beat him by ten lengths. The stable knew that Congress was a far better horse than Jackal and could give him any amount of weight, so the result was tinged with a certain amount of disappointment at what might have happened if Congress had run. By a coincidence there was a runner in the National named Lord Marcus, owned by Mr James Connolly, who finished seventh and was the cause of much amusement at Lord Marcus Beresford's expense.

Although Jackal broke down in the autumn and was shot, and Congress had been a failure, the Prince decided to persevere and requested Lord Marcus to buy more steeplechasers for him. This was duly done, with the pleasing result that the Prince's colours were successful in the Household Brigade Cup at Sandown and the Royal Handicap Steeplechase at the 11th Hussars Kempton meeting. The Scot, ostensibly bought because the Prince of Wales wished to have a runner in the Great Baden Steeplechase, started favourite for the 1884 Grand National, but fell some way from home. During the race a telegram arrived stating that Prince Leopold, Duke of Albany, younger brother of the Prince, had died at Cannes, and immediately after the race the Prince left the course. The Stewards, after much deliberation, decided that the remainder of the afternoon's racing should be held, although several owners preferred, in the circumstances, not to start their horses. Court mourning curtailed the social life of affluent England until the summer, and gave the Prince further time to resent the fact that the Queen and the Government were so reluctant to allow him to play a part in affairs of State. To a certain extent any accusation, however unfair, that the Prince of Wales spent too much time leading the social 'set' should have reverberated in the halls of Balmoral.

At the age of forty-three, cultured, much travelled, the father of five children, with a kindness of manner which charmed and delighted all his associates, and above all else Heir to the Throne, it seemed a very short-sighted policy that he was not permitted to do more for his country. In 1884 his plea to accompany the army of Lord Wolseley on the expedition to rescue General Gordon at Khartoum was refused, although in an effort to mollify his disappointment Lord Charles Beresford was allowed to join his force as an ADC. The truth is that the Prince was compelled to turn more and more towards the society of his friends, many of whom were prominent members of the Jockey Club.

The village of Kingsclere near Newbury will always be associated with the name of John Porter, one of the greatest trainers in the history of racing, who sent out the first of his seven Derby winners in 1868. His Derby candidate for 1883 was St Blaise, owned in partnership by two members of the Jockey Club, Lord Alington and Sir Frederick Johnstone, both personal friends of the Prince of Wales. St Blaise's final trial was witnessed by the Prince, who travelled down by train from Waterloo. Met at Overton station by Porter and St Blaise's owners, he rode out to watch the gallop which satisfied every onlooker that the Derby candidate must have a great chance at Epsom. Later in the day the Prince lunched with Porter at Park Lodge and inspected the stables. St Blaise duly won the Derby and, by doing so, greatly enhanced the reputation of his sire, Hermit, who had won the Derby in 1867 and who was already the sire of the previous year's Derby winner, Shotover, trained by John Porter.

Hermit was owned by the wealthy Mr Henry Chaplin, who had first met the Prince when they were undergraduates. Years later he had achieved unwanted publicity when he became the fiancé of Lady Florence Paget, who jilted him to marry the Marquis of Hastings. The Prince of Wales frequently stayed with Henry Chaplin at Blankney in Lincolnshire, and on one occasion took much pleasure in the prank played upon his host by Chaplin's small son Eric. After his father had gone downstairs to dinner Eric found some Indian corn, used for feeding pigeons from the window, on his father's dressing table. The corn was surreptitiously put between the lower sheet and blanket of his father's bed, which later that night caused great discomfort. At breakfast the next morning the culprit confessed and amidst roars of laughter was presented with a sovereign by the Prince, who solemnly promised him another if the practical joke was ever repeated. On his visits to Blankney, racing was a constant topic of conversation and it is not surprising that the first two yearlings bought by the Prince were sired by Hermit. Both these fillies, the one named Counterpane out of Patchwork, the other Lady Peggy out of Belle Agnes, were sent to John Porter at Kingsclere.

In the middle of May the Prince of Wales went to Kingsclere to see his fillies, and also to see the mighty Ormonde do his final gallop before the Derby. Ridden by Fred Archer, who six months later was to shoot himself in a fit of delirium brought about by constant wasting and by typhoid fever, Ormonde won the Derby on 26th May. Nine days later Archer rode the Prince's filly Counterpane in a Maiden Plate at Sandown, which she won. The Prince was delighted and wrote to his son Prince George from Marlborough House.

> . . . on 4th and 5th I went to Sandown races and you will be pleased to hear that my two-year-old Counterpane won a Maiden Plate. She was ridden by Archer and won easily and I got quite an ovation from the public afterwards. . . .[1]

A fortnight later Counterpane ran at Stockbridge where she was fully expected to win again. Inside the final furlong she swerved, collapsed and died. A post-mortem revealed that she had a diseased heart. It was a sad end, and the Prince of Wales wrote to his son:

> . . . I went to Stockbridge in Hampshire for the Races. My poor little mare 'Counterpane' ran for the Cup – which I think she would have won – but she broke a blood vessel near the heart and tumbled down dead opposite the stand. It was indeed a most sad occurrence and a very rare thing to happen – as the distance was a short one and she had a very light weight to carry. . . .[2]

However her owner was too understanding of the vicissitudes of racing to be amazed, and in reply to a letter of condolence from Henry Chaplin he wrote: 'I must bear it with philosophy, as I know what the glorious uncertainties of the Turf are. . . .'

[1] *George V AA 15/54*
[2] *GV AA 15/57*

The following month the Prince of Wales stayed at the
Jockey Club rooms at Newmarket, and bought two
yearlings. For three thousand one hundred guineas he
purchased a full brother to Paradoz (1885 Derby winner)
and for eight hundred and sixty guineas he acquired yet
another offspring of Hermit, a colt named The Falcon.
Both proved to be useless, The Falcon never winning a race,
and Loyalist, as the expensive colt was named, not even
reaching a race-course, as he proved to be unsound and did
not stand training. In the autumn Lady Peggy won at
Newmarket, ridden by Archer, who a few weeks previously
had sent a signed photograph of himself in the Prince of
Wales's colours to the Prince at Balmoral. Obviously Lady
Peggy's victory pleased the Prince, who wrote:

> . . . We had four good days racing at Newmarket 25, 26,
> 27 and yesterday. On the second day I ran my two-year-
> old filly Lady Peggy in a Maiden Plate and she won very
> easily with Archer on her back. I was also fortunate enough
> to back Sailor Prince who won the Cambridgeshire at
> 22–1. He is the son of Albert Victor so I thought I must
> back him. Ormonde won a handicap yesterday giving
> Mephisto two stone who ran third to him in the Two
> Thousand Guineas this spring. This shows you what a
> wonderful horse he is, and the Duke of Westminster was
> quite delighted.[1]

Eighteen eighty-seven was the year of the Queen's Jubilee
celebrations, and the Prince and Princess of Wales were
largely responsible for the entertaining of the foreign royal
personages who came to England as guests of the Queen.
The next year the Prince and Princess celebrated their
own Silver Wedding, and Marlborough House was inun-
dated with presents. Their five children gave the Princess
a silver model of her mare Viva, and the Prince gave
his wife a cross of diamonds and rubies, her favourite
jewels.

[1] *GV AA 16/13*

During the next two seasons the Prince of Wales had very little success under Jockey Club rules and only two very moderate races were won in 1889 with Gallifet and Shamrock II. It seems probable that the Prince was finding steeplechasing more enjoyable, even though there was an unfortunate incident at Sandown when his horse Hohenlinden, after winning the Grand Military Gold Cup ridden by Captain Roddy Owen, was disqualified on the grounds that the Prince was not an officer in the army on full pay, and the owner of the second horse Mr Abercrombie was quite within his rights to object, although it caused consternation that he chose to do so. Hohenlinden was not quite as good a steeplechaser as had been hoped when Lord Marcus Beresford bought him. Shortly after the Sandown race, having in the meantime won at Kempton, Hohenlinden was presented by the Prince of Wales to the Shah of Persia as an example of an English hunter. Magic, another useful steeplechaser, was bought for the Prince for fifteen hundred guineas. He ran and won at Sandown and the Prince wrote to Colonel Paget:

> . . . You will, I am sure, be interested in hearing that Magic has turned out a capital horse and I must have a fair chance for the Grand National
> Poor Barton had a bad fall at Sandown in the race that Magic won. But he is being nursed by Miss ——— who hopes to marry him next month. . . .

Magic ran disappointingly in the 1888 Grand National, and managed to finish only fifth the following year in which the Prince also ran Hettie. Writing from Croxteth, where he was staying with the Earl of Sefton, the Prince did not seem upset by these reverses and appeared more pleased by the victory of one of his horses a few days later at the West Norfolk steeplechase:

> . . . The West Norfolk steeplechases took place at East Winch on the 15th and we went to them as a duty to the

126

county as the farmers would have been so disapointed. I ran a horse called Reliance in two races (3 miles each time) and he won very easily. . . .[1]

Magic redeemed himself later by winning the valuable Lancashire Handicap Steeplechase.

The year 1890 was important in the racing life of the Prince of Wales, for during the summer Lord Marcus Beresford, who had been acting for the past five years as a Jockey Club starter, was appointed as an Extra Equerry to the Prince of Wales, and from this time onwards the fortunes of the Prince on the Turf improved. Only four insignificant races worth a mere £694 were won, yet Derelict, first foal of Perdita II, ran with promise, and Sir J T Mackenzie gave the Prince a useful horse called The Imp after he had won the Kempton Jubilee. At the end of the Royal Ascot meeting the Prince wrote: 'Alas! The Imp was beaten – but it is sure to win a Race on a future occasion – as there are such good horses running at Ascot that it is not easy to win. . . .'[2]

Further proof of his understanding and patience was shown in a letter he wrote after Hermit, Henry Chaplin's Derby winner of 1867, died at the age of twenty-six:

My dear Harry,
How kind of you to have sent me the hoof of dear old Hermit so prettily mounted, which I shall always greatly value and constantly use as an inkstand. I am also very much touched by the kind expressions in your letter wishing me good luck with my race-horses. Though I can never expect to have the good fortune which attended the Dukes of Portland and Westminster, still I hope with patience to win one or more of the classic races with a horse bred by myself. . . .

from yours very sincerely
Albert Edward

[1] *GV AA 18/2*
[2] *GV AA 18/19*

A month later the Prince of Wales was the central figure in a moment historic in racing history. He described it in a letter he sent to Prince George a few days afterwards from the Jockey Club rooms at Newmarket:

> . . . On the 28th I drove on Baron Hirsch's coach with a large party to the Bushy Paddocks – Hampton Court – where the yearlings bred by Grandmama under Sir G Maud's supervision were sold. Baron Hirsch bought the sister to Memoir for £5,500! – the largest sum ever given and I bought the sister to Sainfoin for £1,000. . . .[1]

Sainfoin, winner of the 1890 Derby, and Memoir, who won both the Oaks and St Leger the same year, were bred at the Royal Stud at Hampton Court. Neither John Porter nor Lord Marcus Beresford thought that La Flèche was worth more than about three thousand guineas, and it was entirely the enthusiasm of the Prince that persuaded Baron Hirsch to go on bidding until his rival the Duke of Portland gave up. La Flèche was not the most beautiful of fillies, but she won £31,153 in stakes. Unbeaten as a two-year-old, she won the One Thousand Guineas in a canter, was desperately badly ridden by George Barrett in the Derby (which she ought to have won, and finished second), two days later won the Oaks, and completed her brilliant three-year-old career by thrashing the colts in the St Leger. One of the greatest fillies ever to have graced the Turf, she ultimately became the dam of John O'Gaunt, sire of Swynford.

Baron Maurice de Hirsch had first sent his horses, the best of which was Vasistas who had won three races in France, to Kingsclere in the spring of 1889. Grandson of a financier who had acquired a fortune in Bavaria, and son of an enthusiastic lover of horses, the Baron was born in Munich in 1831. As a result of various astute business transactions concerning railway enterprises in Germany, Belgium, Holland, Russia and Turkey, the young Baron increased his inherited wealth many times over. At the

[1] *GV AA 18/20*

end of the Franco-Prussian war the Baron settled in Paris where he lived in sumptuous style – although the barriers which certain sections of Parisian Society erected against him were almost insurmountable. In Austria and Hungary the anti-Semitic feelings of the Court made life even more impossible – and in consequence there was nearly a diplomatic incident when in 1891 the Prince of Wales went to shoot at Baron Hirsch's country estate outside Vienna. The shooting was on so prodigious a scale that the Prince adopted several of the methods of rearing birds and introduced them at Sandringham.

Two reasons caused the Baron to close his Paris house. The first was the death of his son, the second the fact that Parisian society were content to ostracise him. When this millionaire Jew came to England it surprised no one that within a short space of time he had become friendly with the Prince of Wales, who was always attracted to anyone with an international outlook, was generous, cultured, a sportsman, and above all else delighted in doing everything on a grand scale. No one will ever know to what extent the Baron was interested in horse-racing – and unkind critics have claimed that his horses were owned only for social prestige. There is a story that even after he had bought the immortal La Flèche, who won three Classic races in his colours – citron jacket with turquoise cap – he did not recognise his own filly when he saw her in her box at Egerton House, Newmarket, where Richard Marsh trained her.

In 1894 Baron Hirsch bought Matchbox from Lord Alington after the colt had run second to Lord Rosebery's Ladas in both the Two Thousand Guineas and the Derby. Lord Rosebery had become Prime Minister on the retirement of Mr Gladstone in March, and in June became the only Prime Minister to have owned a Derby winner whilst in office. This double achievement was so remarkable that a friend in America sent him a telegram of congratulation which read 'only heaven now left'. It was the Baron's intention to run Matchbox in the Grand Prix de Paris, worth almost twice as much prize money to the winner as the £5,450 of Ladas's Derby. The Prince had been elected a member of the French Jockey Club in 1867, and would have liked to go to Paris to see his friend's horse win, even though he was a little dubious as to whether or not an English horse owned by a German Jew might not suffer interference in running. The Prince proposed to have a modest wager on Matchbox, but since the race was run on a Sunday it would have outraged Queen Victoria if the Heir Apparent had been seen at Longchamp. On the day of the race, Matchbox was favourite – although no English horse had won since Minting in 1886 – but was beaten a neck in an exciting finish by Baron de Schickler's Dolma Baghtche.

The Prince of Wales had decided to stay with Mr Arthur Wilson at his home, Tranby Croft, near Doncaster, for the St Leger. On the first evening the host's son thought he saw one of the guests cheating at Baccarat, and the events which followed made a *cause célèbre* in the social world.

The central figure in the case was Lieutenant Colonel Sir William Gordon Cumming of the Scots Guards, who was renowned for his caustic wit. Once, a grandiose doctor, pompously trying to impress, asked him if whilst he had been at Buckingham Palace on guard duty he had noticed the doctor's car. Gordon Cumming, refusing to acknowledge the doctor's social pre-eminence, merely muttered, 'I did not think any of the servants were ill'. Another time when at a dinner party a fellow guest objected to him pronouncing his surname – Gillet – incorrectly and said, 'The "G" in my name is soft as in gentleman'; Cumming replied, 'I thought it was hard, as in beggar.' The law case, which dragged on until the summer of 1891, was sordid, badly managed, and the Prince of Wales was inevitably involved, being subpoenaed as a witness for the prosecution. Ulti-mately the discredited Gordon Cumming retired to his Scottish estate with his American bride. For a time the

Prince became the subject of attacks in many sections of the Press, but a wiser and more restrained article appeared in the *Review of Reviews* for July 1891; almost one hundred years after the affair of Escape at Newmarket:

> The Prince of Wales is now fifty years old and a grandfather. Since his birth, in all churches by law established which comply with the plain ordering of the Book of Common Prayer, the prayers quoted above for Albert Edward, Prince of Wales, must therefore, in the last half century, have been said aloud in the hearing of the worshippers at least 100,000,000 times since first the cannon thundered at the birth of the Heir Apparent to the British throne.
>
> Eight hundred and eighty millions of prayers, and as an answer thereto the baccarat scandal of Tranby Croft!
>
> . . . I rejoice at the protests that are rising, and that will continue to rise against the gambling habit, which is one of the curses of our race. But if we are really in earnest about this matter, it is not with baccarat that we should begin. In England there are only two popular gaming hells – the Turf and the Stock Exchange. To betting and speculation baccarat bears the same relation that in the sphere of temperance Chartreuse bears to beer and gin. To extirpate the use of Chartreuse would not abate by one decimal the sum of England's intemperance and to abolish baccarat and all gambling at cards would not by itself produce any appreciable effect on the serious gambling of our time. . . .
>
> It is well to be zealous about gambling, but it is well also to be consistent, and it is still better to be just. And much of the censure passed so freely upon the Prince was not only inconsistent with the constant daily practice of his critics; it was also cruelly unjust.

A copy of this article was sent to the Prince by the wife of Colonel Arthur Paget, who had been a page at Queen Victoria's wedding, and who had been a friend of the Prince all his life. The Prince, replying from Goodwood wrote:

> My dear Mrs Arthur,
> Many thanks for your letter and for sending me the article

in the *Review of Reviews*. I had seen it some time ago, as I take in the number every month, but am none the less grateful for your kind thought of sending it.

There are many different opinions on its merits and demerits – but I am hardly a judge.

Our party is going off very well. Yesterday the weather was lovely, but today very rainy. There are not as many acquaintances as usual at the races but our stable has done well so far, as we have won 4 out of 6 races, out of which I won 2 out of 3. . . .

Always, yours very sincerely
Albert Edward

The 1891 Flat season opened with the Prince of Wales keeping eleven horses in training – the most he had ever owned, but he was still patient and did not expect immediate success. From Marlborough House on 12th May he wrote to his son:

> . . . On 8th and 9th I went to Kempton Park Races. I ran The Imp the second day in the Jubilee Stakes (worth £3000) but there were 19 runners and he got a bad start and never got through. He won that race last year for old Mackenzie and we had every reason to believe he would win again, being very well, a year older and well handicapped, but my good luck racing has not come yet. . . .[1]

A few weeks later he once more wrote without complaint: ' . . . my two mares, Pierrette and Golden Maze, did not distinguish themselves! I certainly am not lucky with my horses – but one must have patience. . . .'[2]

During the year nine races were won, none of them of any importance, and the following year even less success was enjoyed. It is a curious fact, and inexplicable other than that the horses were of little merit, that John Porter never won an important race for the Prince, and only after the royal horses were sent to Richard Marsh at Newmarket did the Prince enjoy any significant success on the Turf.

[1] *GV AA 19/6*
[2] *GV AA 19/10*

7

Marsh and Persimmon

□□□

RICHARD MARSH WAS born on the last day of the year 1851,
the year of the Great Exhibition in Hyde Park. His father,
a man of Kent, encouraged his eldest son to ride from an
early age, and had no hesitation in agreeing to allow Richard
to accept an invitation to ride Manrico in a Members Plate
at Dover races in 1866, when his son was only fourteen and
a half! Manrico three years previously had won the Lincoln
carrying six stone twelve pounds, and although the Dover
race was only three-quarters of a mile he won by six lengths.
For eighteen months Richard Marsh worked at Newmarket
under the brothers Bloss who sent out Hermit to win the
Derby, and there might have been a chance of his riding
Henry Chaplin's horse at Epsom, as Daley, the stable
jockey, had been claimed to ride another who went amiss
shortly before Derby Day. By this time Richard Marsh's
father had moved to Epsom and here he was joined by his
son who rode several winners before increasing weight
enforced him – as it has so many others – to give up flat
racing and concentrate on riding under National Hunt
Rules. For some years he was associated with the Gloucestershire stables of Golby and Weever, and it was on The Nun,
trained by Golby at Northleach, that he won the Sefton
Handicap Steeplechase at Aintree – his first ride in a
steeplechase!

Every steeplechase jockey suffers severe falls in the
course of his career, and Richard Marsh was no exception.
One of his worst was at Cheltenham when his mount ran
down a flight of hurdles and was hit broadside by the other

runners. Marsh was lucky to escape serious injury, but he broke his arm and his collar-bone. Lord Fitzhardinge kindly had him taken to Berkeley Castle in his carriage, having sent a messenger ahead to warn the local doctor. Unfortunately the doctor was away, and Marsh was compelled to spend a restless and uncomfortable night before his bones were set. Throughout the long hours of his suffering two of the Earl's daughters took it in turns to read him excerpts from *Handley Cross* in the hope that the exploits of Mr Jorrocks would assuage his misery and pain.

Marsh rode in eight Grand Nationals between 1871 and 1881 but was never fortunate enough to win. His final ride on Mr Leopold de Rothschild's Thornfield was his unluckiest, for his horse, described by his jockey who also trained him as 'a beautifully turned bay horse of rare girth, with wide hips, splendid shoulders and altogether a lovely horse to ride', loathed the mud. It rained incessantly from the time Buchanan won the Lincoln until the day of the National, and the course, after three days of torrential downpour, was like a quagmire. Even so, Thornfield finished third. It was Marsh's last ride, as he decided to concentrate entirely upon training.

For some years he had trained at Banstead where Mr Hector Baltazzi sent him a few horses. Later he moved to Six Mile Bottom at Newmarket, before settling at Lordship, which was to be his home from 1876 to 1892. When the lease of the three-hundred-and-fifty-acre Lordship estate was taken over from the previous tenant, Bob Musk, the buildings were dilapidated, but within a short space of time they had been repaired and thirty boxes erected. Marsh's brother-in-law Mr Dan Thirlwell came to live at Lordship and rode many winners for the stable, especially in the 'cerise, french grey sleeves and cap' of Marsh's principal patron the Duke of Hamilton. The Duke remembered quite clearly the first time he came into contact with Thirlwell, for the young jockey's father suggested one afternoon at Sandown that they all should support his two mounts, both of which won at 20–1! Early in his career Thirlwell rode for John Nightingall who sometimes changed the instructions loudly given in the paddock of 'your horse has no earthly chance' to 'don't win too far' whispered in the jockey's ear at the last moment! Whilst at Lordship Thirlwell, Marsh and Robert Anson held a trial for their Grand National candidates which was so secret that it was held at midnight! Only the head lad was allowed to know what was happening, and when the stable boys came to groom their charges at dawn they had no idea that as the clock struck twelve the three horses had been silently led from their boxes and galloped nearly five miles in the moonlight! Thirlwell's outstanding achievement as an amateur jockey was to ride fourteen consecutive winners – a feat unlikely ever to be equalled.

As a jockey and a trainer Richard Marsh's career at this stage was impressive, but no more so than that of many others. He had won three Classics for the Duke of Hamilton with Ossian (1883 St Leger) and Miss Jummy (1886 Thousand Guineas and Oaks), and had proved his ability by winning under both Rules with moderate horses – the test of a good trainer. One of his most notable achievements was winning the Stewards Cup at Goodwood in three consecutive years, 1890, 1891 and 1892, and the 1891 Ascot Gold Cup with Morion, whom the previous year he had trained to win the Royal Hunt Cup. At Royal Ascot in 1883 the Duke of Hamilton, who on Marsh's advice had taken £10,000–£100 that Ossian would win the St Leger, saw his colt beat Ladislas and St Blaise, the Derby winner, who was already showing signs of unsoundness after his hard races at Epsom, and in the Grand Prix de Longchamp. A month later at Goodwood Ossian won two races and, against Marsh's wishes, ran in a third race which he lost by a head. Half an hour earlier Marsh had seen a two-year-old filly owned by Lord Cawdor win a seller at 7–4 on ridden by Archer. It was a race outwardly of no

135

consequence, but if Marsh could have foreseen the future he would have taken more than passing interest in the winning filly – Perdita II.

In 1889 Marsh's lease at Lordship was due to expire, and he was uncertain of his future, for he was at loggerheads with his landlords who wished to renew his lease on terms more favourable to themselves, even though he had spent a considerable amount of his own money in laying out new paddocks and establishing a stud farm. Whilst negotiations were proceeding, Marsh was offered a tenancy of land owned by Lord Ellesmere.

The idea was to create a training establishment which would be the finest in the kingdom, with the proviso that work would not commence until a suitable trainer agreed to accept the tenancy. To finance the cost a sum of fifty thousand pounds was put aside, being the surplus earned by the fashionable sire, Hampton.

Hampton, like other handicappers who ultimately became Cup horses, first competed in two-year-old selling races. He ran for the first time at Oxford in a Maiden Plate which he won, starting favourite. Owned by a Mr Ireland, and as yet unnamed, he next ran at the Hampton autumn meeting, ridden by James Goater, and again won. He was sold for two hundred guineas to Mr James Nightingall, who promptly named him after the Hampton meeting. In the spring of 1875 he won the Great Metropolitan at Epsom, and later was put over hurdles, before he was sent to Robert Peck, who trained him to win the Goodwood Stakes, the Northumberland Plate and the Goodwood and Doncaster Cups. At stud he sired three Derby winners Merry Hampton, Ayrshire and Ladas, and an Oaks winner in Reve d'Or.

The task of building Egerton House took about two and a half years. Gallops were laid out, belts of trees planted, the land turned from arable to grass, and ranges of stabling built. An innovation was a mile-and-a-quarter moss litter gallop copied from one Marsh had admired when he had been hunting with the Duc d'Aumale's boarhounds in Chantilly forest. There can be no doubt that once completed the establishment was superb and on a grand scale. Marsh himself admitted that even as a tenant he needed to make thirteen thousand pounds a year to cover his essential overheads, but nevertheless Egerton House was 'fit for a King' in every respect, when Marsh and his horses took up residence there in the autumn of 1892.

The year 1892 had begun tragically for the Prince of Wales as his eldest son the Duke of Clarence died at Sandringham in January, and for many months the Prince and his family retired from public life. His race-horses were of little account, and it was only in the autumn that he had even moderate success. Writing to his son Prince George, now Duke of York, from the Jockey Club Rooms on 14th October:

> . . . I came here on Monday afternoon and have fair weather, though it blew and rained heavily during the Cesarewitch. Versailles ran in the race but I never expected it would win. However I won a race with my two-year-old The Vigil just before . . .[1]

It was logical that since the Prince spent so much of his leisure time at Sandringham it would be more convenient for his horses to be trained at Newmarket than Kingsclere. The fact that John Porter had been unable to train any of his horses to win an important race did not affect the issue. It is possible that there was some clash of personalities, and it has been suggested that Porter and Lord Marcus Beresford did not see 'eye to eye', but it must have been evident that the distances involved made Newmarket infinitely preferable. There is little doubt that Lord Marcus Beresford and Marsh held each other in high regard, and

[1] *GV AA 19/45*

also that Egerton House was eminently suitable. The first approach to Marsh to train the Prince of Wales's horses was made by Beresford at a meeting at Challis's Hotel in London. To Beresford's surprise Marsh hesitated to accept until he had consulted his principal owner the Duke of Hamilton, with whom he was to stay that night. Marsh was rebuked for his hesitation from three sides, for not only did Lord Marcus smilingly tell him that in olden days he would have been beheaded for such hesitation, whilst the Duke commanded him to telegraph his grateful acceptance immediately, but at a later date the Prince commented upon the incident before congratulating him upon his respect for a good master.

It was a memorable moment when on the first day of January 1893 the eight royal horses arrived at Egerton House. They consisted of two four-year-olds, two three-year-olds and four two-year-olds. A few days later twenty horses owned by Baron Hirsch also arrived from Kingsclere, including the four-year-old La Flèche, one of the greatest mares of all time. In April the Prince, after visiting Egerton House, wrote: ' . . . I left Sandringham on Thursday and spent all day at Marsh's splendid establishment at Newmarket and found my horses very well. . . .'[1]

Hopes that the Prince of Wales's horses would soon triumph were dashed when Marsh started training them in earnest. The truth was that with the exception of Florizel II they were moderate in the extreme. It is staggering to realise that the Prince had been racing for more than eight years and had won less than six thousand pounds in stakes. It would have entitled anyone to feel despondent – especially when horses belonging to his personal friends were winning many races – but he never lost his enthusiasm, and a week after the wedding of his son Prince George to Princess May of Teck he wrote: ' . . . the horses in Marsh's stable have run very badly this week, but they

[1] *GV AA 20/2*

are looking very well and we went over the stables yesterday. . . .'[1]

During the winter he still found time to watch the steeplechasers, and writing from Marlborough House in February stated:

> . . . We elected 10 candidates for the Marlborough yesterday but I was unable to be present as I went to Sandown to see my horse 'The Vigil' run in a hurdle race. It rained without ceasing all day and the ground was so deep and slippery that the horse fell at a fence and lost the race which it had a good chance of winning . . .[2]

'A good chance of winning' – what a hollow phrase that must have sounded to the Prince as he wrote to his son! It must have seemed that the Gods would never relent, but in fact glorious and unexpected fortune lay close at hand, and with horses bred at his own stud at Sandringham.

The Sandringham stud, like many of the buildings on the estate, were made of Carr stone, a brown sandstone quarried locally. When it was decided to create a stud farm, boxes originally used for shorthorns and shire horses were transformed into boxes for the mares, and a further range built for the yearlings. The Prince was fortunate in acquiring the services of Edmund Walker as his stud groom, and no man could have served him more loyally. Walker, who previously had managed a small stud at Newmarket owned by Fred Archer, was appointed on the recommendation of John Porter.

Amongst the ten mares acquired for the stud in 1889 was an eight-year-old named Perdita II. She was bred by Lord Cawdor in 1881 and made her first race-course appearance in her breeder's colours in the First Spring Two Year Old Stakes at Newmarket, ridden by Fred Archer. She started second favourite and was beaten by Lina, a 100–6 outsider owned by Chevalier Ginistrelli, for whom Signori-

[1] *GV AA 20/11*
[2] *GV AA 20/26*

netta was to win the 1908 Derby at 100–1. A week later, at Windsor, Perdita II was no more successful, ran even worse at the Second Newmarket spring meeting, and also without distinction at the Newmarket July meeting. Unbelievably her first success was in a seller at Goodwood! She then ran promisingly at Derby, and was second, beaten by a neck, in the Fitzwilliam Stakes at Doncaster to Whitebine, ridden by Archer, before winning another seller at Newmarket. In the autumn she was bought by Matthew Dawson for five hundred and sixty guineas, on behalf of a Mr Benhold. This purchase money was soon recouped, for she won a thousand-pound Nursery at Derby. She ran nine times as a three-year-old, and won two races, the Great Cheshire Handicap and the Ayr Gold Cup worth in those days only two hundred and ninety pounds to the winner! As a four-year-old she started eleven times, and unluckily never won, even though in six of her races she finished second. The next year (1886) she again won the Great Cheshire Handicap and later dead-heated with Mr Leopold de Rothschild's Middlethorpe for the Liverpool Cup. This was her last victory, and although she ran three more times during the season she never won again.

It is astonishing to look back on her racing career, which by no stretch of imagination could be described as brilliant, and realise that this mare was responsible for virtually all the racing triumphs of the Prince of Wales. Understandably, when Lord Marcus Beresford opened the door of her box for admiring visitors, he prefaced his remarks with 'here is the goldmine'. There seems some discrepancy as to who was responsible for advising the Prince to buy Perdita II, but certainly Matthew Dawson was consulted before one of the bargains of all time was sold to the Prince for nine hundred guineas when the Sandringham stud was founded. Perdita's first foal, by Barcaldine, was Derelict, whose best performance was to finish third in the 1891 Cambridgeshire. Her second foal, a filly named Barracouta, also by Barcaldine, won the Champion Breeders Foal Stakes at Derby on her only race-course appearance as a two-year-old. Perdita was barren in both 1890 and 1892, but in 1891 she produced a colt foal by St Simon named Florizel II – one of the horses owned by the Prince who arrived at Egerton House on New Year's Day 1893.

It was apparent to Marsh that the Prince's horses were very moderate performers, and during the first season that he trained them he was able to produce only two winners, both of them in humble races, the one at Kempton the other at Sandown. However, there was one two-year-old that Marsh instinctively believed to be very much better than the others – Florizel II. Early in the year Florizel II was backward, rather plain and coarse to look at, with forelegs which seemed unsound, but with a perfect temperament. He did not race until the autumn, when he was sent to Manchester, and as expected finished nearer last than first. A fortnight later, intending to give him more experience, Marsh allowed him to run at Newmarket for the Boscawen Stakes. There were only five runners and he was allowed to start at 10–1, which just about represented his chance. To the amazement of everyone, he finished second, beating the odds-on favourite by six lengths. In his subsequent two races he ran disappointingly, and the Prince wrote to his son:

. . . My two-year-old Florizel ran badly but La Flèche won easily yesterday after having been beaten 3 times this year. Old Lord Calthorpe's Stud was sold here yesterday and I bought a Brood Mare and a two-year-old. . . .[1]

Florizel II wintered well, and as a three-year-old gave the Prince his most important victories to date, for he won five races worth £3,499, including the St James's Palace Stakes at Royal Ascot. When he won at Newmarket in the autumn the Prince wrote:

. . . My Florizel race was an excellent one, but those of Coup de Vent and Hamiltrude very indifferent. Nobody

[1] *GV AA 20/16*

expected Sir B Maple to win the Cesarewitch yesterday. Tell Walker I saw my 6 yearlings yesterday morning, and they were all looking splendid, including Safety Pin who was 'cut' a fortnight ago. . . .[1]

It was a very thankful Marsh who sent out Florizel II to win these races, for the remainder of the Prince's horses proved useless.

In 1895 the Prince had nine horses in training, including Florizel II's full brother, a two-year-old named Persimmon. Although the Prince won a race with his filly Thais, another at Epsom with Courtier, and a two-hundred-pound match against Sir Maurice Fitzgerald's Princess Patsy with Safety Pin, his principal successes came with Florizel II and Persimmon. Florizel II won six races, including the Gold Vase at Royal Ascot, the Goodwood Cup and the Manchester Cup. He had become a thoroughly honest, tough stayer, considerably better than a handicapper, with a good turn of speed at the end of his race. He completed a great year by beating None the Wiser in the Jockey Club Cup at Newmarket. After the race the Prince wrote:

> . . . Florizel won the Jockey Club Cup today though he had only to oppose None the Wiser. It will be his last race for a very long time. With the heavy weight Courtier had to carry yesterday he had no chance, but we all backed Polly Marden who won easily, thanks to the handicapper giving him 3 stone 5 lbs less than my horse carried. . . .[2]

As a five-year-old, Florizel II did not win as he developed suspensory ligament trouble, and it was decided to send him to Sandringham as a stallion. He had been the best horse the Prince had ever owned, and had given to his younger brother Persimmon an example of what was expected from a horse who had the distinction of carrying the royal colours. It was an example which Persimmon followed in no uncertain manner. . . .

[1] *GV AA 20/40*
[2] *GV AA 20/62*

142

As a foal, Persimmon pleased all who saw him at Sandringham. Walker, the stud groom, Richard Marsh, the grooms at Welbeck where he was foaled, and the Prince of Wales all believed in his potential ability, although he seemed to have absolutely straight hocks, and was slightly on the leg. Towards the end of August 1894 he went into training at Egerton House. Describing him at this time Marsh wrote: 'I would not claim for him that he was a good coloured bay for the reason that he was inclined to be "mousy" about the muzzle and around the eyes . . . yet he had good black points about his legs and feet. It is what you like to see in a good hard bay horse. Behind the saddle he was indeed wonderful in the remarkable length from hip to hock, and from hip to the round bone. I should be correct in saying that he was just a trifle slack in his back ribs but he girthed rare and well. His shoulders were what may be called strong. I mean that I have seen more perfectly sloped ones. He had a nice clean neck, while his countenance was bold and good. Slightly derogatory to his appearance was a tendency to lop ears, a characteristic undoubtably derived from the Melbourne blood that was in his pedigree.'

Throughout the spring he began to mature, filling his frame and becoming a truly impressive race-horse. Early in May, Lord Marcus Beresford went to Newmarket to see Persimmon perform his first serious trial gallop. Marsh elected to put a four-year-old mare, Rags, into the trial with a light-weight boy on her back. Persimmon, ridden by Jack Watts – giving her chunks of weight – trounced her. It was an impressive gallop by any standards and Lord Marcus was able to report Persimmon's progress with the utmost delight. By the end of the month the ground was hardening up, and Marsh was unable to do more than keep Persimmon on the move, for fear of jarring the horse. Consequently when he made his first race-course appearance, in the Coventry Stakes at Royal Ascot, Marsh was still uncertain as to how good he might be. There had never been any attempt to conceal Persimmon's ability, and not only

143

the Heath onlookers at Newmarket, but everyone else, seemed to know, by repute, that Persimmon was something out of the ordinary. The Prince and his friends saw Persimmon saddled in the paddock and gave their good wishes to Jack Watts, Persimmon's jockey. Starting favourite Persimmon won by three lengths from Meli Melo, and amidst the jubilation were heard many voices remembering that Lord Rosebery's Ladas, the winner of the Coventry Stakes in 1893, had won the Derby the next year, and perhaps Persimmon would do the same. Persimmon's second race was the Richmond Stakes at Goodwood, which he won comfortably, starting at 2–1 on. The Prince was staying at Goodwood for the meeting and naturally was immensely pleased by this victory. It was planned not to run Persimmon again until the autumn, especially as he was now beginning to show signs of sweating-up before his exercise gallops. There was, however, not the slightest doubt that Persimmon was a very high-class colt, who was likely to remain invincible unless there happened to be another horse of similar calibre born in the same year. There was – and on more than one occasion he was to prove a valiant rival.

Named St Frusquin, he was owned by Mr Leopold de Rothschild, and like Persimmon he was sired by St Simon. It was his misfortune to be born in the same year as Persimmon. His early two-year-old career was not especially full of promise, and although he had previously won at Kempton in May and Sandown in June, it was not until his run-away victory in the Chesterfield Stakes at Newmarket in July that racegoers began to appreciate his merit, and wondered whether he, like former winners of this race, Teddington, Cremorne, Bend Or, Iroquois and Ayrshire, would also win the Derby the following year. To everyone's consternation he was defeated in the Imperial Produce Stakes at Kempton, but proceeded to win the Middle Park Stakes and the Dewhurst Stakes. Persimmon was one of those beaten in the Middle Park, and in conse-

144

quence St Frusquin was made winter favourite for the Derby. Persimmon had been coughing for more than a fortnight before the Middle Park Stakes, and unquestionably did not show his true form, but nevertheless St Frusquin's performance in winning by half a length from the Duke of Westminster's Omladina, with Persimmon five lengths away third, was utterly convincing, especially as Omladina had won the Champagne Stakes at Doncaster.

Obviously the forthcoming rivalry of the two St Simon horses was discussed endlessly throughout the long winter months. Persimmon pleased his trainer by the way he was developing even though he was late in shedding his winter coat – a characteristic apparently inherited from Perdita II who every winter looked more like a sheep than a brood mare. Marsh knew that Persimmon was the best horse he had ever trained, but the dreams of what could lie ahead in the 1896 season at times turned to agonising nightmares. The worst of the nightmare was that Persimmon was taking much longer to come to hand than had been expected, and an abscess under one of his teeth did not help his progress. During the Craven meeting he was galloped against two moderate horses. The result of the trial proved that there could be no possibility of Persimmon running in the Two Thousand Guineas, and he was scratched forthwith. Naturally this was a bitter disappointment to the Prince who wrote:

> ... I was also at Newmarket where the weather was very cold. Persimmon is so overgrown that he is only half-trained and will not be fit to run in the Two Thousand Guineas Stakes next week. It is as much as Marsh can do to get him fit for the Derby! and he won't stand knocking about. St Frusquin is what is called a 'set' horse and is now perfectly fit. Thais is looking very well and will I hope run next week.[1]

St Frusquin made his first appearance as a three-year-old

[1] *GV AA 20/75*

in the Column Stakes at the Craven meeting, which he won 'hard held'. After the race bookmakers were reluctant to quote a price against him for the Derby.

Frustrating though it was to all concerned, Persimmon's scratching from the first of the Classics was a blessing in disguise, for if he had run in an unfit state against St Frusquin it might have ruined him for the rest of the season. The Prince was present at the Two Thousand Guineas, and shortly after the race wrote from the Jockey Club Rooms:

> . . . St Frusquin won the Two Thousand Gns Stakes fairly easily today, but who can tell yet whether he will win The Derby. Marsh is doing his utmost to get Persimmon fully trained and we have just four weeks before us. I have been to the stables and seen him gallop. Thais must have a chance for the One Thousand Gns Stakes on Friday but there will probably be a large field. Only 7 ran in the big race today. . . .[1]

Thais, a filly by St Serf out of Poetry, one of the first mares bought for the Sandringham stud, won the One Thousand Guineas, but only just! It was a bitterly cold day with blustery showers, and from the Dip the race was always between Thais and Santa Maura, owned by Mr Douglas Baird. They went past the post so far apart across the course, that no one knew the result for certain until the judge announced that the Prince's filly had won by a short head. It was a very good performance by a game, but highly strung and delicate filly, and the Prince was able to write:

> . . . I am sure you would be pleased at Thais' victory – winning a Classic race and beating a field of 19.[2]

The Prince was saddened by the sudden death of Baron Hirsch on 21st April 1896 whilst staying with friends at Ogyalla, an estate at Komorn in Hungary. The Baron never

[1] *GV AA 21/1*
[2] *GV AA 21/2*

bet and each year gave all his horses' winning stakes to London hospitals. The winnings of La Flèche alone enabled the generous Baron to donate over thirty thousand pounds to this worthy cause, and if she had not been beaten by three-quarters of a length by Sir Hugo in the 1892 Derby the amount would have been considerably more.

The four weeks before the Derby were the most anxious of Marsh's life. He was not by nature over-optimistic but in his own mind he knew that he had a very great chance of winning the Derby for the Prince. Persimmon was a very good horse, but so was St Frusquin. In his heart he believed, with justification, that Persimmon had the beating of all his other rivals, provided that he was fit enough to do himself justice. Early in May, Persimmon seemed to be making the improvement that Marsh both expected and prayed for, and once more it was suggested that Lord Marcus witness one of his gallops. The result was an atrocious trial which left everyone, including his jockey Watts, utterly miserable. There was only one hope, that the trial was too bad to be true.

The trial had taken place on a Tuesday, and the following Saturday a further trial over the same course against the same horses took place. To Marsh's delight Persimmon did everything which was expected of him, and he immediately wired the good news to Lord Marcus Beresford. One more gallop was now proposed, this time in the presence of the owner, his wife and a party of their friends, on 26th May, just eight days before Epsom. For the purpose of the gallop, which took place on the Egerton House moss litter track, the Duke of Devonshire lent his good handicapper Balcamo to ensure a first-class trial. A small stand was erected on the Egerton House lawn for the royal party, from which the spectators were able to watch the trial from start to finish. It was a fine May morning and for once everything went according to plan. Persimmon was as convincing as a potential Derby winner can ever be prior to Epsom, and the royal party were immensely pleased. The only doubt left was how good was the Two Thousand Guineas winner St Frusquin? There was one yardstick which made St Frusquin look uncommonly good – Balcamo. This horse in receipt of twenty-one pounds had been beaten easily by Persimmon in the trial at Egerton House. In the Newmarket Stakes, a fortnight after the Two Thousand, Guineas, Balcamo had finished second to Galeazzo, owned by Mr Leopold de Rothschild, and Galeazzo was vastly inferior to St Frusquin, even though it was common knowledge that St Frusquin disliked firm going, and the going at Newmarket, where he was trained, was getting steadily more firm with drying east winds and no rain. The name St Frusquin, incidentally, had no real significance. Like certain other saints whose names have appeared in the Racing Calendar his history seems obscure, even if it ever existed. A contemporary claimed that the name was a corruption of the French 'futaine', meaning fustian, with the additional prefix 'Saint' to generally mean 'the whole lot', and reminded his readers that Zola once wrote, 'Ah, si ma garce de femme n'avait pas bu tout mon Saint Frusquin', meaning, 'if my jade of a wife had not drunk the whole blessed lot'.

On 2nd June Persimmon was boxed from Dullingham station to Epsom, with Marsh travelling in the box. The usually normal procedure of boxing a race-horse resulted in consternation where Persimmon was concerned. He simply refused to move, lashing out at the crowd of bystanders, and causing his trainer the proverbial forty thousand fits. Eventually, after Marsh had offered a sovereign to every man who helped get Persimmon to Epsom, the horse was virtually manhandled into the box on the waiting train. Once aboard he nonchalantly began to feed, whilst Marsh, keeping his promise, became the poorer by many sovereigns.

It was evident by Derby Eve that only eleven would face the starter on the morrow. St Frusquin's claim to favouritism was obvious to all, although many racegoers were content to rely on Persimmon. Of the remaining nine the critics made out the best case for Mr B S Straus's Tevfel. Mr Straus himself had recently had the misfortune to suffer an accident whilst riding a new-fashioned and still unacceptable machine called a 'bycycle'; Tevfel had his supporters although many were afraid that on his breeding he would hardly stay more than a mile. The Duke of Westminster's Regret, a colt with a very high reputation at home, had been scratched at the last minute, owing to the fact that it was considered the ground was too hard. John Porter's *Reminiscences* were to be published during Derby week, and some wiseacres claimed that if Regret had been a fancied runner Porter would have delayed publication so as to include a chapter upon his most recent Derby winner.

Derby morning broke dull and gloomy in London. The sky was overcast and the dry spell which had made the ground so hard seemed at an end. Showers moistened the earth but did no more than 'wipe a wet sponge on a slate' in the opinion of one commentator. At Epsom Jack Watts rode Persimmon a short canter before going off to Lord Rosebery's house 'The Durdans' to look at brood mares and yearlings. Diffident, brilliant in the saddle, unassuming and at times morose, Watts had already won the Derby three times, on Merry Hampton, Sainfoin and Ladas. For sometime he had contemplated retirement and only the realisation of Persimmon's ability and loyalty and devotion to the Prince had persuaded him to continue riding in 1896. One of his greatest assets was his imperturbability, and on this the most memorable day of his life it did not desert him.

It had been a busy week for the Prince who had been re-installed as Grand Master of English Freemasons, presided at dinners of the 10th Hussars and 2nd Life Guards, and had entertained Trinity Brethren at the Mansion House on the eve of the Derby.

At half past twelve on Derby Day the royal train left Victoria station, with the storm clouds still darkening the scene. The royal party included the Princesses Victoria and Maud of Wales, Prince Charles of Denmark, the Duke and Duchess of York, the Duke of Saxe-Coburg and Gotha, the Duchess of Teck, the Duke of Cambridge and Prince Edward of Saxe-Weimar. The excited Princess Maud had drawn her father's horse in a sweepstake. The clouds still threatened heavy rain when the royal train arrived at Epsom, but slowly, as the afternoon progressed, the light became brighter and before the Derby the sun came out. The scene on the Downs was no different from that of any other year save that, because of the weather, the crowd seemed slightly less than usual. The holiday spirit conquered all, including a fight between a jellied-eel seller and a disgruntled customer who claimed he needed 'seven for threepence'. There were the usual booths and amusements including the girl described as the Champion High Kicker, the African and Zulu Exhibition and young Ted Saunders the midget boxer who weighed three stone four pounds.

The going on the race-course was hard, and the appearance of what little grass could be seen was parched and arid. At 1.30 pm the runners for the first race, the Epsom Town Plate, were sent on their way, with the American mare Helen Nichols winning an exciting race under top weight. Royal Flush, ridden by T Loates, was second, beaten by half a length, and confusion was temporarily caused by the judge hoisting the incorrect number, but this error was quickly rectified. Half an hour later, nine two-year-olds took part in the Stanley Stakes. Zarabanda, owned by Sir Frederick Johnstone, a life-long friend of the Prince, won by a head. There was now an hour's delay whilst paddock critics inspected the Derby candidates. St Frusquin, whose owner was absent, as the day was the anniversary of his father's death, found many adversaries amongst those inspecting him for the first time. 'Short and wanting in scope' were expressions which came to mind, and his peculiar gait was also criticised. Only those who had seen him win his previous races passed over his apparent faults

150

and were content to remember his racing courage and his turn of foot. Tevfel, sweating, but trained to the minute, looked handsome enough to be seen in the winner's enclosure. Knight of the Thistle, whose trainer was reluctant to run him on the hard ground, looked heavy topped and potentially a St Leger horse. On the way to the post the runners appeared to more than one onlooker like 'cats on hot bricks' so gingerly were they moving over the parched course. St Frusquin from time to time lashed out at nearby spectators, but more with joie de vivre than temper. Three of the runners, Earwig, Bradwardine and Persimmon, did not join the parade. By special permission of the Stewards they were saddled at Sherwood's establishment, over by the mile-and-a-quarter starting post. A few moments before the race they moved, coolly and calmly, down to the start, only a short distance from where they had been saddled. In the betting rings it was still a case of St Frusquin being an odds-on favourite, with Persimmon finding many supporters at 5–1, with only Tevfel, of the remainder, having serious backers.

A huge crowd had assembled at the start, and although none of the runners appeared fractious there were several false break-aways before Mr Coventry, the starter, lowered his flag. Gulistan, Mr Leopold de Rothschild's second string who had been kept in the race to ensure a strong gallop, was slowly into his stride after having been reluctant to line up, and it was not until the field had covered two furlongs that he took up the running from Bradwardine and Bay Ronald. At this stage of the race St Frusquin and Persimmon were the last two. When the mile post was reached Gulistan still led, although the field were all closely bunched up behind him with the exception of Toussaint who was already outpaced. St Frusquin and Persimmon were now taking much closer order on the leaders, their jockeys watching every move the other made. Gulistan had shot his bolt within the next furlong and dropped back, a beaten horse. Bradwardine took up the running until the foot of Tattenham Corner, where it was seen that the eau de Nil silks of Bay Ronald were just ahead, with the dark blue, yellow cap of T Loates on St Frusquin almost mingling with the green and cherry of Tevfel and the chocolate and pink of Spook close behind the leader. Persimmon was going easily about two lengths behind the favourite and slightly to his outside. With two furlongs to go Loates drove St Frusquin into the lead, as one by one his adversaries, except for Persimmon, faltered. Tevfel, Bay Ronald, Spook and Earwig all lost ground as the favourite forged ahead. Watts, riding the greatest race of his life, was still gaining ground, although he had not asked Persimmon for a final effort. From the stands it was obvious within the final two furlongs that the winner would be either St Frusquin or Persimmon, with the vital question – could the royal colt catch the favourite? Watts, coolly calculating to a nicety the moment to challenge, urged Persimmon forward. At the Bell the two horses were level, and although St Frusquin never flinched, never faltered on hard going which he hated, Persimmon with his longer stride began to gain the mastery. One hundred yards from the winning post he was a neck in front, an advantage he maintained until victory was achieved. To those who were present and who both understood and loved racing it would have been a memorable and stirring finish between two gallant horses, both ridden par excellence, no matter what the race or the title of the winning owner. When the race was the Derby and the successful owner the Prince of Wales, who had bred the winner at his own stud, the jubilation was incomparable. *En passant* it should be stated that Earwig was third, and Tevfel fourth, the distances being a neck and four lengths between the first three.

As the judge hoisted the winning number 'one' on to his board, all eyes spontaneously turned to the balcony of the Club Enclosure from where the Prince had watched the race. Obviously overcome with emotion, he at first merely acknowledged the cheers which began to increase in acclamation until they were taken up by the multitude at every part of the Epsom Downs. People who could not possibly have seen even a glimpse of the horses and jockeys during the race joined the volume of sound, until even to the modest but elated winning owner the truth must have become apparent. They were not cheering to congratulate an owner upon winning the Derby, they were demonstrating to the best of their ability the fact that they admired and loved Albert Edward, Prince of Wales, and they wished him to understand and realise this. They wanted him to know that they were proud of him and were proud that one day he would be their King. It might be his day, but it was theirs also, because he belonged to them, just as they were to be his loyal subjects. It was a tribute to the personal popularity of the Prince.

All in good time, the Prince, his hat in his hand, advanced to meet his champion. There were smiles, congratulations, tears of happiness, and all the time the crowd roared their approbation. Marsh, who had hacked back from the start whilst the race was in progress, found it almost impossible to force his way through the throngs of spectators, saw nothing of the finish of the race, and was first told the result by jockey Mornington Cannon as he pulled up Knight of the Thistle by the Downs Hotel. Watts allowed himself the ghost of a smile as he rode Persimmon back to join his royal master, and his usually calm countenance had a slightly happier expression than usual. Gradually the police were able to make a way for Persimmon and the Prince, together with the Duke of York, Lord Marcus Beresford and Marsh back to the unsaddling enclosure. Amongst the first to congratulate the Prince were Sir George Chetwynd, Mr H McCalmont, whose Isinglass ridden by T Loates had won the Derby three years earlier, Sir James Miller, the Duke of Westminster and Lord Bradford. It was reported that Marsh's smile was as broad as Berkshire, and Lord Marcus would never be able to wear a hat again. By this time the excited crowd had swarmed on to the course outside the Weighing Room, cheering, shouting their own congratulations, whilst on the Club balcony the Prince was holding a reception to 'all and sundry'. To complete the cup of happiness of the royal party it was the birthday of the Duke of York. There can be no doubt that both Persimmon and St Frusquin were very good horses by any criterion, and equally that even though Loates broke a stirrup iron in the last few strides it made no difference to the result. Later in the day the sunshine was overshadowed by more clouds, there were further showers and revellers who had been drinking the Prince's health in every conceivable beverage were drenched, but nothing could spoil a glorious and perfect day. A telegram was received from the Queen at Balmoral, to which the proud and happy Prince of Wales replied:

> Most grateful for your kind congratulations. The scene after the Derby was a most remarkable and gratifying sight.   Albert Edward.[1]

In the evening the Prince entertained the Jockey Club to dinner at Marlborough House. After an exhausting but wonderful day, it would seem they were all hungry!

DINER DU 3 JUIN, 1896

Turtle Punch	*Tortue Clair*
	Consommé à la d'Orléans
Madeira, 1820	*Petites Truites au Bleu à la Bordelaise*
	Filets de Soles froids à la Russe
Marcobrunner, 1868	*Cotelettes de Volailles à la Clamart*
	Chaud-froids de Cailles à la Lucullus

[1] *Z 458/4*

154

Château Margaux, 1875	*Hanches de Venaison de Sandringham, Sauce Aigre Douce*
	Jambons de York Poëlé au Champagne
	Sorbets à la Maltaise
	Poussins rôtis au Cresson
Moët et Chandon, 1880	*Ortolans rôtis sur Cânapés*
	Salades de Romaine à la Française
	Asperges en Branches, Sauce Mousseuse
Still Sillery, 1864	*Croûtes aux Pêches à la Parisienne*
	Petits Soufflés Glacés à la Princesse
	Gradins de Patisseries Assorties
Chambertin, 1875	*Casquettes à la Jockey Club*
	Brouettés Garnies de Glacés variés
	Gauffrettes

Royal Tawny Port (50 years old): Royal White Port (50 years old): Sherry, George IV: Magnums Château Lafite 1864: Brandy 1848.

Eighteen seventy-five was the greatest vintage in Bordeaux for the past one hundred years, although when the wine was young, it was the opinion of many experts that it would not last. The 1864 vintage was another superb year, but overawed by the greatness of the 1875s, which on Derby evening must have given almost as much pleasure as the events of the afternoon! The next day, the newspaper tipsters extolled their outstanding brilliance at having tipped Persimmon to win. No one admitted to having proposed St Frusquin, and only one was honest enough to admit that Tevfel had been his selection. However he proudly announced that he had 'a grand gem that would atone for this'.

As was to be expected, there were those fatuous enough to attempt to discredit the Prince of Wales's great victory. Their idiotic suggestion were broadsided by an article appearing in the *Racing Illustrated* the week after the Derby:

> It was not likely that the contemptible association of meddlesome busybodies who, with insufferable impertinence, thought fit two years ago to lecture Lord Rosebery on his connection with horse racing, and received such an excellently chosen and telling rebuke for their pains, would forego the opportunity, on the Prince of Wales taking the highest honours of the Turf, of once more parading their bigoted intolerance.
>
> The gratification of the great majority had its origin in the innate feeling of loyalty, which every true-bred Briton, whatever his politics, has at heart for those nearest to the Throne. But it was also largely personal to the Prince, owing to the public appreciation of the fact that as a sportsman and an English country gentleman His Royal Highness had entered the lists in the great national sport against all comers, and had by superior prowess of his representative come off victorious in fair fight.
>
> It has been well said that on the Turf and under it all men are equal. All owners of horses alike, prince, peer or commoner, must conform to the Rules of racing, and submit to the recognised authority by which the great game is controlled.
>
> The huge concourse who saw the most memorable Derby of modern times run for this year, and all other individuals really cognisant of the Turf and its workings need no telling that a more genuine honest, straightforward struggle between two real good horses of two real good sportsmen, was never run. No one present at Epsom with any pretensions to be able to form an opinion of what was going on before his eyes could honestly doubt that the Derby was a perfectly fair run race.

Yet during the last ten days it has not been uncommon to hear certain persons, under the mistaken idea that such hair-brained chatter shows cleverness on their part instead of egregious folly, make offensive innuendoes concerning the Prince and other owners of horses in the race. In the ordinary way such suggestions are best ignored – treated with silent contempt; but as the Turf is a subject in which day by day the public are taking a greater and more intelligent interest, and which the puritanical party are ever ready to malign, it may not be out of place to point out for the benefit of those receiving their first impressions of the sport, why the suggestion that 'Persimmon was allowed to win' – meaning in so many words that the other horses in the race were not doing their best – is false, foolish and malicious.

If no other guide were to hand, the time – two minutes and forty-five seconds, the fastest on record – is in itself alone sufficient to show that the race was true-run. For the other horses in the field to have lain off, to let Persimmon win, would have necessitated an all round slow run race, with the probability if not certainty of St Frusquin finishing at the other end of the field to what he did. Hence, on the face of it, every racing man knows that the suggestion is false.

To insinuate that an honourable gentleman like Mr Leopold de Rothschild actuated as he is with a deep love of the sport, and filled with the keen desire to win the Derby that every true sportsman has, would in any way be a party to such an arrangement, or that such a proceeding could possibly be carried out without his being a party to it, is foolish – utterly foolish; as also is the suggestion that a horse could be ridden out to the bitter end as St Frusquin was in a desperate struggle to stall off the challenge of his half-brother, and yet be so controlled that Persimmon should be 'allowed to win'.

Further to say that 'Persimmon was allowed to win' imputes a direct charge of fraud to the rider of the second. All that need be said on that point is that the jockey has got to be found who can ride a better race than Tom Loates rode on St Frusquin at Epsom, last Wednesday week. Mr Leopold de Rothschild's horse ran as a great good animal giving his running to the last ounce, and while Loates rode him in grim earnest, the horse in the style lovers of racing most appreciate responded with the utmost gameness to every call of his jockey. Hence, to suggest that by any act of St Frusquin's jockey Persimmon was allowed to win – without which act a child can see that the insinuation falls to the ground – is malicious, false, and foolish as well.

But the discordant note before alluded to is not one that comes from such silly slanderers as these. The puritanical Pharisees who day by day thank their God that they are not as other men are, and who in the narrow-minded circles of their own little Bethels preach and prate against the doings of far better men than themselves, having lifted up their voices, have met, and passed resolutions under high sounding titles, whose length is inversely proportioned to their importance, calling upon the Prince to sever his connections with the Turf; which latter they are pleased to term 'the great national engine of gambling'.

It is the same old story. A lot of conceited, self-advertising nobodies see a chance of getting their names in print, and becoming of some importance in their own little locality; therefore, regardless whether men will speak well of them or not, they intrude their bigoted and narrow-minded opinions on the world at large. Some obscure pastor of the Old Tony Weller's 'shepherd' class has addressed a letter of remonstrance to the Prince for participating in a sport which the councils of the nation have legalised, and in which every Englishman worthy of the name is more or less interested.

... Naturally they and all the Puritanical crew are desperately anxious to draw the Prince of Wales away from the Turf, seeing as they do what a blow his patronage of the national sport has struck at their ridiculous organisation. But if there is one thing more than another for which the Prince of Wales has become noted throughout his career, it is for being possessed of sound common sense, and he is not likely to follow the dictation of any man, least of all a man who pursues such very questionable methods of attaining his ends as the secretary of the Anti-Gambling League.

... In fact there is no getting away from the impression that the whole thing is a sham, organised by certain people simply for self-advertising purposes. The Anti-Gambling League, the Non-conformist Conscience, and the South London Evangelical Free Church Council are only different developments of our old acquaintances – the immortal

158

Stiggins and Chadband. All said and done, nothing hits off the character of the average 'shepherd' better than the time honoured conversation held between the Dissenting grocer and his apprentice:

'James.' 'Yes Sir!'
'Have you sanded the sugar?' 'Yes Sir.'
'Have you stoned the currants?' 'Yes Sir.'
'Have you watered the rum?' 'Yes Sir.'
'Then come to prayers.'

To commemorate Persimmon's Derby success, Lord Marcus Beresford sent Marsh the following letter:

June 24 '96

Dear Mr Marsh,

By desire of the Prince of Wales I enclose you a cheque for £800. HRH wishes you to accept a present of £500 for the splendid way you trained Persimmon for the Derby of 1896 in the face of so many difficulties.

HRH also wishes you to give Crisp, the man who 'did' Persimmon £100, £50 also to Leach, the head lad, and £50 to Prince, the travelling head lad, in commemoration of the event. The remaining £100 HRH wishes you to divide amongst the boys in the stable – or if you prefer it to expend that sum on a dinner (or part of that sum), in fact HRH leaves it to your discretion to spend £100 on the boys in any way which you consider best.

Wishing you a continuance of success – for many years.

Believe me,
Yours faithfully,
Marcus Beresford

Two days later Thais ran in the Oaks. She had never looked back after her One Thousand Guineas triumph and Marsh was confident that she would win. To his disappointment she travelled badly, never ate an oat, and by the morning of the race was in a deplorable state. Proof of her condition was that Marsh's head lad, on his arrival from Newmarket, did not even recognise her. Torrential rain in the London area on Thursday night improved the going the following day, and the course was far less firm than it had been for the Derby. By a coincidence there were eleven runners, the same number as in the Derby, and Thais, whose state was not common knowledge, started favourite at 13–8 against. Together with Lord Derby's Canterbury Pilgrim, a lengthy deep-girthed filly of full quality, she did not take part in the parade, but made her way sedately to the starting point. Considering her condition Thais ran well, but inside the final furlong Canterbury Pilgrim stormed past her to win by two lengths, although for a moment the two fillies came so near together that when congratulating Canterbury Pilgrim's trainer, Hon George Lambton, the Prince of Wales suggested that Rickaby, Lord Derby's jockey, had come very close to Thais as he made his challenge. Canterbury Pilgrim, in later years, became the foundation mare of Lord Derby's stud, and became the granddam of Selene, whilst St Frusquin became the grandsire of Gainsborough. Gainsborough and Selene were the sire and dam of a dapper little chestnut named Hyperion.

At Royal Ascot Thais defeated Canterbury Pilgrim in the Coronation Stakes, but both were beaten by the Duke of Westminster's Helm, in receipt of seven pounds. There were rumours that negotiations were afoot to sell to Australia Florizel II, who ran in the Gold Cup and finished third, but the price could not be agreed, and the transaction came to nothing. Also in the Gold Cup was a six-year-old mare Laodamia, owned by Mr W W Fulton, who later in the year was to win the Doncaster Cup, and then started an even-money favourite for the Cesarewitch for which she finished third. To everyone's astonishment she was brought out a fortnight later to run in the Cambridgeshire in which she also finished third, before being bought for the Sandringham stud.

Although one of the topics of conversation at Royal Ascot was the Prince's generosity in adding the Derby prize money won by Persimmon to Princess Maud's dowry, the principal discussion was the proposed meeting of

Persimmon and St Frusquin in the Princess of Wales Stakes at Newmarket early in July. As it was also intended to start Sir Visto, the 1895 Derby winner, notwithstanding his abject display in the Gold Cup, Kirkconnel the 1895 Two Thousand Guineas winner, and the 'talking horse' Regret it was evident that it might become the race of the year – especially as Permimmon had to give St Frusquin three pounds, and more to Troon who had won the St James Palace Stakes so convincingly.

The ten runners were competing for ten thousand sovereigns, of which £9,005 went to the winner, as compared to the £5,450 of the Epsom Derby. The distance of the race was one mile, on a course which was considered ideal for St Frusquin, and the meeting of the two 'giants' was considered even more exciting than when the Derby winners Isinglass and Ladas met in 1894. The early morning was bright and warm, but later the sun disappeared, the sky became dull and menacing with black clouds darkening the horizon. The Prince was staying at the Jockey Club Rooms and was joined by the Princess of Wales, together with the Princesses Maud and Victoria and the Duke and Duchess of York who arrived just before the first race, having left the train at Dullingham.

Persimmon was saddled 'down the course' which was disappointing for his many admirers, and as T Loates, St Frusquin's jockey, was reluctant to allow his mount to stride out freely on the way to the post, spectators were compelled to back their fancies with singular lack of inspection. Surprisingly the Duke of Westminster's Regret making his first appearance of the season, but receiving weight from all his rivals, was made favourite at 7–4 against. St Frusquin was 5–2 and Persimmon 4–1. It was a thrilling race, with never more than a few lengths between first and last. Inside the final furlong Watts drove Persimmon into the lead, but he was immediately challenged by St Frusquin. For a few strides the issue was in doubt, then the three pounds told against the gallant Persimmon, and

St Frusquin courageously held on to win by half a length, with Regret the same distance away third. It was a great race, and an outstanding triumph for the Duke of Portland's sire St Simon. St Frusquin went on to win the Eclipse, but this was his last race of the year as he broke down shortly afterwards. The Prince of Wales saw the Eclipse at Sandown, where the fashions were smart in the extreme, many of the men wearing black top hats and the women in dresses reminiscent of Royal Ascot.

Two days previously at Newmarket, as a result of the death of Baron Hirsch, the incomparable La Flèche was sold. As she walked majestically round the sale ring with her ears pricked, Mr Somerville Tattersall started the auction at five thousand guineas, only five hundred guineas less than she had been sold for at the Hampton Court Paddocks in 1890. Sir Blundell Maple, on hearing the opening bid, promptly raised it by one thousand guineas. Monsieur Edmund Blanc, the leading French breeder who ten years later bought triple crown winner Flying Fox, was one of those content to raise the bidding by five hundred guineas a time until eleven thousand guineas was reached. The bidding then slackened until at twelve thousand six hundred guineas the lovely mare was knocked down to Sir Tatton Sykes.

Towards the end of July the Prince went to stay for Goodwood with the Duke of Richmond. The racing world were stunned to learn of the death from cholera of the beloved Major 'Roddy' Owen, but pleased that the Baroness Hirsch had generously donated five hundred guineas to the Rous Memorial Fund in memory of her husband. There was also considerable comment concerning a case brought by the Anti-Gambling League against the well-known and equally well-liked bookmaker Richard Dunn on the grounds that betting on race-courses was illegal and an offence against the laws of the country. In support of their case two members of the Anti-Gambling League drew sufficient expenses to cover rail fares to Hurst Park, admission

162

charges and losing wagers. Their crusade was reputed to have the support of none other than the Bishop of London, Dr Temple, but the local bench, after deliberating the pros and cons of the issue for nearly ten minutes, dismissed the case! Much to the delight of the racing world.

As St Leger Day approached, it became almost certain that Persimmon would win the Doncaster Classic. St Frusquin was a non-runner, Persimmon had pleased Marsh by the progress he was making at Newmarket, and all seemed to portend another Classic victory for the Prince. From Marlborough House on 6th September he wrote: ' . . . Excellent accounts of Persimmon, so I hope he will be the victor on Wednesday. . . .'[1]

St Leger Day started with heavy rain, made worse by a severe thunderstorm which had earlier split open the heavens, and made the going distinctly soft. Persimmon was a very short-priced favourite at 11–2 on. Again it was disappointing to the crowds surrounding the paddock that the Derby winner did not appear until the last moment. There had been rumours both at Newmarket and Doncaster for a few days before the St Leger that all was not well with Persimmon, but the manner in which he strode down past the stands dispelled any such thoughts. In the race he moved up to the leaders once the straight was reached. From the stands for an instant it seemed that Watts was not confident, and a murmur so often heard, 'the favourite's beat', began to gather momentum. It was a false alarm, for Persimmon, who had been running lazily, strode away to a comfortable victory to the cheers of the delighted crowd. On returning to the winner's enclosure Persimmon was surrounded by no less than six mounted policemen! The following day the Prince wrote from Fryston Hall, Ferry-bridge in Yorkshire:

. . . We had a lovely day for the races on Tuesday, but yesterday a great deal of rain – though during the Leger

[1] *GV AA 21/7*

163

it was fine and bright. I never saw Persimmon look better and he looked a grand horse. The ground was sticky and the day close, but he did all that was asked of him and won by about 3 lengths. There was a dense crowd and the enthusiasm very great, as the Yorkshire 'Tykes' love horses and sport. When I went down to the paddock to look at the horse after the race I was nearly carried off my legs by the immense crowd. . . .[1]

Three days later, whilst staying at the York Club, the Prince wrote:

> . . . I was sure you would be pleased at Persimmon's victory – also Safety Pin's the following day. The latter has 'come on' wonderfully lately since leading Persimmon in his work although Marcus did not fancy him for the Alexandra Plate.[2]

A month later Persimmon won the Jockey Club Stakes at Newmarket by two lengths from Sir Visto. In a manner which would not be tolerated in modern times, Persimmon was saddled in his own stables at Egerton House and, after being walked through one of the gaps in the Ditch, cantered to the post where he joined the rest of the field – which was first class in ability, for it included Kirkonnel, Bay Ronald, Regret and Knight of the Thistle. Ridden with the utmost confidence by Watts, Persimmon won in the style of a really good horse, and considering he was giving over a stone to Bay Ronald and Knight of the Thistle it was a brilliant performance. The race was worth £8,990 to the winner, compared with the £5,540 of the Derby and the £5,050 of the St Leger. In total stakes the Prince won £26,819 in the season, but even more satisfactory was the realisation that Persimmon ought to prove, as a four-year-old, that he was one of the best horses of the century. After the Jockey Club Stakes, His Royal Highness sent Marsh a further cheque for five hundred pounds as a present. On

[1] *GV AA 21/8*
[2] *GV AA 21/9*

164

1st November the Duke of York wrote to his wife from York Cottage at Sandringham about an even more important present:

> . . . Papa wants a photo of both Persimmon and Thais in enamel in a little silver frame for his birthday. I hope to have the photos from Marsh on Tuesday, will you please tell Mary to write to Downey to tell him to come and see me on Wednesday morning at 10.30 and I will explain to him what I want, as there is not a moment to lose. . . .[1]

The year 1897 saw eleven horses, the property of the Prince of Wales, in training at Egerton House, but with the exception of Mousure, a two-year-old filly by St Simon who won the July Stakes, it was a case of Persimmon first and the rest nowhere. At the end of April the Prince wrote:

> . . . Today I went to Epsom – quite a hot summer day which ended in a thunderstorm and rain. I bought Glentilt from C Mowbray last week to lead Persimmon in his work – and as he was entered in the Great Metropolitan Stakes, ran him today. He was second – but ran very well. . . .[2]

Persimmon had grown into a superb-looking horse, whom even the most critical would find impossible to fault. As a three-year-old he was still unfurnished, but during the winter of 1896–7 he filled to his big frame. Marsh was in the enviable position of not having to hurry Persimmon, for it had been decided that the Ascot Gold Cup was to be his first race. About a week before the race Persimmon, carrying nine stone twelve pounds, was tried over two and a half miles against his lead horse the six-year-old Glentilt, who according to Marsh was carrying six stone three pounds. Persimmon put up as good a trial as anyone could have dreamed, and bar accidents the Gold Cup victory was a certainty. It seemed so certain that Lord Marcus Beresford

[1] *GV CC1/197*
[2] *GV AA 21/28*

proposed that Queen Victoria should watch the race – but her arrival in London from Balmoral was delayed and she was unable to honour Royal Ascot with her presence. Nevertheless, Persimmon won the Gold Cup by eight lengths from Winkfield's Pride. Proof of Marsh's genius as a trainer was now apparent, for within a month he produced Persimmon to run for the Eclipse at Sandown over one and a quarter miles. To take a horse who has been prepared for the Gold Cup and within so short a time sharpen him up to compete in a race of almost half the distance is no easy matter. The heat at Sandown was stifling, and the going rock hard, but Persimmon won handsomely, beating Lord Rosebery's Velasquez, who had only been defeated two lengths by Galtee More in the Derby, by a comfortable two lengths.

As a result of Persimmon's victories in the Gold Cup and Eclipse, His Royal Highness generously sent Marsh a cheque for a thousand pounds.

It was intended that Persimmon should have one final race in the Champion Stakes at Newmarket, but the hard ground in mid-summer proved his undoing and he never ran again – being honourably retired to Sandringham stud.

8

Diamond Jubilee

□□□

IF THE PRINCE of Wales needed any further proof of the glorious uncertainty of racing, he was now to receive it. Perdita II had produced an outstanding horse in Persimmon. She also produced Derelict, who performed moderately, and Barracouta, who was a nonentity, and had twice been barren. Her next three foals after Persimmon were a bay colt, Farrant, by Donovan; a bay filly, Azeeza, by Surefoot, and a brown colt, Sandringham, by St Simon, thus a full brother to Persimmon. However Farrant, Azeeza and Sandringham had one factor in common – they were absolutely useless as race-horses! They were not the only ones in the yard who were not paying their way and in October 1897 the Prince wrote:

> . . . The week was very pleasant at Newmarket, though alas Mousure and St Nicholas were beaten. I have sold the latter and he is good riddance. I didn't fancy Dieudonne for the Middle Park Plate – he ought to have a good chance for the Derby now. . . .[1]

Dieudonne, owned by the Duke of Devonshire and trained by Marsh, started second favourite for the 1898 Derby but ridden by Watts could only finish fourth to an unconsidered outsider Jeddah who started at 100–1. Like Dieudonne, Jeddah was trained at Egerton House by Marsh who had always believed that Jeddah, out of Pilgrimage the dam of Canterbury Pilgrim, was a good

[1] *GV AA 21/41*

horse. Earlier in the spring the Prince wrote from the Jockey Club Rooms at Newmarket on April 27th:

> . . . I came here yesterday morning. This place is very full of friends and acquaintances but as for picking winners at the races it is a simple impossibility. Jeddah not running better today in the Two Thousand was also a disappointment. I paid a long visit to Marsh's stable yesterday and saw the horses at exercise this morning. . . .[1]

The summer continued without any worthwhile royal victory and the Prince in slightly disgruntled vein wrote on 4th July:

> . . . It was very unlucky Eventail being beaten at New-market on Tuesday as she ought to have won but M Cannon did not ride her well. I spent 3 very pleasant days there – weather sunny and very hot. Goletta winning the Princess of Wales Stakes was a surprise – Dieudonne was second. Velasquez never looked fit and I didn't back him. I saw Sandringham who is going on well and could stand on the foot where the pastern was split after 3 weeks! so hope he will be able to be trained next year . . .[2]

The pattern of the Prince's life was still such that his participation in affairs of State remained less influential than he desired, and it was not until April 1898 that he presided at a meeting of the Privy Council. His financial affairs were in the hands of Sir Ernest Cassel, who on the death of Baron Hirsch became his business adviser. A cultured German Jew who had amassed a fortune before his fortieth birthday, Cassel was a brilliant financial genius who became a great personal friend of the Prince. His marriage lasted only three years before his wife died, leaving him one daughter, Maud, around whom he centred his entire life. She died of tuberculosis in 1911, and her stricken father declared to a friend that he 'had no further object to go on living for now'. His friendship with His Royal Highness resulted in the nickname 'Windsor Cassel'

[1] *GV AA 21/57*
[2] *GV AA 21/61*

168

being attached to him. His grand-daughter Edwina married Lord Louis Mountbatten. In the course of his career, Sir Ernest Cassel was honoured by many nations for his services, based on his financial acumen, and his decorations included the Japanese Order of the Sun and the Swedish Grand Cordon of the Polar Star. Another to whom the Prince gave his friendship was the Hon Mrs George Keppel, wife of a younger brother of Lord Albemarle. It was a friendship which lasted for the remainder of the Prince's life.

In the autumn the Prince bought a four-year-old mare Nunsuch who had shown useful form in handicaps. She went so well in a trial gallop with Dieudonne that hopes were high that she would win the Cambridgeshire. However the Prince was not convinced of her ability, and wisely wrote: ' . . . Tomorrow is the Cambridgeshire. My mare Nunsuch ought to run well as Sloan the American jockey rides her, but I am not sure if she is quite good enough to win. . . .'[1]

His doubts proved correct, as the mare was hopelessly left at the post. Amends were made two days later when she won the Old Cambridgeshire, again ridden by Sloan, whose sponsor when he arrived in England was Lord Marcus Beresford's brother William who had won the Victoria Cross at Ulundi.

At the end of the year came a tragedy, which was totally unexpected and it was a sad and despondent Prince who wrote from Sandringham on 22nd November:

> . . . You will I know be sorry to hear that my beautiful mare Thais died today. She appeared alright when we saw her on Sunday, but she was very ill yesterday with a stoppage and suffered agonies and died this morning from inflammation of the bowels. Brown, the vet, and Walker never left her but could not save her. The latter is broken hearted, poor man, and she is indeed a great loss. This is an unlucky year for me. . . .[2]

[1] *GV AA 22/7*
[2] *GV AA 22/8*

The year did not, however, end unluckily for Marsh who benefited from the Prince's generosity. In the past he had been given various presents including diamond pins, but now he received a more substantial reward:

Sandringham
12 Dec 1898

Dear Sir,
I have great pleasure by direction of the Prince of Wales to inform you that His Royal Highness has arranged with the four other gentlemen who train with him in your stables, viz The Duke of Devonshire, Lord Wolverton, Mr Larnach and Mr James, to give you, as a mark of their appreciation of your services, a fixed salary of £2,000 a year, in addition to the usual weekly charge for the horses in training.

This salary is to take effect from the 1st January next, and will be paid to you quarterly, £500 a quarter (£100 from The Prince and from each of the other gentlemen above named) the first payment to be made on the 1st April next.

The Prince desires me to say he hopes that this extra fixed allowance of £2,000 a year will cover the heavy rent you are now forced to pay for Egerton Lodge and its splendid stabling.

With my hearty congratulations on what I feel sure is a well earned recognition of your labour, skill and success as a Trainer and with every good wish for the future.

I remain, Dear Sir,
Yours faithfully,
D M Probyn

The next year in itself was no luckier. Fifteen horses in training, and only five minor races won – but there was a bright hope of future glory in the shape of a two-year-old named Diamond Jubilee, a colt by St Simon–Perdita II, who even as an unbroken yearling at Sandringham gave the impression that he was more likely to follow in the footsteps of Florizel II and Persimmon than Farrant and Azeeza. Marsh was delighted with him from the moment he arrived at Egerton House, and always considered him the most handsome horse he trained. There was no genuine vice in Diamond Jubilee, but at the same time he was a 'character' with a will of his own. Not surprisingly it was decided that his race-course début should be the Coventry Stakes at Royal Ascot which had been won by Persimmon on his first appearance four years previously.

His performance was a disgrace, and caused consternation to all, for after lashing out in the paddock, he reared, plunged and attempted to savage his jockey Watts. The starter, Mr Arthur Coventry, on his return to the Weighing Room, stated it was the maddest exhibition by a two-year-old that he had ever seen. His second performance, at Newmarket, was even worse. He threw Watts and careered riderless up the course. Eventually caught, he was mounted by one of the Egerton House stable boys and returned to the start. When Mr Coventry lowered his flag he refused to race, and trailed in an abysmal last. It was an inexplicable display which made some onlookers label him a rogue. In his third race, at Goodwood, ridden by Mornington Cannon he settled down a little better and finished second. In his next outing he managed to win the Boscawen Stakes at Newmarket by a short head. It seemed as though he was settling down, but no one could be certain. In the Middle Park Stakes, once more ridden by Watts, he ran his best race to date, being beaten half a length by Democrat to whom he was giving away three pounds – and Democrat, owned by Lord William Beresford, had won the Coventry Stakes. The Prince seemed pleased and was content to write:

. . . Though D Jubilee didn't quite pull off the Middle Park Stakes he was in wonderfully good form and showed no signs of temper and roguishness. He had to give Democrat 3 lbs for gelding allowances but for the Derby they run at level weights. If he keeps well he must have a good chance for it. This is the universal opinion. . . .[1]

[1] GV AA 22/28

Democrat, who ended his days as Lord Kitchener's charger, defeated Diamond Jubilee again in the Dewhurst Stakes a fortnight later, but once more Diamond Jubilee ran promisingly. Marsh was completely confident of Diamond Jubilee's ability but mistrustful of his temperament. The horse had apparently taken a dislike to Watts, and hardly favoured Cannon. If only a suitable jockey could be found, things might be different.

The autumn of 1899 and the ensuing winter had been an unhappy one for England, for the troubles in South Africa had boiled over into war. The ill-timed and ill-fated Jameson Raid four years earlier had persuaded the Boers of the wisdom of importing arms from Germany and they were far more prepared for the conflict than were the British armies, soon besieged in Ladysmith, Kimberley and Mafeking.

Nevertheless the war seemed so far distant that although it offered excitement and glamour to subalterns and distinguished young war correspondents, life in England was not disrupted, certainly not horse-racing. During the past decade the Prince's interest in steeplechasing had been overshadowed by his interest in racing under Jockey Club rules and his stud at Sandringham, but he was never averse to owning a top-class steeplechaser. Although he had possessed nothing of merit since Magic, at the end of the century he acquired another very useful steeplechaser, Ambush II, sold to him by Mr G W Lushington. Born at Chilham Castle in Kent in 1860, Mr Lushington was one of the leading amateur riders of the era, amongst whose major triumphs was winning the Sefton steeplechase at Liverpool. Unlike so many of his contemporaries he seldom suffered from weight trouble and frequently raced against, and beat, the Irish professional jockeys in races under Jockey Club rules.

For a time he was assistant trainer to John Gubbins at Telscombe, near Brighton, before he bought Conynhams Lodge at The Curragh, where he kept a large string of horses in training. He was a great friend of the Beresfords at Curraghmore and, at the instigation of Lord Marcus, sometimes rode for the Prince of Wales. Mr Lushington was occasionally bidden to look out for a young horse who might prove suitable to carry the Prince's colours.

About 1896, when Persimmon was bringing so much racing glory to the Prince, Lushington found a young horse named Ambush II whom he thought would be ideal. After protracted negotiations with another, who owned a half-share in the horse, the Prince bought Ambush II for five hundred guineas. As a two-year-old Ambush II had been offered for sale at auction for fifty pounds but did not reach his reserve, and later his breeder Mr Ashe tendered him for ten pounds less to a friend to carry him to hounds. This offer was also declined. There was never any intention of training Ambush II on the 'flat' but even so the progress which he made was disappointing. He seemed irresolute and disenchanted with steeplechasing. Yet there was no doubt in Lushington's mind as to his potential ability and he was entered as a five-year-old for the Grand National of 1899. The record of young horses at Aintree was not good, for the stamina and endurance needed to win a steeplechase of nearly five miles came only with age. In February Ambush II won the Prince of Wales steeplechase at Sandown and at Aintree he was not discredited to finish seventh in the National to Manifesto. The following year Lushington thought he had been harshly handicapped with eleven stone three pounds, but decided to train him for the race. Everyone knew that Ambush II was greatly fancied, and the Prince was present – the first time he had been at Aintree since 1889. The Lord Mayor of Liverpool, not an enthusiastic racegoer, attended as did virtually the entire population of Liverpool, as anxious to see the Prince as the Grand National.

Shortly before 1 pm the royal party, who had been staying with Lord Derby at Knowsley, arrived, the Prince wearing a brown bowler.

173

The day augured well when the first race, the County Welter Selling Handicap, horses to be ridden by Liverpool County Stand annual subscribers or gentlemen qualified under the National Hunt rules, professional jockeys six pounds extra, was won by Fiorenza, ridden by none other than Mr Lushington. This was the second time that Fiorenza and Mr Lushington had won at the meeting, for they had won the Toxteth Handicap on Thursday. The second race of the day was started from 'the new fangled' starting machine, and one reporter commented, whilst discussing the favourite: 'his jockey has not as thoroughly mastered the new conditions of the starting machine as Fred Rickaby, but the latter's trouble has hitherto been well rewarded, as he got away today directly the net flew back, and was never headed.'

During the paddock inspection of the sixteen Grand National runners many admiring eyes were turned towards Ambush II and the royal party. It was at Liverpool that the idea originated that sheets marked with the number or name of the horse should be worn by the contestants whilst they paraded in the paddock, and that of Ambush II, worked in the royal colours and coat of arms, was a master-piece. Hidden Mystery started favourite at 75-20, only fractionally shorter in price than Ambush II at 4–1. Lord William Beresford's runner Easter Ogue was a 66–1 outsider, and his brother Marcus was one of the Stewards of the Meeting.

The favourite was knocked over by a loose horse just after crossing the Melling Road on the second circuit, which was a typical Aintree misfortune. After jumping the Canal Turn and Valentines, Ambush II moved up into second place and took the lead before the Melling Road was recrossed. Meanwhile the top weight Manifesto was begin-ning to make up ground steadily under his burden of twelve stone thirteen pounds. It was to no avail as Ambush II, running on strongly, came home a comfortable winner by four lengths with the gallant but exhausted Manifesto losing second place by a neck to Barsac in the last few strides. It was a victory which gave the greatest pleasure to all, and the Prince of Wales received an ovation as he proudly led in his winner. In Dublin, when the news of Ambush's victory was learned, the Irish were equally delighted, particularly as the city was preparing for a visit from Queen Victoria. After the National the Prince returned to Marlborough House, and wrote: ' . . . I wish you could have seen the Grand National yesterday. It really was a splendid sight as no horse could have run better than Ambush. The enthusiasm was tremendous, quite Persimmon's Derby all over again. . . .'[1]

Ambush's subsequent history is that of a very good horse on whom fortune must have thought she had smiled sufficiently. The death of Queen Victoria prevented his competing in the 1901 National. The following year, having won impressively at Kempton and Hurst Park, he split a pastern whilst training for the 1902 National at Newmarket. It had not been thought worth while returning him to Ireland after these victories, as the National was earlier than usual. In 1903 he ought to have emulated Peter Simple, Abd el Kader, The Lamb, The Colonel and Manifesto, all of whom had won the Grand National twice, even though he carried top weight of twelve stone seven pounds. He ran brilliantly, and looked the likely winner as he came to the final fence. Unfortunately on the previous circuit one of the runners had fallen at this fence, leaving a huge gap in it. Ambush II, whether through exhaustion, cunning or laziness swerved towards the gap, jumped the fence sideways, and paying the penalty toppled over. The next year he fell at the third fence, and whilst training at The Curragh for the 1905 National broke a blood vessel in his lung and dropped dead. His trainer decided to cut off both the head and hooves, intending to have the head stuffed and the hooves made into ink-wells. To his consternation no sooner was this done than a royal command was

[1] *GV AA 22/36*

175

received that the skeleton should be sent to Liverpool Museum. Eventually, after much wire and glue were judiciously employed, the skeleton was duly dispatched to the Museum, where it still remains.

Shortly after Ambush II won the Grand National, the Prince went to Belgium and Denmark for Easter. Whilst in Brussels, there was an attempt on his life by a young fanatic. Writing a week later from Copenhagen to his great friend, Henry Chaplin:

> My dear Harry,
> I am most grateful to you for your kind letter of sympathy on the occasion of the narrow escape I experienced in Brussels last week. Luckily the individual was a very indifferent shot, as it is inconceivable that he missed me at two yards! However 'all's well that ends well'. . . . Many thanks for all you say about the Grand National. It is a race I was very proud to win. Indeed I hope that Diamond Jubilee may run well for the Derby, but it would be almost too good luck to expect to win it.
> > Ever yours sincerely,
> > Albert Edward

Although during the 1900 season his other horses won four humble races, it was entirely Diamond Jubilee's year.

Diamond Jubilee had been ridden in all his trial work by Herbert Jones. Young Jones had ridden in forty-three races during the 1899 season, winning two of them, and showing that he had the makings of a first-class jockey. In some inexplicable manner he and Diamond Jubilee had formed an understanding which enabled the jockey to make the royal horse manageable in his gallops. It was assumed that Diamond Jubilee had outgrown his high-spirited two-year-old characteristics, and never occurred to anyone that he would behave improperly if he was not ridden by Jones. The truth took some time to dawn, and until Morny Cannon came to ride him in one of his exercise trials a few weeks before the Two Thousand Guineas, the penny did not drop.

To everyone's alarm, no sooner had Cannon dismounted than Diamond Jubilee knocked him over and attempted to savage him. Onlookers quickly came to Cannon's rescue, and although the jockey was unhurt, it gave Marsh much food for thought. It also made Cannon decide that discretion was the better part of valour and he requested Marsh to find another jockey to ride Diamond Jubilee. The majority of the most fashionable jockeys were already engaged and clearly Marsh was in a difficult dilemma. It occurred to him that if Diamond Jubilee went so well for Jones, then the young jockey, inexperienced though he was, ought to ride the horse; but should he speak his thoughts and suggest that such a step was taken? He knew that Diamond Jubilee, except for his temper, was an extremely good horse, but if an unknown jockey lost an important race, inevitably there would be any amount of criticism. Jones was not a mere stable boy brought from the back streets of an industrial city. His father had been a steeplechase jockey before training for Lord Marcus Beresford, and young Herbert had been brought up in an atmosphere of race-horses since childhood. In view of this, Marsh diffidently wrote to Lord Marcus Beresford proposing that Jones rode Diamond Jubilee in the first of the Classics. The proposal was readily approved, with the happiest of results as Diamond Jubilee spreadeagled his field to win by four lengths. From Windsor Castle the Duke of York wrote to his sister-in-law, Margaret, wife of the Duke of Teck:

> . . . Fancy my father was lucky enough to win the Two Thousand Guineas today with Diamond Jubilee. We are all indeed delighted and I think he has a good chance of winning the Derby now, which would indeed be splendid. Thanks for all your good wishes and kind congratulations on the birth of our third son. . . .[1]

[1] *GV CC 50/520*

The same day the Prince of Wales wrote to his son:

> . . . I know you will have been pleased at D Jubilee's success and I am only sorry you had to be at Windsor instead of here. Little Jones rode the horse admirably and he showed no signs of temper – and won by many lengths. Barring accidents he ought to win the Derby. He runs again on the 16th for the Newmarket Stakes which he will probably win. That is the day Grandmama has fixed for your little boy's christening. I could not be absent on that occasion from Windsor but I want you to write her a line before you leave tomorrow to beg her to have it on the 17th instead as a favour to you – as it really cannot matter to her – and you could also come down for the day to see the race – as when one has a really good horse it is a grievous disappointment not to see him.[1]

This complicated the issue for the Prince of Wales's son, who wrote the next day to his wife:

> . . . I heard from Papa today that Diamond Jubilee runs in a good race at Newmarket on the 16th and of course he is very anxious to be present and has begged me to write to Grandmama to ask her to put the christening off until the 17th as a great favour, which I have done. It was not an easy letter to write as you can imagine. . . .[2]

Fortunately Diamond Jubilee duly won the valuable Newmarket Stakes, though only by a short head, and thus justified the alterations in the date of the christening of the present Duke of Gloucester. As the day of the Derby drew nearer, so Marsh's confidence in Diamond Jubilee increased. There was no horse of the calibre of St Frusquin in the field to beat, and if Diamond Jubilee could adapt himself to the noise and bustle of Epsom Downs he ought, strictly on form, to win.

Thursday 30th May 1900 was a sunny warm day on which Lily Langtry arrived from New York at South-

[1] *GV AA 22/43*
[2] *GV CC 2/171*

178

ampton on the American liner St Louis, and Mr C B Fry scored a hundred and forty-five for Sussex in their match against Surrey before being bowled by Loxwood. In a sporting advertisement A C McLaren wrote from Old Trafford, Manchester: 'I have often been asked, during the last few days, what was the bat I made my runs with against Somerset, and I think it only fair to write and tell you it was one of your own make. For driving power yours are not to be beaten.' On another page binoculars were offered for sale at £2 5s, including a brown sling case. The most important news, however, was that 'Bobs had nearly reached Johannesburg.' The year had opened with the battle of Spion Kop, and as the spring offensive gathered momentum the disasters culminating in Colenso were forgotten. Kimberley relieved, and the sieges of Ladysmith and Mafeking also raised, gave the British people the flavour of victory. The news that the beloved Lord Roberts had only a few more miles to march before Johannesburg was captured made everyone long for an excuse and reason to show their patriotic spirit. They were able to be so at exactly the right moment. . . .

The huge Epsom crowds cheered the royal party, on their arrival, with fervour, as rumours spread concerning the fate of Kruger and the Gold Reef city. News on a lesser scale which pleased racegoers was that the South Eastern Railway Company were shortly to open their new line with a station above Tattenham Corner. Perhaps they were not quite so pleased when an unfancied 10–1 outsider won the opening race of the day. Tod Sloan, the American jockey who was at first ridiculed for his 'monkey on a stick' style of riding which revolutionised jockeyship, won the second race on a little filly of Mr Solly Joel's named Doris. She was so small that eventually she was given by her owner to his brother, Jack, as a present. Exactly eleven years later Doris' son Sunstar was to win the Derby in the famous 'black jacket, scarlet cap'.

In the Derby preliminaries Diamond Jubilee behaved in

exemplary fashion, possibly because it had been decided that his stable companion Frontignan (St Simon–Sweet Muscat) should also run, not so much as a pace-maker, but merely in the expectation that the familiarity of having another horse whom he knew well would help to pacify him. Favourite at 6–4 against, Diamond Jubilee's chief adversaries were the handsome Forfarshire, owned by Mr T R Dewar, and the Kingsclere colt Simon Dale, who had received a typical John Porter preparation and looked fit to run for his life. As Diamond Jubilee strode past the stands on the way to the starting post many waverers, impressed by his smooth action, changed hesitation to confidence and made him their selection. Mr Coventry had little or no difficulty with the fourteen runners, and only the 100–1 outsider Frontignan was slowly away.

In the early stages of the race Dewi Sant, who was eventually to finish last, made the running from Bonarosa and Forfarshire. Coming down the hill to Tattenham Corner Forfarshire seemed to lose his action and at the same time received a bump from Sloan on Disguise II, which completely ruined any chance he might have had. Diamond Jubilee was also affected by the ensuing scrimmage and for a moment became unbalanced, although in the manner of a very good horse, he quickly refound his stride. A quarter of a mile from the winning post Jones gave Diamond Jubilee his head and the horse came clear of his field with his race won. Morny Cannon, on Simon Dale, made an unavailing effort to challenge him, with no doubt his thoughts flashing back to the days in the spring when he had asked not to ride Diamond Jubilee. Long before the race was over the crowds had begun to cheer home the royal victor and as he passed the winning post, hard held, half a length clear of Simon Dale, the applause was thunderous. It was an outstanding achievement for the Prince to have bred the winner of two Derbys in four years, and one would have to go back as far as the victories of the brothers Whalebone and Whisker, both by Waxy out of Penelope, who won in the colours of the Duke of Grafton in 1810 and 1813, to find anything comparable. Congratulated on all sides as he led Diamond Jubilee into the winner's enclosure, the Prince had one surprise still in store for him. To those in the Club Enclosure it was apparent that the crowds out on the course and in the cheaper rings were determined to show their pent-up emotions in some manner, for the Prince's victory seemed completely appropriate at a time when patriotism was at its height. Someone, almost instinctively, began to sing the National Anthem, and as *God Save the Queen* was taken up on every part of the Downs, the people gave vent to their enthusiasm for an historic and memorable scene. Two days later a telegram was received at Marlborough House:

> News of Diamond Jubilee's victory was communicated to me by Stanley during the attack on Brandfort yesterday. Army in South Africa beg to offer respectful congratulations. Roberts.

Shortly after the Derby, worth £5,450 to the winner, Marsh received a letter from Lord Marcus Beresford thanking him for the splendid way in which he had trained Diamond Jubilee and enclosing a cheque for one thousand pounds as a present. As a footnote to the letter, Lord Marcus requested that Marsh put him fifty pounds on anything he fancied for the Hunt Cup. A similar amount was given to Herbert Jones, but the money was invested on his behalf, and he received only the interest.

The plan for Diamond Jubilee's future racing career was to miss Royal Ascot and run in the valuable Princess of Wales Stakes at Newmarket in July. Diamond Jubilee ran well, but was not disgraced to be beaten into second place by Merry Gal, who, although having run second in the Oaks, had never won a race and consequently claimed the maiden allowance, which meant that she carried nearly two stone less than Diamond Jubilee. Amends were made when Diamond Jubilee won the Eclipse Stakes at Sandown, and it seemed that the final Classic was at his mercy. The Prince was unable to be at Doncaster, owing to Court mourning for his brother the Duke of Edinburgh who had died at the end of July, and the news of Diamond Jubilee's Doncaster success came to him at Marlborough House: ' . . . The "tape" in my room has just brought the welcome news of D Jubilee's victory & I am glad I told you to put some money on. I believe he won easily. . . .'[1]

Marsh had great trouble in getting Diamond Jubilee to the post, for the horse was in one of his vilest moods and for a long time refused to allow Marsh to saddle him. Sweating profusely, as was his trainer, Diamond Jubilee lashed out and stood on his hind legs. Eventually saddled, there was still the problem of Jones mounting him, and this required Jones to prove he was an acrobat as well as a jockey. After this inexcusable display of temper, Diamond Jubilee condescended to be on his best behaviour during the race, and won comfortably, thus joining the exclusive and select company of Triple Crown winners. Instead of being retired for the year it was now planned to run Diamond Jubilee in the Jockey Club Stakes, yet another race worth considerably more in prize money than the Derby. In a field of eight Diamond Jubilee failed to finish in the first four, and not surprisingly the Prince wrote from Balmoral Castle: ' . . . Alas, D Jubilee was beaten today – not even placed! so he must have been amiss. I own I am most disapointed. . . .'[2]

Some days later, whilst stalking at Glen Muick, Ballater, he wrote: ' . . . D Jubilee being beaten a week ago was most unfortunate. He had to give too much weight and was "big money" besides. . . .'[3]

Diamond Jubilee had almost completed a long, strenuous season in training, and the most probable cause of his defeat was that he had trained off, although at the weights

[1] *GV AA 22/50*
[2] *GV AA 22/52*
[3] *GV AA 22/53*

he ought to have beaten Forfarshire, whose owner Thomas Dewar had been knighted in the course of the summer. Nevertheless 1900 was a great year for the Prince of Wales who headed the list of winning owners with £19,585 in stakes, and was a fitting climax to his racing career as Prince of Wales. Some years earlier in the Confessional Album to his eldest daughter HRH the Duches of Fife, he had written:

> I am happiest when I have no public engagements to fulfil. When I can smoke a really good cigar and read (must I confess it?) a good novel on the quiet. When I can, like plain Mr Jones, go to a race-meeting without it being chronicled in the papers next day that 'His Royal Highness the Prince of Wales has taken to gambling very seriously, and yesterday lost more money than ever he can afford to pay'. When I can shake hands with and talk to Sir Edward Clarke without it being rumoured that 'the Prince of Wales is violently opposed to the present war'. When I can spend a quiet evening at home with the princess and my family. I am unhappiest when I have a raging toothache, and have to attend some social function, where I must smile as pleasantly as though I never had a pain in my life.

Many of his happiest moments were spent in Paris, surrounded by friends in whose company he could relax. He never forgot those who had served him in the past, such as Brasseur, his old French tutor, or Hortense Schreider, whom he would visit in her old age. It was understandable that, speaking about him, she declared 'Voila un vrai grand Seigneur par example.' The Prince's most intimate friends knew him to be a very good mimic. On one occasion he arrived in Paris unexpectedly and caused consternation to the British Ambassador who was drinking a cup of tea when the Groom to the Chamber threw open the door and announced, 'His Royal Highness, the Prince of Wales.' 'Good God!' exclaimed the startled Excellency, letting his cup smash to the floor as he rose to greet the Prince. Next morning at breakfast the Prince re-enacted the scene, going out, announcing himself, and imitating the Ambassador's 'Good God!' as he dropped the cup.

Always kind and good-natured to those around him, the Prince preferred to glean his information on every subject and topic from experts in the course of discussion rather than by reading, and his keen appreciation enabled him to comprehend the salient features of any problem very quickly. What he found difficult to understand was that his friendship, coveted by so many, could harm those who sought it, by compelling them to live above their means. When he found it necessary to rebuke his friends he did so with charm and grace. At Sandringham, to a guest who shot a hen pheasant when the season was nearly over and the guns were concentrating on the cock birds, he smilingly reproved him with, 'Ah, what a man you are for the ladies.' Seldom was he at a loss for words, but he must have been surprised when the elderly Lord Mark Kerr, a famous and much loved army commander, after speaking with him for some time, said, 'Excuse me, Sir, but would you mind telling me your name. I know your face well, but I cannot remember who you are!' He never tolerated impertinence, nor would he ever discuss the personality of his friends in the company of others. Even to his closest friends he would never tell a *risque* story, even though he had a very great sense of humour.

The Prince of Wales had spent Christmas at Sandringham and early in the New Year came to London to welcome Lord Roberts on his triumphant return from South Africa. Later in the month he stayed at Chatsworth with the Duke of Devonshire. During these days he was constantly given reports on the declining health of Queen Victoria, whose well-being was causing the gravest anxiety.

On 21st January the Prince, together with the Kaiser, who had arrived from Germany the previous day, returned to Osborne. The following evening Queen Victoria died, and her son returned to London for the Accession Council where he informed his audience that as there could only be one Albert – his father – he intended to call himself Edward VII. He was now fifty-nine years of age and King of the greatest Empire in the world. There were those who, unfairly, had criticised him for his mode of life, his friends, his extravagances, including the Turf, and his apparent disregard for the affairs of state. These critics were utterly wrong in their assessment. No one had a greater under-standing of human nature than Albert Edward, no one a wider sense of vision on a grand scale. He was a brilliant organiser, meticulous in his attention to detail, and never shirked hard work. For years he would have loved to have taken an active part in affairs of State to a greater extent than his mother's political advisers would allow. Now he was King, and not only a King who understood his people, but a King who was understood by his people.

Court mourning precluded the royal horses running throughout the year 1901 in the colours of the King. Conse-quently they were leased to the Duke of Devonshire. This did not prevent the King's interest in the horses, for Sir Dighton Probyn wrote to Marsh:

Marlborough House,
9 June 1901

Dear Sir,

I write by command of The King to ask you to write me a short letter the beginning of each week in future, telling me, for the information of His Majesty which of his horses now leased to the Duke of Devonshire are to run during the week. The King wishes you to name the Races they are to run in, and also to say what chance you think each animal has of winning the Race he or she may be entered for.

The King says he is sorry the Persimmon filly did not win the other day – HM hears that Cannon was not in form last week, and that if Rieff had been riding the Filly would probably have won.

I was delighted at the success of Florizel's son!

Although the King is anxious to hear of his own horses in particular (those leased to the Duke) still if there is anything else good in the stable going to win, HM would like to be told of it.

Yours faithfully
D M Probyn

Only two races were won during the year, one of which being the St James's Palace Stakes at Royal Ascot won by Lauzan. Early in May the King wrote from Sandringham: '. . . I went in my motor the other day to Newmarket. It is 50 miles from here and did the journey in 2½ hours. I lunched at Marsh's and saw all the horses. D Jubilee is looking particularly well.'[1]

Unfortunately Diamond Jubilee was a great disappointment to everyone in 1901. Lord Marcus Beresford had decided views on Diamond Jubilee's four-year-old career, and made this clear to Marsh in a letter early in December 1900:

> I saw the Prince last night and told him I thought it would ruin Diamond Jubilee to train him and run him in the Ascot Cup, as the Princess of Wales Plate was 2 weeks after, and he has only Caiman to beat, and I asked him to consult you when he saw you at Sandringham, so back me up, if you agree. Let me know your opinion of the mares & foals after you have seen them.

He was difficult to train and did not run until July, when he was beaten by Epsom Lad in the Princess of Wales Stakes. The King wrote:

> . . . D Jubilee ran for the Princess of Wales Stakes at Newmarket yesterday but was alas! only second. This is the third time I have been second for that race. Of course he ran under Duke of Devonshire's name and colours. He had to give the winner Epsom Lad (who belonged formerly to Rosebery) 8 lbs. . . .[2]

[1] *GV AA 22/63*
[2] *GV AA 23/2*

In the Eclipse at Sandown Diamond Jubilee was again defeated by Epsom Lad, who had improved vastly since his three-year-old days. Epsom Lad's saddle had slipped back during the race and his jockey was compelled to crouch on his horse's withers and grab hold of the saddle, it was a feat which merited success. Diamond Jubilee's defeat resulted in the King woefully exclaiming, 'The Duke of Devonshire is not lucky with my horses.'

In his final race-course appearance Diamond Jubilee managed to finish third in the Jockey Club Stakes, but he was beaten by ten lengths, and it is a sad commentary on a Triple Crown winner that he should go through his four-year-old career without a single victory to his credit. By the middle of the summer, when he bit off a stable lad's finger as he was having his bridle put on prior to the Princess of Wales Stakes, it was evident that his temperament was deteriorating, and at the end of the season he was retired to stud at Sandringham.

Towards the end of the year Marsh received a letter advising him that, since His Majesty had come to the throne, it had been decided that presents should not be given – even from his oldest and closest friends. This caused much consternation to the royal trainer who had commissioned a silver salver with details of His Majesty's racing victories. In the circumstances the salver was presented and gladly accepted.

The problem of a jockey was also causing concern, and Lord Marcus Beresford wrote to Marsh in December:

Dear Mr Marsh,
I had a letter from Sir Dighton asking me the same question about the jockeys, and he said at the same time that he had written to the Duke of Devonshire and yourself. I replied by saying that undoubtedly the King ought to give Jones a retainer of £500 a year as jockey, on the under-standing that if the King's management wished to put up Maher – Cannon – or anyone else Jones must accept the situation. I pointed out that Jones deserved the favour,

187

and that he was an Englishman, and that the appointment would be very popular. I am sure you will coincide with my views in this.

Talking of Jones – it has often occured to me that you might put him in charge of one of your stables, and teach him what he ought to learn – which is to be a trainer eventually. He must look forward a little, and I hope to collect him a nice little pile which will assist him in the future. Do you think you could do this if the opportunity arose? I should be very much obliged to you if you could see your way to do it. We can talk the matter over at Kempton.

Yours truly,
Marcus Beresford

Some of the boxes at Egerton House now became empty, as the Duke of Devonshire wrote to Marsh:

Devonshire House
Piccadilly, W
Dec 12/01

Sir,

I have for some time been thinking of making a change in my training arrangements. My chief reason for wishing for a change is that I should like to have my horses at Beaufort House where I can easily see them. It takes a long time after the races to go to Egerton House and round the stables, and as I have not now the time to do this often, I lose much of the pleasure of owning racehorses by not seeing them constantly. I also wish to have a private trainer who will only have my horses to look after. For these and other reasons I have decided to have my horses at Beaufort House, and Goodwin who now runs the stables there will probably train for me.

Of course I am sorry to put an end to our long connections as owner and trainer, and you will no doubt think that this decision on my part is in consequence of the bad luck I have lately had with my horses, but this is not the case. I think you have probably more horses now than any man can fully attend to, but I know that no one can train a horse better than you can, and also that no trainer can make sure of success.

I do not quite know what is usual about notice in the case

of the removal of horses from a training stable, but I should be glad to consider your wishes on this subject. I should think however that it would be desirable that the trainer who will be responsible for the horses during the training season should take charge of them as soon as possible, and Mr Hamilton will write to you as to what I should propose as to this.

I remain,

Yours sincerely,

Devonshire

9

The King's Derby

□□□

THE YEAR 1902 saw sixteen royal horses in training at
Egerton House, including nine horses sired by Persimmon.
Court mourning over, they once more raced in the royal
colours, but virtually to no avail. In the entire year only
two modest races were won. Early in June, only a few
weeks before his Coronation, the King became ill. In his
Memories of Racing and Hunting the Duke of Portland
remembered that whilst staying for Royal Ascot at
Windsor Castle:

> On the morning of the Gold Cup I received a command
> from King Edward to come to his sitting room. Everyone
> in the castle knew that King Edward was unwell, but I
> was dismayed, on entering the room, to find His Majesty
> in a chair, his face as white as a sheet, and beads of perspir-
> ation on his forehead. 'I have sent for you,' he said, 'to tell
> you how much I hope your colt, William the Third, will
> win the Gold Cup this afternoon. If he does, I am sure it
> will give you extra pleasure to win when you are my guest,
> and in my Coronation year. Don't on any account, forget
> to send me a personal telegram as soon as the race is over.'
> Needless to say I was extremely touched by His Majesty's
> kindness and thought. I thanked him very much, and added
> how extremely sorry I was to see him so unwell and in
> such pain. 'Yes, I feel rather bad,' His Majesty replied,
> 'but don't for one moment think I shall not be crowned
> next week. I have made up my mind to go through with
> it, and nothing will induce me to disapoint my people.'

Kept on a milk diet, and retiring to bed before dinner, the
King managed to survive the remainder of the week,

although constantly in pain. Three days before the Coronation he returned to Buckingham Palace determined to continue with the arrangements, but it proved impossible. His medical advisers explained the seriousness of his illness and after firstly recommending, later insisted on an immediate operation for appendicitis, even though it necessitated the postponement of the Coronation until 9th August. When the King was convalescing on the royal yacht, Mead, a two-year-old sired by Persimmon, won at Goodwood. The Prince of Wales wrote to his wife from aboard His Majesty's yacht *Victoria and Albert*: ' . . . Just heard that a horse of Papa's called Mead won a race today at Goodwood. I believe it is the first race he has won for two years so he is very pleased about it'.[1]

Mead was a better than average horse, and twice in the autumn ran in top class races at Newmarket. Writing to his son, now the Prince of Wales, at the end of October, the King said: ' . . . Mead will, I think, greatly improve as a three-year-old. The first three horses in the Middle Park Plate completely ran him out as they had such a tremendous "turn of speed". . . .'[2]

And a fortnight later:

> . . . The race for the Cambridgeshire on Wednesday and the Old Cambridgeshire today were particularly good. Mead ran 2nd yesterday to a very good horse Rock Sand in the Dewhurst Plate. He is improving every week – and when he is a three-year-old he will I hope be a useful horse. . . .[3]

In 1903 he fulfilled the King's hopes, winning three races including the Prince of Wales Stakes at Ascot, but he was not up to Classic standard, running unplaced in the Derby won by Rock Sand, after being fifth in the Two Thousand Guineas. The King did not see the first of the Classics as he was in Rome, but later in the summer he went to the

[1] *GV CC 3/27*
[2] *GV AA 23/31*
[3] *GV AA 23/32*

191

Eclipse at Sandown and commented afterwards in a letter from Buckingham Palace:

> . . . I had three pleasant days racing at Newmarket but nothing very exciting except Falmouth beating my mare Piari by a short head. I never saw so many people at Sandown in my life as today. The weather was splendid. It was a great race between Ard Patrick and Sceptre and many think that the latter should have won. Rock Sand was only 3rd (infortunately for me!)[1]

It is doubtful if the amount of the King's bet was large, and he was seldom accustomed to give instructions for more than a few pounds to be wagered on his behalf. In a letter from Mount Stewart, Co Down, a few days later, he wrote: ' . . . Please thank Marcus B for his letter rec today, and I quite approve of his racing Perchant and Piari.'[2]

Regretfully neither of these two-year-olds won.

The truth of the matter was that the Egerton House stable was completely out of form. The stable was run by Marsh in the most extravagant manner, but this would not affect the form of the horses – merely the finances of their owners. What might have affected the issue was Marsh's methods of training. It had always been his policy to use his stable lads merely to fetch and carry fodder and water. Tall strong men, some of whom thought nothing of walking four miles in any weather to reach the stables from neighbouring villages, were employed constantly to strap the horses. It is not unreasonable to suggest that this continual strapping by physical giants made many of Marsh's horses irritable and bad-tempered. He had always been attracted by big horses and it needed a tough horse to withstand his training methods. It was his policy to give his horses a half-speed gallop on Tuesdays, a faster gallop on Thursdays and a full gallop on Saturdays. No horse left the stable yard on a Sunday.

[1] *GV AA 23/42*
[2] *GV AA 23/43*

(*Left*) Frederick, HRH the Duke of York (1763–1827), son of King George III. This portrait is by Mather Brown and is reproduced by courtesy of the National Trust, Waddesdon Manor. (*Above*) Sam Chifney, Snr (1753–1808), jockey of the Prince of Wales, the Duke of York's elder brother. The portrait by Abraham Cooper is reproduced by courtesy of the Stewards of the Jockey Club.

Two portraits by Reynolds,
courtesy of the National Trust,
Waddesdon Manor: Ann, Duchess
of Cumberland (*left*), formerly
Ann Luttrell (1743–1809), who was,
according to Horace Walpole,
'very well made, with the most
amorous eyes in the world, and
eyelashes a yard long'. (*Above*) The
actress 'Perdita' Robinson, who
showed the Prince of Wales 'more
affection than either of his parents'.

Every Sunday a clergyman came from Cambridge to take morning service and evensong in the chapel at Egerton House. One of the most popular hymns ended with the exultant cry 'Allelulia' but many of the stable boys led by jockey Herbert Jones persisted in shouting 'Ally Sloper' instead.

Meticulous in every detail of his horses' care, Marsh studied their mannerisms, particularly the way they walked. The attention lavished upon them was boundless, and thoroughly in keeping with the high standards of the establishment. In the house there were a butler and a footman in addition to a cook and kitchen maids, whom Marsh would occasionally upbraid for the incompetence he hated. Once he was so irate with a Hungarian manservant who had accidently upset the pudding he was serving, that he was heard to remark, 'You bloody gooseberry fool!' There were four gardeners, and countless stable lads and apprentices, who were paid less than fifteen shillings per month. Obviously Egerton House was vastly expensive to maintain and inevitably some of the expenses had to be recouped by betting. If the 'coups' failed, then the financial position became strained. None of the owners at Egerton House gambled heavily, but nevertheless they realised that it was imprudent to keep moderate horses under such conditions. Early in 1904 Lord Wolverton wrote to Marsh:

3rd Jan 1904   *26 St James's Place, SW*
Dear Mr Marsh,
Enclosed I send you a cheque for £919 4s 4d, as per a/c. I, like you, am taking a holiday during January, and leave to-morrow for Cannes, but I shall be back for the meeting of Parliament. Under separate cover I send you Weatherby's pass book for the purpose of checking. Please return it to them with instructions to send it to you each month during the racing season for checking purposes. The pass book is instructing. There is a saying that no gold mine pays when it costs £1 to get £1 out, and it is obviously ridiculous to send a horse right up North to win

£100, when it costs the best part of that to get him there and back, but this, of course, will be all put right next year. I shall very likely have a sale in July of such horses as are not quite good enough to win small engagements. Before you are a year older you may hear of an Owners Association for the protection of that unfortunate creature who is fool enough now to race for his own money, pay for the stabling of his horses at race meetings and many other abuses, but this is private.

Y
Wolverton

The next four years saw a complete reversal of the good fortune which Persimmon and Diamond Jubilee had brought to the King. Ironically Sceptre, sired by Persimmon, was proving herself one of the best fillies in the history of racing, and Volodyovski and Doricles, the Derby and St Leger winners of 1901, were both sired by Florizel II. Yet the horses owned by the King could hardly win a race, even though in 1904 he had twenty horses in training, and even more the following year, when the stakes won amounted to a paltry nine hundred and seventy pounds.

Lord Marcus Beresford was at his wits end to know what should be done, and in an effort to rekindle the King's interest in steeplechasing he suggested that His Majesty should buy the New Zealand horse Moifaa who had won the Grand National in 1904. The first news that Marsh learned of the latest acquisition was in a letter from the King's racing manager:

14 Wilton Crescent,
SW
21/2/05

Dear Mr Marsh,
His Majesty wished to be represented in the Liverpool – after Ambush's death – and so I have bought Moifaa. He is the ugliest lightest devil you ever saw; but there was no other horse suitable that could be bought. I asked His Majesty to let you train it, and though you will probably

hate the horse – still, we can't do anything if we don't try.
But you have not much time to improve the looks of a
starved elephant, and keep him going at the same time.
Joe Marsh did something to his teeth some time ago;
you might find out what it was.
If you did happen to win the Liverpool it would do you
some good.
I should like to come down to you on Friday night, if I
might.

Lord Marcus usually stayed at Egerton at least once a
week. Once Marsh's daughter Thora, helping a maid tidy
his bedroom, greatly admired his night-shirts. At dinner
she said, 'Dear Lord Marcus, I do like your night-shirts';
however her anguished father was mollified by Beresford's
prompt reply of 'Not guilty, Dick!'

Although Moifaa had been 'vetted' before the sale was
completed, he was found to have 'gone in his wind' soon
after his arrival at Egerton House. Not knowing of this
calamity, Beresford wrote exuberantly on the subject of
who should ride Moifaa at Aintree:

I have thought of nothing else but the way Williamson
should ride Moifaa in the Liverpool, and from what I
have found out, Williamson must not try and ride the
horse at all. I mean he must let him run his own race to
the Canal turn – and then settle in a good place. If he pulls
him about the first mile, the horse will jump wild and tire
Williamson. When he sees a fence he must go at it. It is
not a horse – it is a great machine at high pressure over
fences – and therefore Williamson must be satisfied to
remain on the horse and guide him. He will try and bolt
into the flat race course, at every opportunity, so he must
be on the look out for that. I should have liked – if you
agreed – to let him up, and trot round again, and jump
them again, so as Williamson may get accustomed to ride
him over his fences.
He ought never to have a horse near him schooling – but
one leading him 50 yards ahead.
Digest all this and see what you think. I have grave
doubts, with the additional strength and go you have put

195

into the horse, whether any man could hold him straight
with one snaffle; any way, he must have a martingale.
Perhaps they starved him because he was a terror when
fresh. He knows the horse as much as anyone.

Another note to Marsh arrived the next day, still in
exuberant mood:

14, Wilton Crescent,
6.45 pm

Dear Mr Marsh,
Just back! I congratulate you heartily on what you have
done to Moifaa. We have got a steam engine! It requires
controlling. We must bit him somehow. Captain Dewhurst
recommends two snaffles – one thick plain – one thick
twisted. (I know 2 do make a difference). It is worth
trying. If we can control him he will win half a mile.

However it was decided that Moifaa should take his
chance at Aintree, and he started favourite at 4–1. Williamson was kicked on his instep a few days earlier, and consequently Dollery had the mount. He was an experienced
steeplechase jockey who had previously won the Grand
National on Cloister in 1893, but even his skill was to no
avail, and Moifaa fell at Bechers Brook. Lord Marcus
Beresford was utterly despondent, and wrote:

Dear Mr Marsh,
I enclose your account with cheque. I have had a rare
blow – and so have you – and I feel I was the cause of
yours.
However, it was not our fault – certainly not yours – I
am hoping to see The King tomorrow, and to tell him
everything.
I have wired to find out if Moifaa is sound enough to be
examined. We must find out where we are. He can't be
bad in his wind, otherwise he would not finish his 4-mile
gallops, and not blow. It must be something else. Dollery
got on well with him, but made too much use of him, and
choked him – with his up in the air jumping to help. He

196

was stone beat after jumping the brook. I never had my number taken down so before. The King was in the worst possible vein of luck with that National – everything went wrong – and his not being well made it worse.

I must apologise to you for putting you in such a position – but you did everything possible to make it a success. We must try Rosemark with Panhard for the Bennington Stakes to see if we can beat Musician.

The King commissioned a statue of Persimmon during the summer which was placed at Sandringham, after he had received sketches from the Prince of Wales suggesting where it should be put, but even this memorial to his Derby winner did not change the luck of the Sandringham stud.

The next year eighteen horses were in training, but there was only a suspicion of improvement when four races were won. In the hope that horses bought publicly would redeem the situation a yearling colt by Cyllene was bought at the Doncaster sales for three thousand eight hundred guineas, but to no avail. Nulli Secundus ran in the Derby, but made no show and the King wrote from Buckingham Palace:

. . . Yesterday I had my usual Derby dinner which was well attended but I missed you very much. There were 22 horses on the card and all ran. Nulli Secundus made a deplorable exhibition of himself – though he looked splendid as he cantered down to the Starting Post – he completely 'turned it up' after the first quarter of a mile. Both Marcus and Marsh are bitterly disappointed as he 'goes' so well at home. I fear he is a rogue and won't try. The winner, Spearmint, won all the way. On 29th I hoped to win the Woodcote stakes with Cynosure for which I gave Londonderry so long a price as a yearling last year, but Rosebery just beat me though he didn't fancy his horse at all. . . .[1]

Nulli Secundus ended the season ignomiously by being beaten by several lengths in a two-horse race. In October the King wrote: ' . . . My week at Newmarket was very

[1] *GV AA 24/47*

197

pleasant but none of the three horses I ran won. The stable is quite out of form this year and my luck especially is simply deplorable.'[1]

Ironically Persimmon headed the list of winning sires for the year, mostly due to Lord Derby's Keystone II who had won the Oaks.

Unbelievably 1907, with twenty-six horses in training, was only slightly less disastrous, and Marsh and Lord Marcus Beresford were at a loss to know the policy to adopt. Royal horses, costing a fortune in training fees, all fashionably bred, well trained and equally well managed, were consistently failing to win races of even the humblest value. Staying at Rufford Abbey for the St Leger the King wrote:

> . . . I won a nice race with Coxcomb on Tuesday and received a tremendous ovation from the Yorkshire 'Tykes'. Yesterday Woolwinder won the Leger in grand style and I am so glad for Baird as I believe he ought to have won the Derby. I backed him to win – also Baltinglass and Acclaim for places, who were 2nd and 3rd, so I did not do badly. Perambulator ran badly yesterday and Slim Lord runs today – but I shall not go to Doncaster again until tomorrow as I am glad to get a quiet day in the country in this glorious weather. . . .[2]

The race Coxcomb won was worth only £345 and yet even this insignificant stake was gladly appreciated after the misfortunes of the previous years. From Doncaster the King travelled to Scotland to stay with the Sassoons at Tulchan Lodge, Strathspey. Tulchan was rented by Arthur Sassoon, who had become one of the King's 'inner circle' of friends. The sumptuous style in which the Sassoons and the Rothschilds entertained the King in their London homes appealed greatly to him, but not as much as their wit, charm and elegance. The visits to Tulchan Lodge were

[1] *GV AA 25/2*
[2] *GV AA 25/21*

198

informal, without the endless repetition of pâté-stuffed quails, rare Eastern fruits and pink champagne associated with the lavish parties given in London, but nevertheless the King looked forward to relaxing in the comforts provided by his immensely affluent friends in the isolation of Inverness-shire. It was whilst at Tulchan in September 1907 he wrote: ' . . . The six horses I have leased from Hall Walker are only yearlings, so we must wait till next year to see how they will turn out. . . .'[1]

William Hall Walker, third son of Sir Andrew Barclay Walker, was born on Christmas Day 1856 – the day on which Lord Marcus Beresford celebrated his eighth birthday, and like Beresford he was educated at Harrow. In his youth he lived in Scotland where a near neighbour and friend was his contemporary, the Earl of Hopetoun. One of their favourite amusements was to collect some of the many Hopetoun gardeners, dress them up as sailors whilst the young Earl donned a midshipman's uniform, and with another gardener dressed in a red coat and carrying a rifle in the bow of the boat, they would row off to the Fife coast. Coming into the harbour of Limekilns they would jubilantly take the fishing village by storm, with young Willie Walker frequently leading the enemy. Without fail the 'battle' would always end in the local public house where the gardeners were regaled with tankards of beer for their trouble. Hall Walker began riding under National Pony and Galloway Racing rules in 1877, and during the course of the next thirteen years rode over a hundred and twenty winners. His very strict father had no sympathy with sport and gave his son an original set of prints after Frith's series 'The Road to Ruin' as a warning to discourage racing activities.

His business interests were centred in Liverpool and from 1900 to 1919 he was Conservative Member of Parliament

[1] GV AA 25/22

for the Widnes division of Lancashire. In 1896, the year of his marriage to a direct descendant of Brinsley Sheridan, his 'blue and white check, cerise cap' colours were carried to victory in the Grand National by The Soarer. The Soarer's acquisition was sheer chance. One day, on a train journey, Hall Walker met the soldier-rider D G M Campbell, who offered to sell The Soarer for six hundred pounds on the condition that he was given the mount in the Grand National. The reason for the sale was that Campbell, like many of his contemporaries, was short of cash. His father refused to pay his debts whilst he still owned a race-horse, and consequently he wanted Willie Walker to buy The Soarer. A further five hundred pounds was required if he won the National. Willie Hall Walker seldom bet, but he had fifty pounds on The Soarer at 50–1 for the National, which gave him a handsome profit on his train journey. The Soarer won by a length and a half, much to the delight of Campbell's regiment – the 9th Lancers – and to his owner, who was described by one newspaper reporter as having cramp in his cheeks from smiling for days afterwards. In his next race The Soarer was ridden in a flat race at Sandown by Willie Walker himself and finished third, and the following day won the Great Sandown Steeplechase.

At the beginning of the century Hall Walker had bought the Tully Stud in Kildare, where he bred the winners of so many important races. His success was phenomenal, particularly since one of his idiosyncrasies was to base his beliefs of his horse's potential ability entirely by references as to whether or not the horse's star was in the ascendancy at the time and date of birth. It might be added that Hall Walker thought that he personally was the reincarnation of Charles II. Whether there was any justification for this belief in the horoscopes of his horses, the fact remains that Prince Palatine was sold simply because the stars did not augur well for him, yet he won the Ascot Gold Cup twice.

On the other hand no one is likely ever to have a more distinguished record than Hall Walker in the Gimcrack Stakes at York. His colours were successful in three consecutive years, 1905, 1906 and 1907, and again in 1909. In 1905 he won five races at Royal Ascot, each of his winners being ridden by Herbert Jones, and at the end of the season was leading owner with £23,687 to his credit. Two years later he was again at the head of the list of winning owners, with countless winners under both Jockey Club rules and National Hunt rules sent out from his racing stables at Russley House in Wiltshire and Sandy Brow near Tarporley, where Mr 'Jock' Fergusson managed his horses. Gamecock, who won the National in 1887, had been trained at Sandy Brow and Mr Fergusson, one of the most brilliant and fearless gentleman riders of the era, had ridden Glen Royal to win the National Hunt Chase for Willie Walker in 1899. There can be no doubt that Colonel Walker, a member of the Marlborough Club, the Jockey Club and the Royal Yacht Squadron, was self-opinionated and at times eccentric, with an unshakable belief in horoscopes.

In 1906 he decided to build a Japanese garden at Tully and for this purpose brought over an expert Japanese gardener, named Eida, and his son, Minoru, which in Japanese means happiness. The elaborate garden was planned to symbolise the Life of Man and took four years to create.

The conception of such a garden was typical of Hall Walker, just as it was a gesture that in 1906 he named one of his foals Minoru, after his Japanese gardener's son.

One of Colonel Hall Walker's characteristics was his generosity, a quality which in 1907 led him to lease six horses bred at Tully to His Majesty. Speaking at the Gimcrack dinner the next year, he said: 'My object in leasing half-a-dozen yearling colts to His Majesty for their racing career was in the first place, seeing that His Majesty had no yearling colts of his own, to save his Master of the Horse, Lord Marcus Beresford, from the anxiety of purchasing in the yearling market for racing purposes, a very onerous and thankless task. Secondly the value of His Majesty's patronage to the Turf continuing must be apparent to all, and it was essential if he was to continue that patronage, he, at least, should enjoy some occasional success.'

The understanding and loyalty to the King which prompted Hall Walker's generosity speaks for itself.

The six yearling colts arrived from Tully in August 1907: They were:

Minoru	by Cyllene – Mother Siegel
La la	by Ladas – La Carolina
Moorcock	by Gallinule – Fair Jean
Calderstone	by Persimmon – Shrewbread
Oakmere	by Wildfowler – Lady Lightfoot
Prince Pippin	by Diamond Jubilee – Goody Two Shoes

The exceptional one was Minoru. 'A good coloured bay with black points, perhaps on the leg, a trifle light about his middle pieces, but with a beautiful head well set on,' was how Marsh described him. His temperament was the exact opposite of Diamond Jubilee and many was the time that Marsh's very young daughter gave him his evening feed of carrots. Minoru inherited his kind nature from his sire Cyllene, one of the best-tempered horses ever born. Although Cyllene's sire Bona Vista had won the Two Thousand Guineas in 1892, his owner did not think it worth while entering Cyllene for the Classics. Cyllene proved the folly of this decision by winning over seven thousand pounds in stakes as a two-year-old, his principal victory being in the National Produce Breeders Stakes at Sandown. As a three-year-old he won the Newmarket Stakes and in 1899 the Ascot Gold Cup. His first offspring ran in 1903, and the next year Cicero and Polymelus showed that he was getting outstandingly good stock, whilst Minoru, Lemberg and Tagalie were to enhance his reputation in

202

later years. Minoru's dam was Mother Siegel one of the last mares from the Blankney Stud owned by His Majesty's great friend Mr Henry Chaplin. Colonel Hall Walker bought Mother Siegel when she was in foal to Cyllene.

Minoru won only one race as a two-year-old at Epsom, but he was runner-up in the Coventry Stakes at Royal Ascot and also ran with promise at Newmarket. Great hopes had been placed in the spring on the three-year-old Perrier who started a short-priced favourite for the Two Thousand Guineas, but he ran miserably, and even worse in the Derby. After the Two Thousand Guineas, the Prince of Wales wrote to his wife from the Jockey Club rooms:

> . . . We were all terribly disapointed yesterday that Perrier was only fifth for the big race. The weather was awful just before the races started, we had a deluge of rain which lasted an hour and the course was like a snipe marsh. Neither Marcus nor Marsh could find any excuse for the horse except the very heavy going. They were both much upset. I fear he has not much chance of winning the Derby, but he might improve a great deal in the next month and the Epsom course might suit him better. Sir Ernest Cassel was elected a member of the Jockey Club yesterday.[1]

The year had opened tragically when Persimmon died at Sandringham of a fractured pelvis. It was a bitter sadness, tinged with the disappointment that whilst Persimmon had sired such great Classic horses as Sceptre, Keystone II, Zinfandel, Perola, Prince Palatine and Your Majesty, he could produce nothing of Classic ability from the Sandringham mares. Shortly after Persimmon's death the future King George VI, then a boy of twelve, wrote to his mother from York Cottage, Sandringham: ' . . . Is it not sad about poor Persimmon's death? Grandpapa must be so sad.'[2] Two months later Persimmon's own sire, St Simon, died suddenly as he was returning from exercise.

[1] *RA GV CC 4/3*
[2] *RA GV CC 5/64*

In January, Mr Larnach, owner of Jeddah, decided to curtail his racing interests and wrote to Marsh:

Dear Marsh,
First let me thank you and Mrs Marsh very much for your kind good wishes. I am quite sure that you will take an interest always in my horses, and hope that you will. I hate changes always, and feel that the end of a 12 years' association is a very sad thing for us all, but I find that now I have my daughter out it is quite impossible for me to look after or take an interest in so many things, and am obliged to curtail my troubles, which I am sure you will understand.

To me the long association has had some very happy times, but also some very sad ones; one of the greatest pleasures of my life came to me when we won the Derby with Jeddah, but I also have had the greatest sorrow of my life in the loss of my dear wife, and life has lost most of its interest for me ever since.

You also I know have passed through varying times in the 12 years, and no one, I can assure you will be more pleased when you win, or watch your horses winning with greater pleasure than I shall, and no one can wish you good luck more sincerely than I do. You have the kindest hearted and the best of employers in His Majesty, and I know will do your very best for him.

It is very kind of you to say what you do of myself. I can only say that all through my life I have tried to 'run straight' and to do to others as I would they should do to me, which is I think the only right way. So few in these days really care for their horses or for the racing itself. You and I know many who race for all sorts of reasons, racing itself the least of them; alas! what would those fine old sportsman, like the late Lord Falmouth, Admiral Rous, etc, think of present day racing – they would be horrified.

I have made the cheque into round numbers, as I know just how a little ready money may be useful; accept it with my best wishes for good luck to you in the near future, and with many thanks for doing your best with my horses.
Yours sincerely,
J W Larnach
I shall come and have a look at your string sometimes, and see if we cannot pick out a Derby winner.

Of the horses bred at Sandringham in training at Egerton House in 1908, only the filly Princess de Galles proved a money-spinner. A beautifully proportioned filly by Gallinule out of Ecila, she did not run until July when she won the Chesterfield Stakes at Newmarket, beating Battle Axe who had previously defeated Minoru. She cantered home in the Ham Stakes at Goodwood, and ought to have won again two days later, but her jockey was caught napping, and was beaten a head by Lord Rosebery's Attic Salt. Later in the year she won two more races at Newmarket, to bring her winning stakes to over three thousand pounds. Perrier, who had run so abysmally in the spring, was unable to act on the hard ground as he was a heavy-framed horse without the best of legs and in consequence was taken out of training for the year.

After the Newmarket October meetings, His Majesty usually stayed with Sir Ernest Cassel at Moulton Paddocks. Every morning whilst he was there the Jockey Club still-room servant was brought in a fly to Moulton to cook the King either a bloater or a herring for his breakfast. He always insisted that no one could cook a bloater as perfectly as she did. He enjoyed the pleasure of eating, and although he drank only a glass of milk when he rose at 7 am, he would eat a substantial breakfast at about 10 am, after having meticulously dealt with a mass of correspondence. There is a story that on one occasion at the Hotel de Palais at Biarritz he sat down to dinner, after having declared that he was not hungry. Long after his guests had lost their appetite, the King was still happily and contentedly eating, and when the fruit was served he exclaimed with disappointment, 'Is there no cheese?'

Frequently when he dined out at Newmarket – especially with Mr Rothschild at Palace House – crowds would gather to watch both his arrival and departure. In order that the visits should become more private, the Chief Constable fell back upon the ruse of stationing police outside Palace House when, in fact, the King was dining elsewhere.

205

The King holidayed in Biarritz during March and early April of 1909, and whilst there received Asquith who had come out to kiss hands as Prime Minister on the death of Campbell-Bannerman. One month later, after an exhausting State visit to Berlin, which he undertook only with reluctance, the King returned to Biarritz, having caused his family and his medical advisers alarm by appearing tired and ill.

Minoru, however, had wintered well, even though Marsh had very little idea of the horse being up to Classic standard. The season augured well when Vain Air won two unimportant races in the first week of the Flat season. Minoru, of whom Lord Marcus Beresford seemed to have only a moderate opinion, went to Newbury to run for the Greenham Stakes, which he won decisively. The next race was won by Oakmere, another of the horses leased from Hall Walker, but the King was unable to be present at the meeting, and so missed seeing this double success.

Minoru's next race was the Two Thousand Guineas, in which Marsh expected he would run well, but felt he had no chance of winning with Bayardo in the line-up. Bayardo had won every race for which he had competed in 1908 and was considered to be one of the best horses seen on a race-course for many years. Owned and trained by Alec Taylor at Manton, it seemed that he had the 'Triple Crown' at his mercy, bar an accident. However in the spring of 1909 there were persistent rumours that all was not right with the champion. In fact Bayardo, who suffered from shelly feet, loathed the firm going and equally loathed the dry, bitterly cold weather of the early spring. When he ran in the Two Thousand Guineas, starting an odds-on favourite, he was only a shadow of his real self, and finished fourth to Minoru, who won impressively by two lengths. It was almost an outstandingly successful week for the royal horses, for in the One Thousand Guineas Princess de Galles was beaten only by a length by Mr L Newmann's Electra, with four lengths between second and third. It

206

was a very promising effort, and on all sides racegoers were beginning to wonder if their beloved King would win both Epsom Classics. Heartfelt wishes arrived from all corners of the globe. From Canada, Earl Grey wrote:

> Your Majesty
> Sir,
> There are so many subjects on which I should like to be graciously permitted to congratulate Your Majesty upon of greater importance, that I hesitate to trouble Your Majesty with an expression felt by everyone who takes an interest in racing in Ottawa over Your Majesty's winning the Two Thousand.
> When Your Majesty won the Derby with Persimmon I was at Bulawayo – I can remember as if it were yesterday the thrilling pleasure that vibrated through that small but big-hearted community. When the cable that the Prince of Wales had won the Derby arrived – Weston Jarvis was also at Bulawayo at the time, and between us out of a feeling of loyalty for Your Majesty we broke the local booky.
> Weston Jarvis will be staying with me for the Toronto races at the end of May and I hope it may be our happy privilege to experience another similar thrill of loyal exhultation on May 26th when I look forward to hearing at another point of Your Majesty's Empire, far distant from both London and Bulawayo, the glad tidings that the King has again won the Derby. . . .
>
> Grey.[1]

Derby morning was dismal and sunless, with heavy rain ruining the journey for those who travelled to the course other than by train. At the Oval the Surrey *v* Essex match was abandoned. At Epsom everyone longed for Minoru's victory, but although he remained favourite in the betting, there was a great deal of money for both Bayardo and the American-bred Sir Martin, who had been sold some weeks before the race for the huge price of fifteen thousand pounds to Mr Louis Winans. Sir Martin was trained by Joe

[1] *RA W 8/72*

207

Cannon at Lordship, almost next door to Egerton House, and the stable lads had often seen him working in the mornings. They were not impressed, and his characteristic of racing with his head so low as to be almost between his legs was the cause of much comment.

The royal party arrived shortly before the first race, the Queen dressed in her favourite colour, mauve, with a matching hat, whilst the Princess of Wales, who was celebrating her birthday, had chosen a smart blue ensemble. Mr H J Joel's Sun Cloud won the opening contest, defeating a colt bred by St Frusquin and ridden by the King's jockey Herbert Jones. In the second race His Majesty had a runner who only managed to finish sixth, but it was some consolation that the winner was sired by Persimmon. There was an hour's interval before the Derby which enabled the critics plenty of time to view the horses as they paraded in the paddock. Mr Walter Raphael's pair Louviers and Brooklands were the first to be seen. Brooklands had his ears back and appeared sour, but Louviers, who had lost the disfiguring marks on his hocks, was as 'fit as a fiddle'. Diamond Stud, sired by Diamond Jubilee, and running in the colours of Mr J Buchanan, seemed a perfect picture of a race-horse, but was showing signs of temperament. Sir Martin looked bright in his coat beneath a huge colourful American rug, whilst William the Fourth, who had not been on a race-course since the previous October, attracted many by the manner in which he walked autocratically around the paddock. Bayardo looked very impressive, but it was to Minoru that all eyes were turned. Marsh tried to keep his charge away from the huge crowds, and at one moment bent down, picked a bunch of grass and gave it to Minoru in an effort to distract his attention. The betting between Minoru, Bayardo and Sir Martin was close, but during the final minutes before the start, Sir Martin ousted the King's colt from favouritism.

The fifteen runners were quickly on their way, with Brooklands taking up the running from his stable companion

208

How to ESCAPE Winning.

Rowlandson's comments on the Escape Affair. The figure on the right in
each caricature is the Prince of Wales

How to ESCAPE Losing.

(*Above*) HRH the Prince of Wales acknowledges the 1900 Grand National victory of his horse, Ambush II. Five years later *(below)*, the Prince, now King Edward VII, awaits the parade of the 1905 National runners (Photos by W W Rouch)

Louviers, followed by Sir Martin who was being tracked by Minoru and Bayardo. At the mile post Brooklands dropped back beaten and Louviers went on from Sir Martin, Diamond Stud, St Ninian and Electric Boy. Jones had settled Minoru down, and was allowing him to find his stride before moving up to join the front rank. Nearing Tattenham Corner a disaster occurred which altered the complexion of the race, for Sir Martin struck into the heels of another horse and fell. From the stands it was uncertain for a moment as to what had happened, until it was realised that the 'black, white and red hoops' of the favourite were missing. In the ensuing mêlée Bayardo and William the Fourth were the chief sufferers, but Minoru, next to the rails, seemed unaffected by the incident. Half-way up the straight the race was between Minoru and Louviers. Bayardo had got back into his stride but was unable to challenge, and although William the Fourth was gallantly trying to get on terms with the leaders, his efforts were unavailing. Minoru and Louvier came on towards the winning post racing neck and neck. Neither flinched, the crowd roared their excitement, and the two jockeys rode as though inspired. For a split second it seemed that Minoru was going to draw ahead, but Louviers and his jockey, Stern, who had been brought over from France, had other ideas; and held on tenaciously. One hundred yards from the post Minoru was inches in front, but by infinitesimal amounts Louviers was reducing his lead. As the two horses flashed past the post the hubbub of noise suddenly slackened and breathlessly the onlookers awaited the judge's verdict. In their hearts they dreamed of seeing the number 'ONE' hoisted into the winner's frame; they would have settled for a dead-heat; and if 'ELEVEN' was put up, they would have acknowledged that Minoru had been gallant in defeat.

The seconds before the result was announced seemed eternity, and then the pent-up emotions of the racegoers swept through the sound barrier as the hoped-for magical

'ONE' was hoisted. The King of England had won the Derby. Tears of happiness mingled with a combination of loyal pride and relief from tension made many an exultant spectator dry of throat. As the cheering crowds swarmed on to the course the King and the Prince of Wales came to the entrance of the unsaddling enclosure. The noise was deafening, and for a moment Minoru and Jones were lost amongst a host of patriots. The jockeys of Bayardo, Phaleron and Brooklands dismounted and slipped into the Weighing Room saluting the royal party as they passed. As Minoru, unperturbed by his tumultuous reception, eventually forced his way through the crowd, racegoers tried to pluck hairs from his tail. The King, always courteous and considerate, even in such exultant moments, was heard to remark, 'Please do not touch him or he will kick.'

As he led his third Derby winner into the enclosure of honour, smiling and almost overcome with emotion, the thoughts of everyone were centred upon the fact that the King of England had won the Derby. Over and over again the joy of the occasion was savoured as the King stood alongside Minoru and acknowledged the cheers of his loyal subjects. There was a cheer too for Mr Raphael as he came forward to greet his gallant loser, and one wishes that the sporting manner in which he accepted the judge's verdict of a short head could have enabled him, in some miraculous way, to have foretold that three years hence he too would lead in his Derby winner. Whilst the ovation continued Martin, the jockey who had come crashing to the ground when the favourite fell, was brought back in an ambulance. Badly bruised, he managed to raise himself on his right elbow and add his congratulations as he was carried away.

Elated but tired, the King returned to Buckingham Palace for tea. In the evening he gave the customary banquet to members of the Jockey Club before joining the Queen and the Princess of Wales at a dance given by Lord Farquhar.

Throughout the evening severe strain was put upon the secretarial staff and the special telegraphic department at the Palace, as telegrams began to arrive continuously from every part of the Empire. Marsh, too, received many letters, one being from John Porter:

Harrogate

Dear Dick,
I am sorry I was not able to get to Epsom to witness your success. I have had a touch of rheumatism lately, so I am here for 3 weeks going through the water cure and beastly stuff it is.
I heartily congratulate you on winning the Derby again for the King, it will repay you for the trouble and anxiety you have passed through this last two or three years with a lot of bad horses. I have passed through it myself, so know what the feeling is; it is not so much the bad horses that trouble you but the ingratitude of some of your employers, who made a great fuss of you during your success but quit you like rats from a sinking ship when you are out of luck.

With kind regards to Mrs Marsh,
I remain,
sincerely yours,
J Porter

There were great expectations that Princess de Galles would win the Oaks, but it was not to be. At the start, Electra, the 5–4 favourite, lost so much ground that her supporters knew their fate before the fourteen runners had covered a furlong. Her misfortune seemed to make the chance of the King's filly even greater, but she was not a true stayer and in the final furlong Mr William Cooper's Perola came past her to win by two lengths. Princess de Galles redeemed herself by winning the Coronation Stakes at Royal Ascot where Minoru enhanced his reputation by impressively defeating two opponents in the St James's Palace Stakes. This victory frightened away the opposition when he next appeared, and he won minor races at

Goodwood and Newmarket. The ultimate test of his ability was to come in the St Leger. The supporters of Bayardo had always thought he was a better horse than Minoru, and were convinced that he had not shown his true form in either the Two Thousand Guineas or the Derby. At Royal Ascot he had won the Prince of Wales Stakes in the style of a very good colt, before beating Louviers at level weights in the Sandringham Foal Stakes at Sandown. On his next appearance he trounced the previous year's St Leger winner in the Eclipse. Everyone knew that the contest between Minoru and Bayardo at Doncaster would prove decisively whether Bayardo's supporters were justified in their claims.

The King, after returning from Marienbad, stayed at Rufford Abbey near Ollerton for the St Leger meeting. Marsh was completely satisfied with Minoru's preparation for the race, and although realising Bayardo's merit, believed that the King's colt would win, although this opinion was not held by many of the Egerton House stable lads. The general public thought that Alec Taylor's colt was superior and made Bayardo an odds-on favourite. Their wisdom was correct, for Bayardo won in fine style, with Minoru trailing past the post in fourth place. It was heart-breaking for the royal party, and not surprisingly it was a sad King who wrote from Tulchan Lodge:

> . . . I knew you would be quite as disappointed as I was at Minoru not winning the St Leger. I certainly thought that he would have fought it out with Bayardo instead of which he ran a 'bad fourth', and appeared to have lost his form completely. Having been in training since March he may have got a bit stale which would account for his running so badly last week but I believe Marcus wishes to run him on Saturday at Newbury so we shall see if he is better. I was also disappointed at Princess de Galles being beaten by Mr Newman's Electra but the latter outstayed the former. . . . [1]

[1] *GV AA 25/64*

Bayardo went on to win six more races as a three-year-old, and in 1910 won both the Chester Vase and the Ascot Gold Cup. Minoru, once more victorious as a three-year-old when he won at Newmarket, failed to train on the following year, and showed Marsh that he had passed his zenith. He ran without distinction in the City and Suburban, and was then taken out of training. Returning to the stud at Tully he stood at ninety-eight sovereigns. Two years later he was exported to Russia, but not before he was mated with Gondolette. The resulting filly foal Serenissima was the grandam of Hyperion. The ultimate end of Minoru is uncertain, but Sir Charles Markham claims that he shot Minoru with a revolver to prevent the stallion being tortured by the Bolsheviks. Another story is that Minoru, and also Aboyeur, were harnessed to a cart and driven from Moscow to Novorossiysh where they joined the British Military Mission and eventually found their way to Serbia. If this is true it was an epic journey, with two Derby winners covering nearly fifteen hundred miles in double harness.

Minoru's victories in 1909 helped the King to be second on the list of winning owners, with £20,144 to his credit. In the course of the summer there had been some mention of curtailing his racing activities, but these matters had been satisfactorily sorted out, largely due to the persuasion of Lily Langtry, with the result that in 1910 there were twenty-two horses in training at Egerton House including two bought at the Doncaster sales the previous autumn. They seemed a promising collection, including some of Persimmon's last stock, and there were hopes that at least one of the three-year-olds would be up to Classic standard.

In March His Majesty's Bahadur, ridden by Major D G M Campbell, who had ridden Colonel Hall Walker's The Soarer to win the National, finished third in the Grand Military Gold Cup at Sandown; and steeplechase enthusiasts hoped that the King was reviving his interests in sport under National Hunt Rules. Like Nulli Secundus, who had won a hurdle race for his royal master at Aldershot, Bahadur had originally been in Marsh's charge, but as a young horse he had proved totally lacking in ability. The King did not witness the steeplechase at Sandown, as on doctor's orders he had gone to Biarritz. Breaking his journey in Paris, he went to the theatre, where he saw a 'stupid and childish' play which did not amuse him in the least. He was tired and irritated by the political situation at home which he felt might necessitate his return to England at any moment. He remained in Biarritz until 17th April when he returned to Buckingham Palace, where in the course of the next two days he saw Asquith, Kitchener and Morley, before spending the week-end at his beloved Sandringham. After lunch on Sunday he happily inspected his horses.

Back at Buckingham Palace on Monday he seemed listless, with his doctors diagnosing bronchitis, whilst the Queen was returning post-haste from Corfu. Not until Friday did the British public learn in their newspapers that their King was gravely ill. Dick Marsh, passing through London on his way to Kempton Park, went to Buckingham Palace to ask Sir Francis Knollys if His Majesty's filly Witch of the Air should run in the Spring Two Year Old Plate, and was told that the King had given express instructions that she should compete, as should Minoru in the Jubilee the following day.

At Kempton spectators, stunned by the news of their King's illness, were uncertain whether to cheer or be silent as Witch of the Air won her race by half a length. At five o'clock the telegraphed message, detailing her victory reached the Palace, where the Prince of Wales mentioned her success to his father. A few moments before midnight the King died. The world learned of his death from an official bulletin issued early the following morning:

214

Buckingham Palace
6 May 1910
11.50 pm

His Majesty breathed his last at 11.45 tonight in the presence of Her Majesty Queen Alexandra, the Prince and Princess of Wales, the Princess Royal (Duchess of Fife) the Princess Victoria and the Princess Louise (Duchess of Argyle).

Signed F H Laking MD
James Reid MD
Douglas Powell MD
Bertrand Dawson MD

In his diary, the new King wrote:

> I have lost my best friend, and the best of fathers. I never had a word with him in my life. I am heart-broken and overwhelmed with grief, but God will help me in my great responsibilities, and darling May will be my comfort as she has always been.

Three days later Lord Marcus Beresford wrote to Dick Marsh. His letter summed up his respectful love and affection for King Edward VII:

> Dear Mr Marsh,
> I have just seen our Gracious King and Master for the last time, and anything more calm and beautiful I never saw. He looks 20 years younger than when I last saw him, and as if he had just heard that Witch of the Air had won her race. We have lost the best master that ever lived.
> It will be an enormous consolation to you to feel that you were associated with all the record-breaking triumphs which adorned the life of His Late Majesty on The Turf, and the crowning success of The Derby of 1909 will stand out in Turf History as the greatest training feat that ever was accomplished. His last words were expressions of delight at hearing Witch of the Air's victory – so you have the extra satisfaction of having been the means of giving him a pleasant thought to finish up his great life. Nothing ever pleased him so much as winning a race, and receiving the congratulations of his people after wards.

I must take this opportunity of thanking you for your unswerving devotion which you always extended to me during 18 years of difficulty which owing to your skill, were crowned with success – which may be equalled, but never surpassed. No more loyal servants ever served their sovereign than yourself and Walker.

And so ends the pleasantest chapter of your life – and of mine.

Believe me,

Yours gratefully,

Marcus Beresford

10

'A Most Regrettable Scandalous Proceeding'

□□□

PRINCE GEORGE FREDERICK ERNEST ALBERT, second son of the Prince and Princess of Wales, was born at Marlborough House on 3rd June 1865. President Lincoln had been assassinated six weeks earlier and eighty-year-old Lord Palmerston, whose racehorse Iliona had won the Cesarewitch in the same year that the Prince was born, was to die at his home in Piccadilly four months later.

There was only eighteen months' difference in age between Prince Albert Victor and Prince George and the two boys were inseparable as they grew up. It had been the intention to send Prince Albert Victor to Wellington College, of which the Prince of Wales was a Governor, whilst Prince George entered the Royal Navy – but on the advice of their tutor, Rev John Dalton, their parents agreed that both boys should become cadets in the naval training ship, *Britannia*. The reason for this decision was that Prince Albert Victor (Eddy) was not so robust as his younger brother, to whom he was greatly attached, and it was considered unwise to allow them to follow separate careers. Consequently in June 1877 they joined *Britannia* where the twelve-year-old Prince George made greater progress than his delicate brother who found it difficult to concentrate for long on any subject.

Full of high spirits Prince George loved his new life, and was quite prepared to admit that he was the culprit when the First Lieutenant found a marline-spike in his bed. The Prince of Wales, always a believer in Kipling's 'What do they know of England who only England know', advocated that after leaving *Britannia* his sons should tour the world. The *Bacchante*, four thousand tons, commanded by Lord George Scott, with a complement of four hundred and fifty, including seven naval cadets, was chosen as a suitable ship for the Royal Princes, who spent the next three years visiting almost every corner of the globe, including South Africa, South America, Australia and Japan.

In 1883 Prince George was appointed a midshipman on the *Canada*, and during the next eight years saw service on *Thunderer, Dreadnought, Alexandra* and *Northumberland* before being given his first command – Torpedo boat 79.

It seemed as though the Royal Navy would remain his career, until on 14th January 1892 his brother died at Sandringham, only a month after his engagement to Princess May of Teck had been announced. Queen Victoria wrote to Lord Tennyson: 'Was there ever a more terrible contrast? A wedding with bright hopes turned into a funeral.' Utterly distressed by his brother's death, Prince George had now to be groomed as Heir Presumptive. He was created Duke of York and, after a short course at Heidelberg University, he returned to England where he took his seat in the House of Lords. There had been considerable speculation as to which of her uncle's titles would be revived by Queen Victoria for her grandson, but Prince George's new title was acclaimed even though there were some who discreetly remembered that the last Duke of York had been extravagant and profligate. Twelve months later, on 6th May 1893, to the delight of both the Royal Family and the British public, the engagement was announced between the Duke of York and Princess May.

The wedding ceremony, performed in the Chapel Royal, was followed by a honeymoon spent at York Lodge, Sandringham. Queen Victoria attended the wedding, and for the rest of her life showed the greatest affection towards her grandson and his wife. Their mode of life, more subdued and unostentatious than that of the Prince of Wales, met with her outspoken admiration and approval. Although the Duke of York, like his father, was not an avid reader, he found solace in his collection of stamps. He also enjoyed the solitude of the family estate at Sandringham where he could spend days shooting. As the years passed, his reputation as a brilliant shot became universal. No member of the Royal Family has ever shot with such success, and accounts of his prowess at Sandringham coverts, with such names as Grimston Car, Folly Hang and Ugly Dale, are still discussed with amazement and awe. Queen Victoria died in January 1901, and the following March the Duke and Duchess of York began their world tour in the *Ophir*, which did not end until November. The tour, planned the previous year, had been given royal consent shortly before the Queen's death. Nine days after the end of the tour the King conferred upon his son the title of the Prince of Wales. At London's official Guildhall welcome-home banquet, replying to Lord Rosebery, the Prince made his wise and famous 'wake up England' speech.

With the King and Queen now installed at Buckingham Palace, the new Prince and Princess of Wales moved from St James's Palace to Marlborough House, which was their London home for the next nine years. During these years, when the Prince's father was enthralling the world by the splendour of his reign, the Heir Presumptive diligently prepared for his ultimate role of King.

Less than three weeks after the death of King Edward VII, Richard Marsh received a letter from Sir Dighton Probyn:

Dear Mr Marsh,
Thanks for your letter. I heartily congratulate you, and our young King also, that he purposes carrying on King Edward's Racing Establishments at Newmarket and Sandringham, in the same way as his great father did.

219

I am delighted that you and Lord Marcus are 'as you were' and poor old Walker too. Good luck to you all.

In great haste to catch our last post.

Yours faithfully

D M Probyn

Marsh was relieved that he had been commanded to 'carry on' for there were twenty-two royal horses in the stable. Leased to the Earl of Derby for the remainder of the season, they proved a very moderate collection. Although King George V had not owned race-horses during his father's lifetime, this had not precluded his great interest in the sport. A better judge of a horse than King Edward VII he was also more knowledgeable concerning the form shown by both the royal horses and the others trained at Egerton House. He enjoyed a modest wager which seldom exceeded ten pounds on his own horses, and meticulously kept an account of his betting transactions, which usually showed a small profit at the end of each year. In a letter to Queen Mary he wrote, 'I made the acquaintance of Lord and Lady Wilton, and gave them some good advice about betting. They assured me that they would only bet in very small sums. . . .'[1]

In the first two years of King George V's reign his horses were not successful, and Pintadeau's (by Persimmon) victory in May 1911 was the only occasion on which the royal colours were seen in the winner's enclosure. On dismounting in the unsaddling enclosure Herbert Jones proudly remarked, 'Now I have ridden winners for two Kings.' In the Derby Pintadeau ran a respectable fourth to Tagalie, owned by Mr Walter Raphael, whose horse Louviers had lost only by a short head to Minoru three years previously.

That evening the King gave his customary dinner to members of the Jockey Club. Fifty-five sat down to dinner, with Prince Kinsky on the King's right, the Duke of

[1] *GV CC 4/206*

Richmond on his left and opposite him the Duke of Devonshire, Earl Rosebery and the Earl of Sefton.

The celebrations surrounding the King's Coronation in June 1911, followed by his journey to India for the Delhi Durbar, left little time for relaxation, and his visits to racecourses were infrequent. It was apparent, however, to his advisers that he enjoyed his days at Newmarket when he saw his horses at Egerton House either before or after racing, and equally that he had no intention of curtailing his racing activities. Writing from the Jockey Club Rooms in May 1912 he told the Queen, 'Unluckily yesterday morning April Princess's foal was running about in the paddock and slipped up and broke her leg and had to be destroyed.'[1]

The Derby in 1913 was one of the most dramatic in the history of the race. The King's Anmer, named after a village on the Sandringham estate, was a 50–1 outsider with little chance of success. Nevertheless as the fifteen runners started to round Tattenham Corner, Miss Emily Davison, a leader of the Suffragette movement who had previously been imprisoned for her views, dashed on to the course and brought Anmer and his jockey Herbert Jones crashing to the ground. It was an act of utter foolhardiness which did nothing for the Suffragette cause. Luckily neither Anmer nor Jones was badly hurt. When Herbert Jones was brought back in the ambulance, the stretcher on which he was lying was found to be too wide to allow it to pass through either the Jockeys' Room door or the passage leading to the back of the stand, so the royal jockey was unceremoniously dumped on the ground outside the Weighing Room in full view of all whilst it was decided how to get him to the local hospital.

Miss Davison received a fractured skull and died in Epsom Hospital the following Sunday. The most remarkable fact of the incident is that Miss Davison managed to single out the horse whose jockey was wearing the royal

[1] *RA GV CC 4/489*

colours. In the opinion of many, including Steve Donoghue who was riding in the race, it was purely coincidental that Miss Davison brought down the King's horse, who happened to be nearer last than first at the time. If the misguided woman had elected to rush forward a few seconds earlier a far greater catastrophe would have occurred.

Another theory, and conceivably the right one, is that the unfortunate Miss Davison, who knew nothing about horse-racing, had no intention of bringing down any of the Derby runners. By the time Tattenham Corner was reached there was a considerable distance between the leaders and the stragglers at the rear and Miss Davison, imagining that all the horses had passed, could have been attempting merely to cross the course. This theory is to an extent sub-stantiated by Jones's comment that, just before Anmer was brought down, he saw an expression of absolute horror on the Suffragette's face.

As Anmer was struggling to his feet, a desperately close finish to the Derby was in progress, with the favourite Craganour beating the 100–1 outsider Aboyeur by a head with Louvois (a full brother to Louviers) a neck away third. Whilst Craganour and his owner, Mr Ismay, stood in the winners' unsaddling enclosure receiving the congratulations of their friends, it was learned that the Stewards objected to the winner on the grounds that he had interfered with the runner-up. After a considerable time, with opinions and tempers, enflamed by the warmth of the day and the tension of the moment, causing many altercations amongst the crowds assembled outside the Weighing Room, the Stewards announced that Craganour was disqualified and placed last. In his private diary King George V, who on Derby Day wore a Brigade of Guards tie and a white carnation with his grey morning dress, wrote:

> We all left for Epsom at 12.40 to see the Derby. The police say it was the largest crowd that has ever been seen there, the road was blocked and it took us some time to get on the course. It was a most disastrous Derby. Craganour,

the favourite, won by a head, from Aböyeur (who had made all the running) and was led in by his owner Mr Ismay, but was afterwards disqualified for bumping and boring by the Stewards, and the race given to Aboyeur (100–1) with Louvois 2nd and Great Sport 3rd. I ran Anmer, just as the horses were coming round Tattenham Corner, a Suffragette (Miss Davison) dashed out and tried to catch Anmer's bridle. Of course she was knocked down, and seriously injured, and poor Herbert Jones and Anmer were sent flying. Jones unconscious, badly cut, broken rib and slight concussions; a most regrettable scandalous proceeding. In the next race Leo Rothschild's horse Felizande fell and broke his leg and had to be destroyed. His jockey was not hurt. It was a most disappointing day. . . . I gave my usual dinner to the Members of the Jockey Club, at 8.30 and we sat down 61. I talked to a great many of them afterwards.

It was a very eventful Derby Day, and although Whalley, the Anglo-Indian jockey who rode Felizande, was only bruised, it should be mentioned *en passant* that the father of W Saxby, who rode Louvois, fell out of bed and broke his neck that evening.

Jones, battered and angry with women in general, and Suffragettes in particular, was discharged from hospital two days later. He found on his return to Newmarket that many letters on the subject of Anmer's fall had been sent to him. One, from an influential member of the Church of England, suggested that if Miss Davison died it would be a Christian act if Jones attended her funeral. Jones, usually the kindest of men, was not amused at this proposal, and his reply made this abundantly clear.

At Egerton House, Jones had the enviable reputation of being the man to whom anyone could turn if they were in trouble. Marsh, aristocratic in demeanour, was considered too awe-inspiring and unapproachable by his staff, but financial problems, or those involving the relationship of the stable lads with the local girls, invariably found their way to Jones. Often money was provided so that a few sticks of furniture could be bought to set up a home for a newly wed couple. Jones was responsible also for equipping a Boy Scout group at Newmarket. One of the first to enlist in 1914, he was stationed at Norwich. One Sunday a visiting Brigadier told him to look after his charger whilst he went to lunch and warned Jones that the horse was strong-willed. Jones could not resist the opportunity of mounting the animal – with the result that after lunch the Brigadier came out of the Mess to see the disobedient Lance-Corporal Jones hacking around the parade ground. His shouts of 'look out, the bloody fool will be killed!' were hushed when it was explained that the horseman had already ridden two Derby winners.

The futile and tragic action of Miss Davison was followed up at Royal Ascot by the antics of a madman who ran on to the course, brandishing a revolver in one hand and a flag in the other, whilst the race for the Gold Cup was in progress. In trying to avoid him Tracery, the second favourite and the 1912 St Leger winner, fell. In his diary King George wrote:

> Neither horse nor jockey were hurt, but the man fractured his skull, and they trepanned him in hospital. He is a lunatic, who wished to commit suicide, and not a suffragist, but it caused great excitement.

It was a memorable year for racing, for not only did it see the début of a grey two-year-old trained by 'Atty' Persse named The Tetrarch, but also the Stewards of the Jockey Club decided that 'in the interests of the English Stud Book, no horse or mare can be admitted after this date, unless it can be traced without flaw on both sire's and dam's side of its pedigree to a strain already accepted in the earlier volumes of the book'.

In August the King's two-year-old Brakespear won at Newmarket and the King wrote in his clear and bold hand-writing to Queen Mary: 'Brakespear won the first race and everyone was very pleased. Today is another warm day, but there is a strong wind, and if it is like this at Cowes

224

it will be ideal.'[1] Brakespear ran without distinction in the Derby the following year, and was the last horse to run in the royal colours in the Derby until Resinato in 1924.

By the end of June 1914, the gloom of the news from the Continent was beginning to seriously disconcert the peace of mind of the people of England. Tragedies of the past two years, such as the loss of the *Titanic* and the death of Captain Scott in the Antarctic, and more recently the assassination of the King of Greece, were overshadowed by the murder of Archduke Ferdinand at Sarajevo. Horse-racing was of little importance compared with events which were to disrupt the world until Armistice Day 1918.

Nevertheless, during the last days of halcyon peace in the summer of 1914 a two-year-old colt Friar Marcus, who was immeasurably superior to those who had raced in the royal silks since the days of Minoru, ran in the colours of King George V. Bred at Sandringham he was sired by Lord Rosebery's 1905 Derby winner Cicero, out of Prim Nun, by Persimmon out of Nunsuch. Dick Marsh described Friar Marcus as 'a perfect model of what a sprinter should be, that is to say, he was short-coupled and very strong in the back, quarters and arms. He had a beautiful head and neck, the best of shoulders, while his joints were all that they should be.' Friar Marcus made his racing début at Newmarket. He was not mentioned in any of the morning newspapers and the stable hoped that they might bring off a minor betting coup. To their chagrin they found the bookmakers had installed him as favourite, but they were compensated to some extent as he led the field of twenty-four runners from start to finish to win unextended. He started coughing soon afterwards and Marsh was compelled to scratch him from his Royal Ascot engagements. When not fully recovered, he won the Prince of Wales Stakes at Goodwood by a head – beating the following season's Oaks winner Snow Marten – and completed his two-year-old career by winning the Rous Memorial Stakes and the Middle

[1] *GV CC 4/116*

Park Stakes at Newmarket. Naturally hopes ran high at Egerton House that Friar Marcus would win the Two Thousand Guineas, but his trial gallops proved conclusively that he stayed hardly more than six furlongs. He was allowed to take his chance in the first Classic, but ran exactly as his trainer had predicted, and by the Bushes was a beaten horse. There was no question of training him for the Derby and it was agreed that he should be kept entirely for sprint races. He duly won the Great Eastern Handicap, the Queensberry Handicap, and as a four-year-old the Crawfurd and Chesterfield Handicaps, under top weight, before being retired to stud at Sandringham.

In the autumn of 1914 the war precluded many race-meetings, and those arranged for Kempton, Stockton, Hurst Park, York, Derby, Ayr and Newbury were abandoned. In September the Jockey Club decreed that racing should continue where possible, but by the summer of 1915 it was realised that only at Newmarket could meetings be held until the end of hostilities. This decision was modified later, and in 1917 there were forty fixtures, at Brighton, Newmarket, Manchester, Stockton and Windsor. The subsequent year this number of racing days was increased to fifty-three, proving that even in wartime there was racing as usual. England had been at war when the Darley Arabian left Aleppo on his sea voyage, in the charge of Captain William Wakelin of the *Ipswich*, in 1704; she had also been involved throughout the eighteenth century in conflicts such as the War of the Austrian Succession, the Seven Years' War, and the War of American Independence, but racing never ceased, neither did it during the Crimean War and the Boer War.

At Christmas 1915, Colonel Hall Walker sold his famous Tully Stud, together with his training stables at Russley Park, to the nation. It was a momentous event in the history of English racing, and the Colonel's generosity was munificent.

News of Colonel Walker's offer was first made public at

the end of October – on the same day as thousands of lovers of sport mourned at the funeral of W G Grace, and Tod Sloan was deported, travelling 1st class to America with Mlle de Herlys, for running a house in the West End of London at which gaming had taken place especially when it was frequented by young army officers! In a letter to the Press, Colonel Walker stated:

> My offer to the Government is being considered and I have not yet had a reply. I have every reason to believe it will be accepted, but failing acceptance the stud will be submitted for sale at Newmarket on Dec 3rd.

Later, he stated:

> The comprehensive scheme of a national stud suggested by my offer to the Government was met with some difficulties in departmental etiquette, and the long delay in deliberating upon it has caused me to assume that it was impossible to carry it through in time. The offer is therefore withdrawn.

With typical Government indecision nothing was done until the last moment, and, on the morning of 3rd December, Mr Somerville Tattersall announced at the sale ring that he regretted any inconvenience caused to prospective buyers of Colonel Hall Walker's horses catalogued to be sold later in the morning, but they were all withdrawn in consequence of the Government's acceptance of the Colonel's generous gift. He added that the only intimation that the Government had cared to give their benefactor was a telegram delivered to the Jockey Club Rooms at a quarter to eight on the previous evening! Eventually the price for Tully was agreed at £47,625 and a further £18,000 for Russley Park.

Since the Colonel established the stud at the turn of the century, horses bred at Tully had won the Derby, the One Thousand Guineas twice, the St Leger twice, the Ascot Gold Cup twice, the Gimcrack Stakes four times and the St James's Palace Stakes five times. He now gave his entire bloodstock including six stallions, forty-three brood mares, ten two-year-olds and nineteen yearlings, as well as three hundred and eight head of pure and half-bred short-horn cattle to his country. The Government, in accepting the bloodstock on the understanding that the breeding of high-class horses was in the interests of the British Army, placed the stud under the control of the Ministry of Agriculture, who appointed Sir Henry Greer as Director. An agreement was reached whereby the yearlings not sold at auction were leased to Lord Lonsdale for their racing careers.

No one will ever know the real reasons why Colonel Walker decided to dispose of his Tully Stud, even if the Government did not accept his offer. There are two possible solutions. The first is that he was worried about the political situation in Ireland, and foresaw the events which led to the 1916 Easter Rebellion. The second, which seems more in keeping with his eccentric and egotistical character, is that he was dissatisfied with the manner in which some of his horses were being ridden by jockeys who did not follow his instructions and decided impulsively to abandon racing.

A year later Friar Marcus was retired to the stud at Sandringham in 1917. His stock were strong good-looking offspring who fetched substantial prices in the sale ring, even though they seldom showed signs in their racing career of more stamina than their sire. From 1923–1933 Friar Marcus was always in the first twenty winning sires, with Lemnarchus, Beresford and Brown Betty, the 1933 One Thousand Guineas winner, the best of his stock. His greatest claim to fame came through his daughter Friars Daughter, the dam of both Dastur and Bahram.

Whenever King George V was free to do so, he loved to stay at Sandringham, set amidst the rhododendrons, silver birches and pine trees of the Norfolk coast, spending many hours discussing with his workers the management of the thirty-thousand-acre estate and stud. The entrance to the stud farm, only a few moments' walk from the mansion, is dominated by the magnificent, larger-than-life statue of Persimmon, whilst inset in a nearby wall are plaques commemorating Florizel II and Perdita II. Above the green-tiled box where Diamond Jubilee was foaled on 12th March 1897, the Norfolk reed thatch kept the stables cool in summer and warm in winter for the mares who, at the end of the First World War, included Saint's Mead, Vervaine, Princess de Galles and Vain Air. Vain Air's dam, Vane, a sister to Flying Fox, had been bought at the Duke of Westminster's executor's sale in 1900. Souvenirs of past victories are accumulated in the small racing museum in the Sandringham stable yard where the stuffed head of Persimmon still vies with the racing plates of Ormonde for pride of place. The sheet worn by Ambush II on Grand National Day is another trophy, but the most historic and unusual is the silver plaque given by John Porter to the King's parents on their twenty-fifth wedding anniversary. Inset into the plaque are hairs from the tails of such famous Classic winners as Ormonde, Isonomy, Geheimniss, La Flèche, Orme, Flying Fox, Common, Blue Gown, Shotover and Sainfoin.

Not until 1922 were the King's colours carried successfully in any post-war races of importance. Weathervane (Lemberg – Vain Air) won the Greenham Stakes at Newbury, and the following year the Royal Hunt Cup ridden by Staff Ingham – to whom His Majesty presented a whip at Goodwood to commemorate the Ascot triumph. London Cry (Call of the Wild – Vervaine) won the Prince Edward Handicap at Manchester and three other races before winning the 1924 Goodwood Stakes, and Bowood ran up a series of victories in minor races. John Green, however, ran badly on several occasions and his owner wrote in his diary after Goodwood, 'John Green ran like a PIG.' Lancer, bred at the National Stud, won the St Leger in the colours of Lord Lonsdale, only a day after news of the disaster in the new Haig coal pit at Whitehaven cast a gloom over the Yorkshire miners at Doncaster.

Lord Marcus Beresford, although believing that the Sandringham-bred horses were at long last likely to prove successful, decided in the autumn of 1921 to buy a foal by the fashionable sire Son-in-Law, to augment the home-bred yearlings. He selected a colt out of Castelline, a Cyllene mare, and paid the modest price of seven hundred guineas for him. It was fitting that this colt, named Knight of the Garter, should prove a great asset to the King, for his purchase was one of Beresford's final acts as racing manager to the King before his death in December 1922. One of the last letters Lord Marcus Beresford wrote to the King was from his home at Englefield Green on 14th November:

> Sir,
> Your Majesty's two horses ran well to their form. It is quite a treat to have two such game, staying horses. Considering they have both been at it since March – I think they have done wonderfully well. I always have Your Majesty's horses ridden out (other people do not!) and consequently we do not get well handicapped – but I am sure it is the right example to set – the British public back Your Majesty's horses – both ways – and very seldom lose by doing so, and when the colours do win it is immensely popular.
> I beg to remain – Your Majesty's humble and loyal subject.
> Marcus Beresford.[1]

After Lord Marcus Beresford died, Dick Marsh wrote:

> A man more delightful, more staunch and loyal and devoted to their Majesties, whom he loved to serve, never came into my life. He brought sunshine into the lives of all he cared to be interested in, for God had given him a rare and ready wit such is vouchsafed to so few men. . . . There was no finer judge of a horse or racing. He understood the breed of a thoroughbred and had gained his knowledge partly from that which was instinct in him, and also from having been educated in a keen school.

Commenting on this sad moment, the King, in a letter to his

[1] *GV AA 67/3*

230

aunt, Princess Louise, Duchess of Argyll, wrote: 'Poor Marcus Beresford's death was a great shock to me, although I knew he had a bad heart; he will be a great loss to me. . . .'[1]

The problem of a successor to Lord Marcus Beresford was soon solved by the appointment of Major F H Fetherstonhaugh, whose wife Beatrice was a cousin of Lord Wolverton, with whom the King frequently dined when he stayed at the Jockey Club Rooms in Newmarket. Every year, unless other commitments interfered, the King stayed at Newmarket for at least one of the Spring Meetings and again for either the Cesarewitch or Cambridgeshire meeting in the autumn.

Major Fetherstonhaugh brought a more realistic approach to the question of where the royal horses should race than Lord Marcus Beresford, who believed that it was infra dig for horses carrying the royal colours to run in humble races. In consequence the King began to have considerably more success, and in 1923 won nineteen races with twelve horses. Owing to the illness of his aunt Princess Helena, the King did not go to the Derby, but this did not prevent his congratulating Mr Ben Irish, owner of Papyrus, whom he insisted on receiving at Buckingham Palace two days later.

During the summer Knight of the Garter won the Eglinton Stakes at York, and the Coventry Stakes at Royal Ascot, was unluckily beaten at Goodwood and then won again at Nottingham. This Nottingham race was the last occasion on which 'Bert' Jones rode in the royal colours. Knight of the Garter wintered well, and there were great hopes that he would figure prominently in the Two Thousand Guineas. To everyone's disappointment he ran like a complete non-stayer and was a beaten horse at the Bushes. In his diary, the King mentioned the Two Thousand Guineas result in a typical entry:

Wednesday 7 May. Jockey Club, Newmarket. At 8.0 rode with Fether. Saw my horses canter near the July course, a

[1] *VIC ADD Mss A/17/1355*

nice morning, lovely air. Worked and read after breakfast. Went to the races, a great many people to see the 2000 Guineas run. Diophon 1, Bright Knight 2, and Green Fire 3. There were 20 runners. Knight of the Garter Wragg up was 7th. I fear he can't stay a mile in the best company and that pace. Weathervane was just beaten a neck in the Bretby Handicap. I am not in luck just now.'

In the weeks before the Derby, Knight of the Garter proved to Marsh that his Guineas form was utterly wrong, and hopes ran high at Egerton House that he would redeem his reputation at Epsom. Then catastrophe struck in the shape of the dreaded heel-bug and all thoughts of running him either in the Derby or in any other race during the forseeable future were dashed. The King gave his customary dinner to the Jockey Club on the evening of the Derby – won in 1924 by Lord Derby's Sansovino – and proposed Lord Derby's health. On the back of his menu card Colonel Hall Walker – now Lord Wavertree – wrote 'Dinner to members of the Jockey Club on the occasion of Lord Derby winning the Derby with Sansovino by Swynford out of Gondolette sold to him by Lord Wavertree for that purpose'!

At Royal Ascot Weathervane failed only by a neck to win the Hunt Cup for the second year. On the Friday, Sir Dighton Probyn, who had given loyal service to the Royal Family for over fifty years, died at Sandringham aged ninety-one. The King's disappointment over Knight of the Garter was alleviated by Runnymede's success at Newmarket on the July course.

> . . . A lovely warm day yesterday; it was delightful at the races and not too many people there. I was cheered up by Runnymede unexpectedly winning the July Stakes, the best race of the day worth £1,789, but I had not a shilling on him, he is an improving horse so I hope he may win me some more races. I also had a good sale, in the morning, I sold six horses that were not worth keeping for £2,700. Quite a good day for the racing account. Went to see the

horses at the stables after the race. I rode early this morning.

Lord Marcus had suggested the name Runnymede:

... If we only have an open winter I hope to get as many of Your Majesty's horses out – as we possibly can – early next year. I have a splendid name for the foal by Hurry On out of Saints Mead: Runnimede – if Your Majesty approves. If it is taken we might call it Runnimede II. I am not sure if it is spelt with an 'i' or a 'y'.[1]

In the autumn Dick Marsh, trainer to two Kings, was approaching his seventy-third birthday when he received the following letter from Sir Frederick Ponsonby:

Dear Mr Marsh,
I understand that Lord Lascelles contemplates buying Egerton House as the Newmarket residence of Princess Mary and himself. This will necessitate considerable changes and as the King would never expect you as it were to make a fresh start under such altered conditions, I feel that this is a favourable opportunity for you to consider the advisability of placing your resignation in His Majesty's hands, and as Major Fetherstonhaugh finds that the present arrangement does not work satisfactorily and regards a change indispensable, the King would look for a younger man to succeed you whose position with regard to Major Fetherstonhaugh would of course not be the same as that which by your age, standing and experience you have occupied. These views are entirely shared by Lord Lascelles.
His Majesty naturally much regrets the necessity for the proposed change. For not only have you been personally associated with all that concerned the King's racing, in which His Majesty has enjoyed the benefit of your advice and knowledge, but it was owing to your skill and experience as a trainer of King Edward's horses that his late Majesty was so successful on the Turf.
But I cannot doubt for the above reasons, added to that which alas! we must all recognise, increasing years, you

[1] *GV AA 670*

233

will admit the reasonableness of the suggestion and then help to make matters easier and avoid all pain for both the King and yourself by expressing a wish to retire.

Yours faithfully,

F Ponsonby

It is understandable that Marsh, who had been training at Egerton House for over thirty years, and had been so close a friend of Lord Marcus Beresford, was finding it difficult to adapt himself to Major Fetherstonhaugh's new regime, and in any circumstances it would have been a difficult state of affairs if the King's racing manager and his trainer could not work in unison. Consequently at the end of the year Marsh left Egerton House, after a career which had established his reputation as one of the greatest trainers of all time.

In the early spring of 1925 the nation's interest in Sir Alan Cobham's feat of flying over the Himalayas was distracted when the King became ill, and did not resume his official duties until the end of May. In consequence he did not see Runnymede win at Newmarket and Chester before running unplaced in the Derby. He was a handsome colt, a little below top class, and later in the season finished third in the St James's Palace Stakes at Royal Ascot and the Gordon Stakes at Goodwood. During the Ascot meeting the King presented Richard Marsh with the MVO in his room in the Royal Stand, on the same day as Aloysia won the Queen Mary Stakes in the royal colours.

Runnymede's victory at Newmarket in the Brandon Handicap was the first winner sent out from Egerton House by the King's new trainer – William Jarvis. Born on 21st June 1885 he was the son of the W Jarvis who trained Cyllene for Sir Charles Rose. Sir Charles Rose had bought his first race-horse at the Hampton Court sales in 1888, a yearling filly by Hermit out of Land's End which he named Distant Shore. Distant Shore eventually went to her owner's stud at Pangbourne, and her third foal Arcadia became the dam of Cyllene – the sire of Minoru.

For many years Sir Charles Rose was Liberal MP for the Newmarket division of Cambridgeshire – and was very popular with his constituents even though he was a shy and awkward public speaker. At one political meeting he was known to have said, 'The Chair's place is in the Chairman.' Sadly he died from a heart attack in 1910 only a few hours after making his first flight in an aeroplane. He was young Willie Jarvis's godfather, and hoped that Willie would become a member of the Stock Exchange after he left Cranleigh. However, there was too much love of racing in his blood – as there was also in that of his brothers Basil and Jack – and although too tall to ride as a jockey, he went to assist his uncle James Ryan whose only son had died of typhoid. After the death in 1911 of his uncle, Willie Jarvis started training on his own account at Green Lodge, Newmarket. It never entered his head not to enlist at the outbreak of the First World War, in which he served with the South Notts Hussars and the 23rd Middlesex Regiment, and not until 1919 was he able to start training again. It was a hard struggle, but the words 'trained by W Jarvis' began to appear in the sporting papers. His wife, the sister of Frank and Fred Butters, did much to encourage him in these difficult years. When the offer to succeed Dick Marsh at Egerton House was first made, it caused much heart searching in the Jarvis household. Many trainers would have been glad to accept, but Jarvis was chosen, largely on the recommendations of the Hon George Lambton. Egerton House had now been acquired by the Earl of Harewood and his wife, the Princess Royal, and it was proposed that a new trainer's house be built for Jarvis. Mrs Jarvis did not like the three possible sites and suggested that the small entrance lodge be enlarged instead. Plans were drawn up and work started. One day in the course of discussion with the architect, Mrs Jarvis explained how sad she was that her fine staircase could not be incorporated in her new home. The architect suggested that, as the Royal Palace at Newmarket built for King Charles II was being demolished, the magnificent staircase should be installed in the trainer's house at Egerton. This was duly done. On his first visit of inspection of Jarvis's new home, King George V placed his hand on the staircase banister and smilingly said, 'I wonder how many times Nell Gwynn climbed these stairs.'

Jarvis took many of his own stable lads to Egerton House with him, and the extravagances of the Marsh regime were greatly curtailed. Sunday Chapel still continued for the lads, and Jarvis docked half a crown from their wages if he found them absent from evensong. The stable light-weight jockey Billy Alford had the misfortune to stammer and stutter, and it was a typically understanding kindness of the King that, when he went around the stables speaking to many of the lads as they groomed their horses, he merely smiled and shook Alford's hand. Jarvis noticed that on these visits, which the King loved, he always admired the Sandringham-bred horses, but the few horses in the yard which had been bought on his behalf at public auction he passed by without comment.

Many of the horses that Jarvis inherited at Egerton were moderate, and although some of them ran at Goodwood, they ran badly. In his diary the King wrote:

> Rained from early morning with sea fog till 4.30 in the afternoon which made it most unpleasant at the races and at times you hardly saw anything at all.

And the next day:

> Had three horses running today – none of them got a place even. Heaps of people at the races in spite of the weather. After tea motored over to Lavington Park where Lord Woolavington showed me his stud. Hurry On and Captain Cuttle are both fine horses. . . .

The year ended sadly for the Royal Family when Queen Alexandra died at Sandringham on 20th November.

Nineteen twenty-six began ominously with the General Strike which did not end until May. On a happier note, King George's daughter-in-law presented him with his first grandchild on April 21, and a week later he wrote from the Jockey Club Rooms:

> I had a nice ride on the heath early this morning, with Mary, in spite of slight drizzle and saw the horses at work. Colorado (Derby's horse) winning the Two Thousand today was a great surprise, he beat the favourite Coronach, by 5 lengths, & I should think barring accidents he is sure to win the Derby. I ran three horses today, Runnymede was 2nd & Jovial Monk was 3rd. I lost my money. . . .[1]

The remainder of the year brought little success for His Majesty's horses, but a yearling filly by Captain Cuttle out of Stained Glass named Scuttle was greatly pleasing her handlers at Egerton House, and the King was as delighted about her as he was that the Australians had been defeated in the Test Match by 289 runs. Scuttle's dam, Stained Glass, had fractured her pelvis when she fell in an exercise gallop whilst in training, but fortunately it was decided to save her for the Sandringham Stud.

In March 1927, the King went to Aintree for the Grand National, which was won by Sprig ridden by Ted Leader and owned by Mrs Partridge. Sprig, who started favourite, was trained by Ted Leader's father. Mrs Partridge, who was seventy-three years of age and kept Sprig in training in memory of her son who was killed in the First World War whilst serving with the Shropshire Yeomanry, visited Liverpool Cathedral on the morning of the race; and in the evening gave the customary celebration dinner at the Adelphi Hotel. In many of the villages near her home in Herefordshire people were returning from the day's hunting when they heard the church bells ringing to announce that Sprig had won. A local church dignitary was mightily displeased at this outward display, but was told

[1] *GV CC4/251*

by one of his younger and more sporting clergy that Mrs Partridge was an immensely popular local benefactor and that if Sprig should happen to win the National the following year, then undoubtedly the bells would again ring, for all Sprig's winnings were given to charity. Another reason for the importance of Sprig's Grand National is that it was the first occasion on which the BBC broadcast a horse-race. The commentator was Mr Meyrick Good of *The Sporting Life*, and he broadcast the race standing next to King George V, whom he respectfully reminded that any comment uttered whilst the race was in progress would be heard throughout the world. All went well until the last fence when, on his own admission, Mr Good so far forgot himself as to shout into the microphone, 'Come on Ted, you'll do it!'

During the Flat season, although Tutbury gave consistent pleasure to King George V by running six times, winning at Goodwood and Manchester, and being placed on the other four occasions, it was Scuttle who gave both her owner and the Egerton House stable most hope for the future. She was inclined to be temperamental, and never seemed to give of her best in home gallops, but nevertheless as a two-year-old she was second in the Queen Mary Stakes at Royal Ascot, won the Fitzwilliam Stakes at Doncaster, the Berkshire Foal Plate at Newbury and the Cheveley Park Stakes at Newmarket. The previous afternoon, Major Fetherstonhaugh, in an effort to help racing journalists, went to the Press Room and told the assembled correspondents that Scuttle had done an abysmal final gallop. In consequence no one tipped her. Ironically she won by a short head at 5–1.

Her first race as a three-year-old was the nine-furlong Brandon three-year-old handicap which she won by three-quarters of a length under top weight. The form looked useful, and was not discounted when Physic Bell who had been second to Scuttle ran with promise on the opening day of the Two Thousand Guineas meeting. Magnum

Bonum was first in the Thurlow Handicap to give His Majesty another humble victory, but one which augured well, showing that the Egerton House horses were in form. The next day King George wrote to Queen Mary from the Jockey Club Rooms: 'Scuttle is very well and I am in great hopes she will distinguish herself on Friday, but she has a lot of good ones to beat.'

Flamingo, trained by Jack Jarvis, won the Two Thousand Guineas, and the flying machine Tiffin spreadeagled a field of twenty-eight in the next race as she sauntered home to win by eight lengths on her race-course début.

Scuttle, after giving a great deal of trouble at the start, won the One Thousand Guineas by a length from Lord Dewar's Jurisdiction, ridden by Gordon Richards, who had never before been placed in a Classic. A memorable occasion, it was the first time a reigning monarch had both owned and bred a Classic winner. The King wrote in his diary:

Friday 4 May. *Jockey Club, Newmarket.*
Lovely morning. I rode with Mary & David (he is staying at Egerton House) and we saw the horses at work. I then showed David my rooms, the first time he has ever been to Newmarket. Racing began at 1.0. Gauntlet ran 4th in Friday Sweepstake. There were 14 runners in the One Thousand Gns which Scuttle won by 1 length from Jurisdiction, with Toboggan 6 lengths behind. It was a most exciting race, she was very fractious at the post and got a bad start. Childs rode an excellent race and brought her up to win easily at the end. She started favourite at 15–8. Everyone was delighted, and she got a great reception. I am very proud to win my first Classic and that I bred her at Sandringham. She is certainly a very game little filly.

The day before the One Thousand Guineas Joe Childs had told Willie Jarvis's young daughter Bridget that he thought Scuttle would win. Bridget in her prayers that night added as an afterthought that if Scuttle won she would do three somersaults. Children were not allowed in the Members' Enclosure at Newmarket, but the somersaults were duly executed with happy abandon in one of the cheaper rings. Spectators who witnessed this charming exhibition of *joie de vivre* missed an even greater one as the thirty-four-year-old Prince of Wales caught hold of his sister, the Princess Royal, and jubilantly danced a few steps as Scuttle passed the winning post.

There was much talk at the dinner given by the King on Derby Day to the members of the Jockey Club about Scuttle's chances in the Oaks, in two days' time. She ran exceedingly well, but Lord Derby's filly Toboggan had made great improvement since Newmarket when she had finished third to Scuttle and Jurisdiction, and was a convincing four lengths' winner, Scuttle second and Mr Tattersall's Flegere a further six lengths away third. Coincidentally, when Lord Derby's father had won the Oaks with Canterbury Pilgrim in 1896, the royal horse Thais had been relegated to second place, and also had started favourite. The King wrote in his diary:

> Raining this morning, it cleared up at 10.0 and became a nice day with sun. We all went to Epsom to see Scuttle run in the Oaks. She started a hot favourite, evens, but she was beaten by Toboggan (belonging to Eddy Derby) by 4 lengths with Flegere 6 lengths behind. It was a great disappointment to me, there was no excuse; perhaps she didn't like coming down the hill. We returned home wiser but certainly poorer.

At Royal Ascot, Scuttle finished third in the Coronation Stakes to Toboggan, ran badly in the Falmouth Stakes at Newmarket and was second in the Nassau Stakes at Goodwood giving the winner over a stone. Retired to Sandringham, she lost her first produce, a colt foal by Friar Marcus, as a yearling, and her next two offspring Fairlead and Canvas, both fillies, were of little account. It was yet another piece of bad luck for the stud when she died after foaling her second colt in 1934.

Joe Childs, who rode as first jockey to King George V, spent the early part of his life in France. Apprenticed to Tom

Jennings at Newmarket, he won the Great Metropolitan at Epsom in 1902 and the Goodwood Cup the same year on Perseus, trained by Dick Marsh at Egerton House. He rode his first Classic winner in 1912, when he won the Oaks by three lengths on Mirska, and during the course of the next twenty years won fifteen Classics on horses such as Gainsborough, Coronach, Solario, Fifinella and Hurry On. In his youth he was hot-tempered, but by the time he donned the royal racing silks he had become one of the finest jockeys ever seen in England; and was immensely proud of the fact that he was the King's jockey. Whenever he won a race for the King he would insist on drinking a half-bottle of champagne in the jockeys' dressing room, and toasting 'Your Majesty' as he raised the glass to his lips.

During the last few weeks of 1928 the King became seriously ill, and bulletins were posted outside Buckingham Palace as to the state of his health. By February 1929 he was sufficiently recovered to convalesce at Craigwell House, near Bognor (in future to assume the additional title of 'Regis'). Much of the year was spent quietly at Windsor and Sandringham, and it was not until the following May that he once more attended Newmarket races – the day after Miss Amy Johnson set out on her lone flight to Australia in her Puss Moth. At this Newmarket meeting the King had his first experience of Tote betting, and after expressing interest to know precisely how the Tote operated, and what would be the Tote procedure if he wished to make a bet on the next race, was handed a Tote ticket. History does not record if it was a winning one. Throughout the summer months, although the King's horses were not distinguishing themselves, a yearling colt was showing signs of promise at Sandringham. Sired by Lord Derby's Pharos out of Vervaine, and thus a half-brother to London Cry, he had been named Limelight. In his first four races as a two-year-old, his début being at Newmarket followed by another race on the same course, then Doncaster and Goodwood, he ran with sufficient promise to show that he might be a good horse one day. He won his next two races, at York and Doncaster, before ending the season by being beaten a short head and three-quarters of a length in a Newmarket Nursery Handicap, for which he started favourite.

His Majesty had suffered another racing setback in July 1931 when Major Fetherstonhaugh died. The news of his death was given to the King at Goodwood just after he had heard that both Sutcliffe and Duleepsinghyi had scored centuries in the Test Match at the Oval. It was a sad week as, at Cowes two days later, the King saw the second mate of his racing cutter *Britannia* swept into the sea and drowned. For nine years Major Fetherstonhaugh had managed the King's racing interests with considerable success. His widow, a great personal friend of the Royal Family, continued to advise and help from her home at Exning, where she looked after some Australian 'splendide' parakeets presented to the King. Her husband's successor was Brigadier-General H A Tomkinson.

Fifty-year-old Henry Tomkinson had a distinguished military career. The third son of the Rt Hon James Tomkinson, PC, MP, he was educated at Eton and RMC Sandhurst before joining the Royals in 1901. He served in the South African War 1901–2 and in the First World War, and won the DSO and Bar. A great polo player, he was included in the English team against America in both 1914 and 1921. His father had died after breaking his neck whilst riding in a race at the House of Commons point-to-point steeplechases in 1910 – the race being won by Colonel Hall Walker riding Buttercup. His grandfather Major William Tomkinson, who had served under the Duke of Wellington in the Peninsular Campaign and at Waterloo, was one of the three dashing Cheshire brothers:

Were my life to depend on the wager
I know not which brother I'd back
The Vicar, the Squire or the Major
The Purple, the Pink, or the Black.

242

The other brothers were Vicar of Davenham and Squire of Dorfold.

One of Brigadier Tomkinson's first decisions as Racing Manager was to suggest that the stud fees of the nineteen-year-old stallion Friar Marcus were reduced, in an attempt to help those owners of modest means who wished to send their mares to him. In consequence the fee was reduced from £199 to £98, even though at the Doncaster sales five of his yearlings fetched 5,620 guineas, an average of 1,124 guineas. Throughout the remainder of King George V's life, Tomkinson annually wagered half a crown with Sir Philip Hunlike, sailing master of His Majesty's yacht *Britannia*, as to whether the King's horses or his yacht gave him the more victories.

Limelight was a temperamental colt, and his victories in 1932 and 1933 were in no small measure due to the brilliant handling he received from Joe Childs, who found great satisfaction in having mastered a horse who, having given of his best in a race, would attempt to bite his jockey as he dismounted. Early in 1932 Limelight won twice at Newmarket before winning the Jersey Stakes at Royal Ascot. Later in the summer, after finishing last in a race at Newmarket, he broke down and did not run again as a three-year-old. Unfortunately he was never entered for the Derby, a race he might have won, for the winner April the Fifth was not a great horse.

The King, notwithstanding the immensity of his official duties, found time not only to enjoy his racing, but to show a profound understanding of every aspect of the sport. In September 1932 he wrote to his new racing manager from Balmoral:

My dear Tomkinson,
Thanks for your letter telling me that you had bought the yearling by Winalot – Skip Bridge for £1400, it seems a lot of money, I only hope he will prove as good as he looks, lucky he came up for sale when the prices were low, as I see the last three days they fetched much more. Hope

243

Jarvis liked him too. Did Lady Chesterfield breed him? I know she used to have several nice mares. The Leger was a surprise. I mean the Aga Khan having 4 horses in the race, all in the first 5. I hear they called it the Indian Circus. I hope Limelight is going on well and is back at work now. I see you did not accept him in the Cambridgeshire, he would have had to give Firdaussi 2 lbs. I wonder what the handicapper thinks of it now.[1]

This letter was followed up by two others to his manager – known to his friends as 'Mouse':

Balmoral, 15 Sept 1932

Thanks for letting me know you had bought another yearling by Foxlaw – Reef for £500. I hope he may turn out well, you think he will make a better 3 year old but I am glad you believe that the other one ought to win races next year. How would Grand Slam do for the Winalot colt if the name is not already taken? I wonder if Mrs Fethers would think it suitable. Just got your telegram that the ground is too hard to run Fox Earth at Yarmouth today. I am sorry as he might have won, but you were quite right. Glad to hear Limelight is cantering again & I trust he may be quite fit by next month. . . .[2]

And a week later:

Balmoral, 23 Sept

I was delighted to get your telegram saying Fox Earth had won by a neck. Sharpe must have ridden a good race. He certainly stays well, but I thought he was difficult for a boy to ride. Hope The Abbot may do a good gallop tomorrow and that he may run next week. Very difficult to find a name for the Winalot colt, I don't think I like Goulashe – too foreign. Hope Jarvis was bucked up by winning two races on one day. A nice change.[3]

In February 1933, Lord Wavertree died in London and three months later Dick Marsh died at his home at Great

[1] *GV AA 67/11*
[2] *GV AA 67/12*
[3] *GV AA 67/13*

Shelford near Cambridge. Their deaths severed two links in the history of royal racing.

Limelight began his four-year-old career by a splendid victory in the Newbury Spring Cup. A furlong from home he seemed to have no chance, but Childs, riding with outstanding skill, weaved his way through the field until he caught Solenoid in the last few yards to win by a short head. It was a wonderful success, the best part of which was that it showed Limelight had fully recovered.

In his next race he was beaten at Newmarket, before running in the Hardwicke Stakes at Royal Ascot. The King's horses, not for the first time, had been running disappointingly, but their owner neither complained nor criticised those responsible for their care, whatever his private opinion might have been. At the start of the Hardwicke, Limelight was not on his best behaviour and Childs, sensibly soothing and pacifying him, appeared almost to be in sympathy with Limelight's churlishness.

It showed great understanding on Child's part, for if he had attempted to manhandle his mount in an effort to prove his mastery, Limelight would have become resentful and might have refused to start. In the race Limelight settled down and came into the straight just behind Nitischin ridden by 'Brownie' Carslake and Donna Sol ridden by Eph Smith, both of whom were still full of running. Gallantly Limelight overhauled them and in a finish which thrilled the Ascot crowds Limelight just managed to force his head in front as the winning post was reached.

The scenes in the unsaddling enclosure, as King George V came from the Royal Box to greet his courageous winner, were amongst the most tumultuous ever seen at Ascot, for the British public love nothing more than for their Monarch to win an important race with a gallant horse.

A fortnight after the excitement of Royal Ascot, Childs nearly completed a hat trick for the King at the First July Newmarket meeting. Having won on Fox Earth and The Abbot he mounted Whitehead, sired by Triple Crown winner Gay Crusader, fully hoping for a third victory – but Whitehead was a very moderate animal and despite the artistry, skill and determination of Childs, he was beaten a head by Owers, ridden by Tommy Weston.

At Goodwood The Abbot won again, but then broke down, and the King wrote to his manager:

> *24 Aug 1933*
>
> Thank you for your letter telling me the five colts arrived safely on Monday. I took leave of them on Sunday and agree with Jarvis in thinking that Curraghmore and Firestone are the best. I only hope they may do well in training. I am very sorry to hear that The Abbot has developed a thoroughpin which will anyhow prevent him running again this season, I fear. How unlucky, but it may yield to treatment. I see Fox Earth will carry 7.12 in the Ebor next week which will enable Gordon Richards to ride him. Corady mustn't be allowed to get above himself and you must give him more work if the going is soft enough. If Limelight is well I should certainly like to run him in Duke of York Stakes especially as it would not mean a penalty for the Cambridgeshire should he win. . . . Harry showed me his yearlings and foals at Harewood on Tuesday. I didn't think they were anything wonderful, I wouldn't certainly exchange them for mine. . . .[1]

A month later, the King wrote again:

> *17 Sept 1933*
>
> Glad to hear from your last letter that the yearlings have settled down and have been backed. Will it ever rain again? The ground must be like iron now everywhere. Hyperion must indeed be a good horse, Derby tells me he won at Doncaster as easily as he won the Derby. The yearling sales were a great improvement on the last two years and several fetched quite big prices which shows that some people still have some money left. Hope you have got rid of Catherine Wheel. He is certainly no use to me. Glad you have had Whitehead cut, it was the only thing to do. I see that Bulteel has been even more unkind to Limelight

[1] *GV AA 67/17*

246

in the Duke of York Stakes than Fawcett in the Cambridgeshire. 9.7 is a big weight and there are some pretty good
horses in the race. Do you think it is worth running him
especially as the ground is so hard, but of course it may
rain before then. . . .[1]

Limelight, now a great favourite with the general public, did
run at Kempton and put up one of the finest performances
of his career when he won by a length and a half, giving
the second horse, Shrewton, thirty-eight pounds. As at
Royal Ascot, racegoers cheered to the echo their beloved
King and his courageous horse. Limelight's final race before
retiring to stud at Sandringham was in the Cambridgeshire
in which he finished fourth to Sir Abe Bailey's Raymond. A
few days later both Childs and Jarvis were presented with
silver cups by the King at Buckingham Palace.

The 1934 season opened tragically for the King when Fox
Earth broke down, and he wrote to Brigadier Tomkinson:

> *Windsor Castle, 13 April 1934*
> What a bombshell. I had hoped that Fox Earth might have
> won one or two races this year and now he will probably
> never run again. It is certainly very bad luck. I trust for
> the moment that my bad luck is over as this is the 3rd
> case. I should think if we got a decent offer for him to go
> abroad as a stallion it would be wise to accept. Just got your
> telegram that Slam was again unplaced, I fear he is not
> much use as a race horse. . . .[2]

The summer months slipped by with the usual visits to
Epsom and Royal Ascot. The King thought Colombo
slightly unlucky to lose the Derby and he, like every other
lover of horses, was overwhelmed by an event on the last
day of Royal Ascot. Included in the nine runners for the
Queen Alexandra Stakes – the longest race in the Jockey
Club calendar – were Nitischin, defeated by Limelight in
the 1933 Hardwicke Stakes, but nevertheless a Cesarewitch

[1] *GV AA 67/18*
[2] *GV AA 67/21*

247

winner, Harinero, the 1933 Irish Derby winner, Dark Dew, a French challenger with useful form on the Continent, Loosestrife, ridden by Gordon Richards, and above all others Brown Jack, now a ten-year-old, attempting to win this historic race for the sixth consecutive time. In the betting ring many believed that the gallant old warrior was facing defeat and impertinently offered 3–1 against his chances; odds which were gladly accepted by his legions of admirers who compelled his price to shorten until he took his rightful place as favourite at 6–4.

Turning into the straight, with only three furlongs still to race, Brown Jack moved into the lead closely pursued by Solatium with the other runners toiling hopelessly in the rear. To everyone's consternation the young Solatium refused to surrender, and it was not until the final furlong that Brown Jack struggled clear, with the daylight he was placing between himself and Solatium seeming utterly precious to his devoted worshippers in the Grandstand. No horse has ever captured the public's favour as much as Brown Jack, and as Steve Donoghue – himself an idol to his supporters – brought Sir Harold Wernher's champion back to the unsaddling enclosure, there was hardly a dry eye on the race-course. When Sir Harold Wernher was received by the King in the Royal Box the members of the royal party were as enchanted as all others that Brown Jack's career should have ended in so memorable a way.

In August the King, who happily announced the betrothal of his son Prince George, created Duke of Kent in October, to Princess Marina, received letters from his racing manager regarding the mares at Sandringham. He replied from Balmoral on 23rd August 1934:

> Many thanks for your letter. All you say about the mares and fillies interests me very much and of course I am very keen to improve the stud in every way I can. I should like you to discuss the matter with Mrs Fethers and let me know what she thinks. I see both Palma Bay and Picardy are supposed to be in foal to Limelight so would it not be

better to give them another chance and see what their foals were like before getting rid of them? The other two, Shanogue and Sunset Gun, might go. I think Mrs Fethers would probably agree with me. Certainly if you could get a well-bred yearling filly at a reasonable price you might do so at Doncaster. I am sure you are right in saying that it is no good breeding from mares who only produce very moderate animals which won't win races especially in a small stud like mine. I want you and Mrs Fethers always to work together and you both to advise me. I also own that I was not greatly impressed by the foals, with one exception, Polonaise, but it was the first time I had seen them, and some of them not yet weaned. I do hope you will soon get some rain and be able to train Fairlead seriously but on no account are you to take any risks with her. We have plenty of time to settle about the mares, but you can try and get a nice filly at Doncaster. . . .[1]

Even whilst he was busy shooting the King found time to consider the future of his stud, and studied the Doncaster Sales catalogue with meticulous care:

Balmoral, 2 Sept 1934
With regard to the fillies of the Sledmere Stud, no 9 by Fairway has a defective eye, is of course beautifully bred, and would be most useful at the stud, but probably not for racing, but she might fetch a reasonable price and so would be worth buying, or you might find another at the sale. I will leave it to you. I suppose really I am buying for the stud and the eye does not matter. Very likely if she is not trained she will produce better ones than if she was. . . .[2]

In a subsequent letter he suggested that three thousand pounds would be a sufficient price to pay for the yearling. Later he wrote approving the suggestion that Limelight be sent to Egerton House in October:

Balmoral, 16 Sept 1934
I am very glad that Whitehead took it into his head to win yesterday at Ripon, but I suppose it is not much use keeping

[1] *GV AA 67/22*
[2] *GV AA 67/23*

him. The prices given for yearlings were enormous and I suppose we are lucky to have secured a Blandford filly so cheaply, even if she does not win races she ought to be useful at the stud as she is well bred, we haven't got a Blandford before. I was very pleased Blank won, it must have been an exciting race, anyhow Harry has got a three-year-old which can stay 2¼ miles. I fear it must be getting very hard at Newmarket, and not good for Fairlead: don't run any risks with her, it is next year I am thinking of. I think your idea of getting Limelight to Egerton House for the two meetings in October a very good one and it will enable people to go & see him and I hope send mares to him. There must be an awful lot of money about, as even the Fairway filly with defective eyesight V Sassoon was going up to £4000 to get her. I suppose the yearlings were a better lot than usual, they fetched £100,000 more than last year.[1]

Fairlead, of whom he had such high hopes, was sired by Fairway out of Scuttle, but never lived up to her superlative breeding. Unlike his father, King George V had never been a devotee of racing under National Hunt rules, and Whitehead was the first horse he proposed to race in the winter months, although the next season Marconi was also sent hurdling:

Certainly I would like to run Whitehead over hurdles this winter, if you think he is good enough. Who would train him? Delighted to hear that Fairlead is doing and going so well and that you, Jarvis and Childs are pleased with her. I trust this may continue and that you will soon have rain to make the ground less hard. Yes, I think Parity quite a good name for the Blandford filly[2] and see it is not taken. Yes I was pleased to see that the only Friar Marcus yearling[3] at Doncaster fetched such a good price.[4]

[1] *GV AA 67/25*
[2] *Filly by Blandford out of Paritat, bought from Capt J B Fitzgerald for 1,300 guineas.*
[3] *By Friar Marcus out of Tangelo, sold to Mr J V Rank for 2,600 guineas.*
[4] *GV AA 67/26*

Nineteen-thirty-five, year of the Silver Jubilee celebrations, meant an exceptionally busy time for the King, but in the midst of all the planning and preparations, he was still able to maintain his racing interests. Writing to Tomkinson from Compton Place, Eastbourne on February 27th:

I am glad Fairey is cantering again and that Fairlead is having her violet ray treatment which I hope will help her on. Poor old Magnum Bonum he rendered good services to the stable for many years. About jockeys. We are alright for this season with Childs and Fox. I quite agree that either Gordon Richards or Fox would be the best for me. First have a private talk with Fred Darling before doing anything, and if he made no objection you could sound Gordon Richards and failing him you could speak to Fox. In either case they would ride only my horses and not for the stables. Gordon Richards might like to ride my horses but one never knows, and he would not have to break with Beckhampton as I really have so few. I like Fox, he is a fine rider in spite of his age. Anyhow these two are absolutely straight, and always try to win, you can't say that about them all. I should think £1000 retainer for Richards would be right. . . .[1]

Once more the summer months sped by and after the happiness inspired by the Jubilee celebrations, the world was shocked by the earthquake in Quetta, when thirty thousand lives were lost, the death in a motor accident of Queen Astrid of the Belgians, and the invasion of Abyssinia by the Italians.

At King George V's annual Derby dinner, the Jockey Club had presented him with a painting by Lynwood Palmer of Limelight. He had no horse in training of any real merit in 1935, although Bahram's Triple Crown victory naturally pleased him. Freddie Fox, who had ridden Bahram in both the Two Thousand Guineas and Derby, was thrown, and badly bruised and concussed

[1] *GV AA 67/28*

in a race at the Doncaster meeting, and consequently Charlie Smirke deputised for him on Bahram in the St Leger:

> Many thanks for your letter of 14th. Poor Fox, what bad luck, glad you gave him my message. I trust he will make a good recovery, but he certainly will not ride again this year. Yes, try and get Gordon Richards when Childs can't ride the weight. Would it not be worthwhile for Childs to ride both Canvas and Fairey even if he has to carry a few pounds extra, anyhow it would be better than a bad jockey at the weight. Glad that both Canvas and Fairey are doing well, what a pity I shall not be able to see the former run her first race. You did quite right to get rid of Bonnie Dundee to go to India, I never like Buchans. Yes, try Parity at a longer distance. Bahram must be a jolly good horse, and I am glad he is out of a 'Friar Marcus' mare. The Aga Khan only gave £250 for her at one of the Doncaster yearling sales, that was indeed luck, and sent her to Blandford. £500 is indeed an enormous fee, but I suppose he is worth it. . . .[1]

On 16th November 1935, 'Midge' Richardson rode Curragh-more to win at Derby. It was an unimportant race, but it was to prove King George V's last racing victory, for he died before the commencement of the next Flat season.

Although destiny ordained that he should reign for twenty-five years, when the world, both politically and socially, was in turmoil, he loved nothing better, when affairs of State allowed, than to stay informally at the Jockey Club Rooms in Newmarket. On Sunday 12th January 1936, writing in his diary at Sandringham: '4° of frost; walked to church, 11.30. The Bishop (of Wakefield) preached. In the afternoon we went to see the mares and yearlings.'

At five minutes to midnight a week later he died, and the British Empire mourned an immeasurably kind and conscientious King. Writing in the *Household Brigade*

[1] *GV AA 67/30*

Magazine, Brigadier Tomkinson stated:

Racing may be only a sport, but to the enthusiastic and keen owner, it does bring out the traits in a man's character to a very remarkable degree. Particularly in this case, when ill luck dogs a stable, and everything goes wrong, and I regret to say that this did certainly occur to a very marked degree, particularly in the last two years of His Majesty's reign. There is no greater mistake than to imagine that the late King raced only from a sense of duty and did not care for it. On the contrary, he loved a day's racing, particularly at Newmarket, and no owner was keener or took a greater interest in his horses than he did. It was not only in the racing that he took such an interest, but even more so in the breeding and welfare of the young stock. Constantly when in London, he would say to me how anxious he was to get down to Sandringham to see the foals that had just arrived, and how the yearlings had done since he was last there. Certainly on his arrival there, his first tour of inspection was to go very carefully all around the stud. His quite remarkable consideration and sympathy for the feelings of all about him extended to his horses as well. After having been all round the Sandringham stud, and no doubt being somewhat fatigued, he would say, 'Now we must go down to Wolferton to see old Friar Marcus. The old boy might feel neglected if we did not go to see him.'

11

... and the Sport of Queens

☐☐

WITHIN A MONTH of the death of King George V, Brigadier Tomkinson received a letter from Lord Derby giving his views on the future of the royal horses:

> ... The more I think of it the more alarmed I am at any prospect of His Majesty not continuing to race. It would be a fatal blow to what after all is one of our biggest industries and with the decline of racing the value of our bloodstock for export purposes would be diminished to a degree that I do not think anyone would care to contemplate. At the present moment it is the thoroughbred horse market of the whole world and anything that was done which injured it would bring very disastrous consequences.
>
> ... It is outside the province of these remarks but I would suggest to His Majesty that, at all events at first, the Stud and the number of horses in training should be diminished to such an extent as to enable one person to supervise both. I would further strongly urge that the paddocks at Wolferton, which must be horse sick as they have had horses continually on them since the days of Persimmon, should be closed for 2 or 3 years and the Stud brought to Hampton Court.
>
> I would further suggest the weeding out of several of the mares who would probably fetch fair prices and perhaps with the money so obtained buy any suitable mare that came into the market. If the stud was reduced to about 10 mares that would give His Majesty quite enough foals to go on racing with every year and I think I could guarantee that the services of the best stallions in this country and even in France would be at the disposal of His Majesty free of all charge.
>
> Under these circumstances and especially if Limelight makes good, the Stud could be run not only at no loss but at a profit.

When the Earl of Derby wrote these words he could not have foreseen the momentous events of 1936. The new forty-one-year-old King had enjoyed riding ever since his childhood, although in his memoirs he claimed that he had been brought up 'in the atmosphere of game and guns at Sandringham and in Scotland' and 'the manly accomplishment that I coveted above all others, therefore, was to be a good shot rather than a good man to hounds'. His first day's hunting had been with the South Oxfordshire Hounds whilst he was an undergraduate at Magdalen. He rode his first point-to-point winner in March 1921, when he won a race at the Pytchley on his own horse Rifle Brigade. There were thirteen competitors and the Prince put up three pounds overweight. His younger brother, the Duke of York, was also present at the meeting. After the race, which Rifle Brigade won by a length, the Prince was overheard to remark, 'I was amazingly lucky to win', to which a bystander replied, 'it was amazingly good horsemanship that did it'. Shortly after the point-to-point the Prince presented the horse to Colonel 'Taffy' Walwyn, who had been responsible for breaking Rifle Brigade as a yearling.

For the next seven years as the Prince of Wales he caused consternation to some Government leaders who considered the fact that he rode in point-to-points and the hunting field to be both reckless and dangerous. He was on safari in Tanganyika in 1928 when he learned that King George V was seriously ill. Hurrying home he found his father weak but much improved in health. It has been suggested that the first words that the King whispered to his son were 'did you shoot a lion, David?' Nevertheless the importance of his duties as Heir Presumptive now compelled him to take an interest in the safer sport of golf. It is probable that he would have continued the racing activities of his father once he became King, but the historic events of 1936 left little time for him to show his interest. In fact 1936 proved a successful year for the royal horses, as Fairey (Fairway – Polish Air) won the

Waterford Stakes at Ascot, Fairlead (Fairway – Scuttle) won at Sandown and Canvas (Solario – Scuttle) won at Doncaster. More important were the victories of Feola, bought as a yearling from Lord St David's stud. After winning at Kempton and Newmarket she ran second to Lord Derby's Tideway in the One Thousand Guineas and third to Lord Glanely's Lovely Rosa in The Oaks. In due time she became the dam of Foretaste, Knight's Daughter, Hypericum, Kingstone, Above Board, Reprimand and Angelola – the dam of Aureole.

On a cold gloomy night a fortnight before Christmas, HMS *Fury* left Portsmouth harbour with the eldest son of King George V aboard. The Abdication crisis and his new responsibilities could have left little time for the new King, George VI, to consider his race-horses, but within a week of his Accession, Lord Derby, so loyal and generous a friend to the Royal Family, was writing to Brigadier Tomkinson: 'Nobody could be more pleased than I am to see that the new King is going on both with the Stable and the Stud.'

From Sandringham King George VI found time to write, on 28th December, to Brigadier Tomkinson:

My dear Mouse,
I hope I may call you by this name?
Many thanks for your letters. Your last one only reached me today, so I did not know why Fairlead did not run on Saturday. The heavy going does not seem to suit our horses.
I want to come down to Newmarket one day next month to see Jarvis & the horses when we can meet and have a talk. I have accepted the free services offered by Ld Derby (3) the Aga Khan (3) Sir Abe Bailey (2) for this year. Ld Glanely has not written to say the offer still holds good. As I do not know him well I don't expect he will write to me. I understand that there was a question of selling Limelight. This matter will have to wait until we can talk it over. Also his first foals are 2-year-olds this new year aren't they? We must wait and see if they are going to be of any

use. I may have to sell him as I shall want some cash to make the Stables & Stud square on legal grounds.

I shall certainly take a great interest in Racing, but of course at the moment I know nothing about breeding or anything else so you must teach me.

I am so glad that you will go on being my manager, & I hope that we shall have a good season to start off with.

Yours very sincerely
George RI

The King's hopes that his fifty-six-year-old manager would be of great help were dashed when Brigadier Tomkinson died in a London nursing home exactly a year after the death of King George V.

Three months later at Liverpool, Jubilee, bred by King George V, won the Molyneux Stakes to give King George VI his first racing victory. Jubilee's dam, Judith, had been bred by Captain Charles Moore, who was appointed to succeed Brigadier Tomkinson. Two day's after Jubilee's success the King and Queen, who were staying at Knowsley as the guests of Lord Derby, saw Royal Mail, trained by Ivor Anthony and ridden by Evan Williams, win the Grand National. It was the first time that the King and Queen had attended a race-meeting since their Accession.

In the first two years of the Second World War there were few racing opportunities for royal horses trained at Newmarket by Willie Jarvis, who died in January 1943. On his death Captain Cecil Boyd-Rochfort took over as trainer, and in the next four seasons made a brilliant start to King George's racing career by winning with Fair Glint, Knight's Daughter, Kingstone, Rising Light and Hypericum. Meanwhile in 1942 Big Game and Sun Chariot, leased to His Majesty from the National Stud and trained by Fred Darling at Beckhampton, were proving to be two of the best racehorses ever to have carried royal colours. Only Big Game's defeat by Watling Street in the Derby prevented every Classic being won by His Majesty's horses. Three years later the final substitute Derby was run at

Newmarket. There were hopes that Rising Light, cleverly named as he was by Hyperion out of Bread Card, bought by King George VI for 1,550 guineas in 1938, would win for the King, but he could only manage to finish fifth to Sir Eric Ohlson's Dante. The King, in naval uniform, the Queen, and Princess Elizabeth in ATS uniform, were present. This was the first Derby that the Princess had seen, and only the second time she had been to a race-meeting. She had been given her first pony, a Shetland named Peggy, by her grandfather King George V when she was four years old, and had learned to ride under the tutelage of Horace Smith at Holyport. During the war years she followed the exploits of her father's horses with great interest, and was delighted that she was allowed to read the training reports. In the spring of 1942 she accompanied her father on a visit to Beckhampton to see Big Game and Sun Chariot at exercise. Sun Chariot was on her worst behaviour and charged into a ploughed field, where she went down on her knees roaring like a bull, much to the embarrassment of her rider – Gordon Richards. After the royal party had left, Gordon admitted to Fred Darling that it was the first time that he had ever polished his boots again for the second lot.

It was evident to all that Princess Elizabeth was greatly attracted to the sport of racing, and amongst her wedding presents were prints of Newmarket, binoculars, a saddle from the Worshipful Company of Saddlers, and also a filly foal named Astrakhan, given to her by HH Aga Khan, who considered a racehorse to be an eminently suitable wedding present for a Royal Princess. In 1949 whilst eagerly awaiting Astrakhan's début the Princess registered her racing colours – scarlet, purple hooped sleeves, black cap. Unfortunately Captain Boyd Rochfort was caused much anxiety by Astrakhan who proved difficult to train as she had weak forelegs. When HH Aga Khan learnt that the filly might never be strong enough to race, he proposed that another filly should be chosen. A beautifully bred yearling by

Stardust out of Bellinzona was selected, named Marsa; but she had little ability and died in 1951 without ever having been placed in the first three. Meanwhile Boyd-Rochfort persevered with Astrakhan, who made her début in the Sandwich Stakes at Ascot in October 1949. The Princess had hoped to fly from Scotland to see her filly run, but fog prevented the journey being made. Astrakhan ran creditably to finish second to The Golden Road ridden by Gordon Richards. Subsequently in the spring of 1950 she was third at Windsor and won at Hurst Park, before being taken out of training after failing to gain a place in the Oaks Trial Stakes at Lingfield.

On the same day that Marsa was transferred to the Princess, the steeplechaser Monaveen was bought by Peter Cazalet on behalf of the Princess and her mother. The real instigator of this purchase was Lord Mildmay who had been a guest at Windsor Castle for Royal Ascot. Lord Mildmay, admired by many as the last of the Corinthians, had so enthused over the sport of steeplechasing that it was agreed that Cazalet should try to find a suitable horse for his royal patrons. Monaveen, described by Sir Martin Gilliat as 'a medium sized, wiry, light-framed horse with excellent bone', had been bred in Ireland. His sire Landscape Hill was also the sire of the famous steeplechaser owned by Lord Mildmay – Cromwell. At the time Peter Cazalet bought him from Mr Dal Hawkesley, a well-known trainer of greyhounds, Monaveen was an eight-year-old who had won three steeplechases and had run promisingly in the Grand National. The sale price was reputed to be one thousand pounds.

On a sunny October afternoon at Fontwell Park, Monaveen ran for the first time in the colours of his new owner. There were only three runners and the Princess jokingly pointed out that, bar a fall, her horse was at least certain to be placed. Monaveen started favourite at 100–30 on, and won easily. Thus Fontwell Park, an unpretentious but charming Sussex course, had the honour of being the first race-course on which the Princess's colours were carried to victory. Naturally everyone connected with Monaveen was delighted, although knowledgeable race-goers did not feel that this modest success made the horse a world-beater. Lord Mildmay, doyen of amateur riders, went so far as to pretend that he would have been too nervous to ride Monaveen in public. Before the end of the year, Monaveen had shown that he was capable of greater achievements than his Fontwell success. In November the Princess and her sister, Princess Margaret, saw him finish second in the Grand Sefton at Aintree to the great steeple-chaser Freebooter, and then proceed to win at both Sandown and Hurst Park. The Hurst Park victory on the last day of the year was very impressive, for he defeated such crack horses as Wot No Sun and Roimond as well as Freebooter.

Peter Cazalet was convinced that Monaveen was potentially an Aintree horse, and his training during the first three months of the new year prepared him for the 1950 Grand National. The King and Queen in addition to the Royal Princesses were at Liverpool to see Monaveen run. The Press made reference to Ambush II and King Edward VII, and even without the loyal patriotism, which influenced racegoers' judgement, the form book gave the royal horse an undeniable chance. Princess Elizabeth, believing, like so many other owners in lucky mascots, wore the same hat as she had worn when her horse won at Hurst Park. Monaveen led at Bechers Brook on the first circuit, but a mistake at the Chair fence in front of the grandstand put paid to his chance, although he battled on gallantly to complete the course and finish fifth to Freebooter. Tragically he was killed at the water jump at Hurst Park on New Year's Day, when attempting to win the Queen Elizabeth Handicap for the second time. The Princess was in Malta and did not see the race, which was broadcast. HM Queen anxiously asked if the broadcast would have been heard in Malta, as she felt that her daughter would have been upset to learn the news of

Monaveen's death over the wireless. Raymond Glendenning assured her that the broadcast was relayed only in Britain.

In the previous spring the Royal Family, like all other lovers of steeplechasing, were saddened by the death of Lord Mildmay, drowned near his Devonshire home. When his horses came up for sale, HM Queen bought Manicou on whom Lord Mildmay had won six races. During the autumn she registered her colours of blue, buff stripes, black cap, gold tassel, which for generations had been the racing colours of the Earls of Strathmore. The blue in the first set of silks seemed paler than expected, and it was discovered that they had been copied exactly from a set fifty years old. A new set was quickly ordered. It was an historic occasion when Manicou won at Kempton Park in these colours, for it was the first time that a Queen had won a race since the days of Queen Anne. The French-bred Manicou went on to win at Sandown and again at Kempton where he won the King George VI Steeplechase, before breaking down and being retired to stud. His name should remain immortal in racing history as the horse that gave Queen Elizabeth an insight into the wondrous sport of steeplechasing. When King George VI died it was tacitly agreed that she, now HM Queen Mother, would concentrate on racing under National Hunt rules, whilst HM Queen would maintain royal interests under Jockey Club rules.

Court mourning precluded the royal colours being seen on the race-course for some months after the King's death, and in consequence when Choir Boy won at the 1952 Second Newmarket spring meeting it was in the colours of the Duke of Norfolk. Stream of Light's victory in the Lancashire Oaks in early June was the first occasion on which the royal silks were publicly seen in the winners' enclosure since the Queen's accession. The Queen did not attend Epsom for the Derby or the Oaks, but at Royal Ascot the pageantry as she drove up the course, with her postilions in their scarlet and gold livery, cast the thoughts of many back to the day when Queen Anne had inaugurated the meeting. Her obvious enjoyment of racing was further proven when she went to Goodwood in July. To everyone's delight Gay Time, ridden by Gordon Richards, won the Gordon Stakes in the royal colours. Gay Time had been sold by Mrs J V Rank to the National Stud, and the Queen decided to lease him for the remainder of his racing career. The decision was made whilst the Goodwood meeting was in progress, and Mr Peter Burrell, Director of the National Stud, only just managed to get the news to the race card printers in time for them to include correctly details of Gay Time's new owner on the race card.

The Queen was at Balmoral during September, but nevertheless she travelled to Doncaster for the St Leger, in which unhappily Gay Time could finish no nearer than fifth to HH Aga Khan's Tulyar. Later in the autumn a two-year-old filly, High Service, won a humble race at Birmingham, appropriately on the same day as Her Majesty opened the new session of Parliament. Also during the autumn Noel Murless moved from Beckhampton to Warren Place at Newmarket. Warren Place had been built originally at immense cost by Sam Darling, and after the Second World War even further improved by the Gaekwar of Baroda. This move on the part of Noel Murless meant that all the royal horses whether home bred or leased from the National Stud were now centred at Newmarket, only fifty miles from Sandringham.

It was the wish of all that one of the horses trained by Murless or Boyd-Rochfort would prove a champion for the new Queen, particularly as Gay Time, who had turned out to be an unsatisfactory bargain, had been sold to the Japanese Government for less than half the price of fifty thousand pounds that the National Stud had paid for him. For once the Gods, or those who rule the Destiny of Man, relented, and a chestnut race-horse named Aureole brought glory and honour to the royal colours. Sired by Hyperion out of the royal mare Angelola – herself a daughter of the brood mare Feola and thus a sister to Hypericum – Aureole was brilliantly named by Her Majesty. Remembering that Angelola's sire was Donatello II, she proposed that the dapper little foal should be named after the golden discs around the Italian sculptor's marble saints, which symbolised glory. Aureole's début was delayed until the Ebor meeting at York when, to the surprise of many, he won the valuable Acomb Stakes. This victory augured well, but the royal colt's antics at the start of the Middle Park Stakes later in the season and his subsequent six lengths defeat by Royal Challenger took some of the gilt off the gingerbread. Although the colt wintered well, he seemed to take a dislike to the Limekiln's gallop and caused his trainer much worry, even though it was evident that he possessed great ability.

The Queen watched the Two Thousand Guineas in which Aureole was unplaced behind Nearula – but was absent when he won the Lingfield Derby Trial Stakes convincingly. Four days before the Derby at Epsom, an event of far greater importance occurred when Her Majesty was crowned in Westminster Abbey. It would have been a fitting climax to the Coronation celebrations if Aureole could have won the Derby – but the newly knighted Sir Gordon Richards and Pinza beat him by four lengths. No one in the world of racing could begrudge Gordon Richards a Derby triumph, after so many years of frustration, least of all the Queen who, as she congratulated him in the Royal Box, expressed the hope that the following year he would ride her intended runner Landau. This colt, by Hyperion out of Sun Chariot, had shown infinite promise when winning at Brighton. Later in the year he was also to win at Doncaster, but unfortunately his temperament was a little uncertain. At Royal Ascot, Choir Boy won the Royal Hunt Cup, but Aureole, who had been coughing, could only manage to be third in the Eclipse at Sandown, before once again being defeated by his rival Pinza, this time in the King George VI and Queen Elizabeth Stakes at the July Ascot meeting.

Although as a three-year-old Pinza seemed to have his measure, there was a belief that if Aureole's unruly temperament could be curbed then he might become a champion. Consequently a course of treatment under the supervision of Harley Street consultant Mr Charles Brook was suggested. The treatment appeared successful, and the Queen travelled from Balmoral to Doncaster for the St Leger with high hopes of success, especially as Pinza had broken down and been taken out of training. Once again the irony of racing fortunes was hammered home by Aureole, who never really settled down in the race, and finished third to his stable companion Premonition, owned by Brigadier W P Wyatt and also trained by Boyd Rochfort. In October Aureole competed for the Cumberland Lodge Stakes at Ascot. His usual jockey W H Carr could not do the weight and Eph Smith was given the mount. Aureole won stylishly, and Smith, who had requested that he be allowed to ride Aureole at exercise at Newmarket so that he could become familiar with the colt who now had a reputation for being 'rather a handful', was convinced that he would make a top-class four-year-old.

His view was correct, for in 1954 Aureole after winning at Kempton and triumphing in the Coronation Cup at Epsom, proceeded to emulate Limelight by winning the Hardwicke Stakes at Royal Ascot. Aureole suffered a minor eye injury a few days before the meeting which enabled Eph Smith to quip to Her Majesty, when asked if he thought he would win, 'Well, Ma'am, we are rather handicapped. The horse is blind in one eye and I am deaf.' In July Landau, who had disappointed in the Derby, finished third in the Eclipse. In the next race the Queen watched her two-year-old filly, Abergeldie, in the paddock and wished Gordon Richards good luck as he mounted. Within moments of being led from the parade ring Abergeldie had shied, then reared and fallen, pinning the champion jockey beneath her, his pelvis fractured. This accident hastened his decision to retire from the saddle and turn to the equally exacting profession of training.

The following Saturday, at Ascot, Aureole ran his final

race when he won the King George VI and Queen Elizabeth Stakes. The fact that the race was run in appalling conditions, the course soaked after torrential rain, did not detract from the infinite pleasure of this outstanding swan song. By his victory Aureole proved himself the best horse in Europe, and in three seasons had won £36,220 – almost three times as much prize money as Persimmon had collected by his victories in the Derby, St Leger and Ascot Gold Cup. There were tentative suggestions that Aureole would be invited to compete in the Washington International at Laurel Park in the autumn, but the Queen decided that he should be retired to stud at Sandringham. However there was still a possibility that a royal horse might be sent to America instead of Aureole, for Landau had restored his tarnished reputation by winning the Sussex Stakes at Goodwood. This redemption was somewhat marred by his failure to win a four-horse race at Newmarket in the early autumn; in fact in this race he was not even placed! Sportingly the Queen agreed that he should accept the American invitation, although his chance was not rated highly. Flown across the Atlantic he developed a heel infection which dissipated his chance even more, and no one was surprised when he finished last. On a happier note it should be recorded that the racing silks carried by Landau in the Laurel Park race are now displayed in the US National Museum of Racing at Saratoga Springs. Landau was subsequently sold as a stallion to Australia.

In 1954, Her Majesty graciously consented to become patron of the Jockey Club, the National Hunt Committee and the Thoroughbred Breeders Association. Few men have greater knowledge and understanding of every aspect of horse-racing than the Queen, and her patronage is acclaimed by all. Unlike King George V and her great-grandfather King Edward VII, who occasionally bet in modest amounts, the Queen never bets, although she takes pleasure in attempting to select winners both on form and critical paddock inspection. Her generosity to those in the world of racing who work on her behalf is boundless, and there are many jockeys who treasure above all else the royal tie-pins, cuff-links and silver cigarette boxes which have been given to them. The Queen, being an exceptionally accomplished horsewoman, enjoys riding over the racecourse at Ascot, and during Royal Ascot week she and her Windsor Castle house guests frequently can be seen in the morning riding at speed past the five furlong gate towards the winning post. In 1968, as an added attraction for her guests, she arranged a small exhibition of 'raciana' taken from the Royal Archives, including letters from Sam Chifney.

After the excitement and glory of Aureole in 1954 the subsequent year was uneventful. In the spring of 1956 the Queen went to Aintree to see her mother's horses Devon Loch and M'as-Tu-Vu run in the Grand National. The record books will show that both the Queen Mother's horses were unplaced, but for those present at the meeting the sight of Devon Loch collapsing some fifty yards from the winning post with his nearest rival toiling in his wake will be one of the unforgettable tragedies of steeplechasing – far more tragic than the fall of Ambush II at the final fence in the 1903 National when he was apparently full of running and in the lead. The 1956 National was also historic as the Hammer and Sickle flag flew from one of the grandstand flagpoles as a compliment to Mr Malenkov, who on his visit to England insisted on seeing the race.

At Kempton Park on Easter Saturday, High Veldt won the Two Thousand Guineas Trial in the Queen's colours and later was second to the incomparable Ribot at the July Ascot meeting. In the St Leger High Veldt ran badly, but the Queen's visit to Doncaster was not in vain. On the eve of the St Leger she went to the sales and inspected some of the yearlings in the company of her racing manager, Captain Charles Moore. Captain Moore had served in the Irish Guards and, at his home, Mooresfield in Co Tipperary, had bred Zionist, second to Manna in the 1924 Derby. He was racing manager to King George VI and Queen Elizabeth for more than twenty-five years, and must rank alongside Lord Marcus Beresford as not only one of the most charming of men, but also as one to whom great credit must be given for the success of the royal racing fortunes. The Queen considered that two of the yearlings at Doncaster were suitable to introduce new blood into the royal studs, and they were duly bought at auction. No one knew, however, not even the leading bloodstock agency who had been instructed to bid, that these yearlings had been personally chosen by the Queen. Both were fillies, the first, bought for four thousand guineas, being by Petition–Danse d'Espoir and bred at the famous Yorkshire stud owned by Sir Richard Sykes at Sledmere. The second filly, who cost fifteen hundred guineas, was by Luminary–Whoa Emma. They were named Petronella and Stroma. Petronella proved a disappointment, but Stroma turned out to be a very astute purchase. At the end of her racing career she was retired to the royal paddocks. In 1961 she produced Canisbay by Doutelle, who before his untimely death had sired such top-class horses as Pretendre, Dites, Fighting Ship and Audrey Joan. Canisbay did not race as a two-year-old, but made a successful début when he won the Wood Ditton Stakes at Newmarket in the spring of 1964. The following year he won the Eclipse Stakes at Sandown for the Queen. He is now one of the stallions at the Royal Stud at Sandringham.

The first hat-trick in the Queen's colours occurred at Haydock Park in the spring of 1957 when the two-year-old Pall Mall made a winning début, Atlas won the Haydock Park Stakes in record time, and Might and Main won the last race of the day. A hat-trick of a different kind came the following year when Doutelle won the Two Thousand Guineas Trial at Kempton, for Alexander – now a leading South African sire and High Veldt – had won this race the two preceding years. Doutelle was one of the best horses ever bred at the Royal Stud. He made a winning début in the Granville Stakes, and his victory in the Guineas Trial at Kempton the following spring brought fresh hopes of another Royal Classic victory. These hopes were strengthened when he won the Derby Trial at Lingfield. At Epsom he finished tenth behind Crepello but there may have been some excuses for him as it was a rough race, and not only was he badly bumped and baulked, but he also damaged a pastern. This injury kept him off the race-course until the autumn when he won the Cumberland Lodge Stakes at Ascot. As a four-year-old he won the 1958 John Porter Handicap at Newbury, beat Ballymoss at Chester and was third to Ballymoss in the King George VI and Queen Elizabeth Stakes before being retired to stud at Sandringham. Colonist II, who had run in the colours of Sir Winston Churchill and had won thirteen races worth £11,937, was bought at this time ostensibly to act as a 'teaser' for Doutelle. Colonist II seemed to be endowed with the same battling qualities as his owner. Appropriately on the day that Sir Winston Churchill was elected to the Jockey Club, Colonist II won the Jockey Club Cup at Newmarket. Doutelle's brother Above Suspicion (Court Martial – Above Board), after winning the St James's Stakes at Royal Ascot and the Gordon Stakes at Goodwood for the Queen, was sold as a stallion and now stands at the Cloghran Stud near Dublin.

Nineteen-fifty-seven was another great year for the Queen's horses, for in addition to Doutelle's victories Noel Murless saddled Carrozza to win the valuable Princess Elizabeth Stakes at the Epsom spring meeting, and a month later, ridden by Lester Piggott, won the Oaks. It was a desperately close finish with Carrozza and the Irish filly Silken Glider passing the winning post virtually inseparable. There was little doubt that Silken Glider was ahead a few strides beyond the post, but no one knew until the judge gave his verdict after consulting the photo of the finish that the royal filly had held on to win by a short head. For Piggott and Murless, who had ridden and trained

Crepello to win the Derby two days previously, it was a wonderful double; for Her Majesty, a moment when she was able to understand by her own experience the patriotic acclaim which had greeted her great-grandfather as he led in his Epsom Classic winners, for Carrozza's success was the first Royal Classic winner at Epsom since Minoru in 1909.

By the end of the year the Queen headed the list of winning owners with a total of £62,212, achieved from victories in thirty races. At Royal Ascot not only did Pall Mall win the New Stakes, and Michelino and White Flake win at the Heath meeting on the Saturday, but Almeria won the Ribblesdale by five lengths. Almeria's breeding is typical of the vicissitudes of racing and how bargains can be acquired. At the Newmarket July sales in 1943 a batch of mares were sold by the executors of the sixth Duke of Portland. Prices were very low due to the war, and Captain Charles Moore bought one of the mares – a twelve-year-old named Santorb in foal to Winterhalter – for four hundred guineas, for the Royal Stud. The foal was useless, but Santorb's next foal, by Hyperion, was Avila who won over six thousand pounds in stakes as a three-year-old. Sent to stud Avila produced Sierra Nevada, Alesia, Spanish Court and Almeria, who after winning at Royal Ascot went on to win the Yorkshire Oaks and the Park Hill Stakes at Doncaster. It was intended to retire Almeria to stud at the end of her three-year-old career, but eventually she was put back into training as a four-year-old. By the end of 1958 she had a decided will of her own, and in the Doncaster Cup she blatantly refused to go past her stable companion and pacemaker Agreement who proceeded to win at the undignified odds of 25–1. Agreement also won the Doncaster Cup for the Queen in 1959 but this time at odds of 7–2. Agreement is now a hack at Windsor, and is a particular favourite of Princess Margaret, who frequently rides him. Occasionally he has found himself back on a race-course, but in an unusual capacity – that of starter's hack at the Ascot meetings!

In 1958 Pall Mall's victory in the Two Thousand Guineas gave Her Majesty another Classic victory. Unfortunately a heavy cold prevented her, on doctor's advice, from seeing the race and leading in her second Classic winner. Pall Mall had been unimpressive when fourth to Aggressor at Kempton on Easter Saturday, and although he had won the Thirsk Classic Trial, his trainer Boyd-Rochfort fancied him at Newmarket less than his other runner, the American-bred Bald Eagle. Malapert, Pall Mall's dam, had been bought by King George VI for a hundred guineas at the 1949 Newmarket December sales. She never won a race, or bred a winner, prior to being sold at the 1955 Newmarket December sales for nine hundred and ten guineas in foal to Palestine. Luckily for the Queen her chestnut foal, also by Palestine, was retained – that foal being Pall Mall. Pall Mall was ultimately sold and now stands at the Bally-kisteen Stud, founded in 1901 by theatrical impresario George Edwards.

The good fortune which enabled the Queen to enjoy great success on the Turf during the first decade of her reign, waned in the first part of the second decade. Inexplicably nothing seemed to go right, despite the patience, care and attention lavished on her race-horses. Yet her enthusiasm never waned, and despite the disappointments brought by the sudden death of Doutelle, there was always the consolation of the success at stud of Aureole and the exploits of his offspring throughout the world. In May 1967 Her Majesty made an informal and private visit to the stud farms of Normandy. Her French hosts, including Baron Guy de Rothschild and M Francois de Brignac, showed her such famous stallions as Exbury, Baldric, Nasram and Sicambre, and were as appreciative as all others of her knowledge of the bloodstock industry. A year later in July 1968 she sent Hopeful Venture – a son of Aureole – to race at Saint Cloud in the Grand Prix. Hopeful Venture's victory was a momentous occasion acclaimed by the French racegoers, and may well be the forerunner of more victories in the royal colours of 'purple, gold braid, scarlet sleeves, black velvet cap with gold fringe' both on the Continent and in America. Royal race-horses have had many triumphs and disappointments throughout the past four hundred years, but few victories more popular than Hopeful Venture's in France. It ranks with the achievements of Persimmon, Diamond Jubilee, Scuttle and Limelight – all of whom had the honour and distinction of having been 'bred for the purple'.

APPENDIX I

Foundation Mares at the Sandringham Stud

Mare	Breeding	Breeder	Vendor	Year Born
Lilian	Wingrave–Lady Blanche	G Savile	Lord Wolverton	1869
Skelgate Maid	Speculum–Habit	G S Thomson	G Savile	1875
Fluster	Young Melbourne–Makeshift	Lord Wolverton	Lord Wolverton	1875
Marie Agnes	Macaroni–Belle Agnes	Sir Tatton Sykes	C Chomeley	1877
Hazy	Hermit–Fog	C G Carew Pole	F Archer	1880
Fanchette	Speculum–Reticence	T E Walker	Lord Wolverton	1880
Poetry	Petrarch–Music	Duke of Hamilton	Duke of Hamilton	1881
Perdita II*	Hampton–Hermione	Lord Cawdor	Lord Cawdor	1881
Cyclopedia	Blair Athol–The Martyr	J J Mackenzie	J J Mackenzie	1883
Lady Peggy	Hermit–Belle Agnes	Sir Tatton Sykes	Sir Tatton Sykes	1884
Welfare	Doncaster–Lily Agnes	Duke of Westminster	Duke of Westminster	1884

* See following page for Stud and Turf record

Perdita II

STUD RECORD

1888	Bay or brown colt Derelict	by Barcaldine
1889	Bay filly Barracouta	by Barcaldine
1890	Barren	to Minting
1891	Brown cold Florizel II	by St Simon
1892	Barren	to Galopin
1893	Bay colt Persimmon	by St Simon
1894	Bay colt Farrant	by Donovan
1895	Bay filly Azeeza (died)	by Surefoot
1896	Brown colt Sandringham	by St Simon
1897	Bay colt Diamond Jubilee	by St Simon
1898	Slipped foal	to St Simon
1899	Bay filly Nadejeda	by St Simon
	and died after foaling	

TURF RECORD

1883	Won Selling Stakes, Goodwood	£112
	Won Sweepstake, Newmarket	127
	Won Chesterfield Nursery Stakes, Derby	975
1884	Won Great Cheshire Handicap	455
	Won Ayr Gold Cup	290
1885	No victories	Nil
1886	Won Great Cheshire Handicap	460
	Dead heat with Middlethorpe for Liverpool Cup	650
		£3,069

Fees Earned by King Edward VII's Stallions

	PERSIMMON		FLORIZEL II		DIAMOND JUBILEE	
	fee 300 gns		fee 100 gns to 1901 200 gns in 1902 300 gns from 1903		fee 300 gns	
	Public	Private	Public	Private	Public	Private
	£	£	£	£	£	£
1897	——	——	2,520	315	——	——
1898	6,930	1,575	3,497	315	——	——
1899	10,710	2,520	4,226	105	——	——
1900	10,395	2,520	4,147	315	——	——
1901	10,560	2,835	4,410	210	——	——
1902	11,025	2,205	9,030	——	7,560	1,890
1903	11,340	2,205	13,230	315	11,655	1,260
1904	11,025	2,205	11,079	315	10,290	630
1905	10,920	1,260	10,762	315	8,085	945
1906	11,970	1,265	11,917	——	7,140	315
1907	12,495	945	5,932	630	——	——
1908	——	——	5,460	1,260	——	——
1909	——	——	1,890	630	——	——
	107,370	19,530	88,100	4,725	44,730	5,040

APPENDIX IV

Mares at Sandringham 1935

ON THE DEATH of HM King George V the following twenty brood mares were at the Royal Stud at Sandringham:

Blairtoi (1922): By Santoi out of Blair Bridge, by Bridge of Earn. Bred by Mr P H Madden. Bought by Lord Woolavington as a 4-year-old for 1,100 gns. Purchased for King George when carrying a foal, Keen Air, by Coronach, at the December Sales of 1933 for 250 gns.

Catherine (1926): By Swynford out of Neuve Chapelle, a half-sister to Friar Marcus by Sunstar out of Prim Nun, by Persimmon. Bred by King George.

Convent (1932): By Friar Marcus out of Shanogue, a William the Third mare who also produced Jacobite, Patrick, Colleen, Shandrydan and Shamrock, and was from Isleta, by Isinglass. Bred by King George, who bought her dam for 1,700 gns from the Compton Stud in 1923.

Fairy Story (1926): By Captain Cuttle out of Fairy Glen, a Torpoint mare. Fairy Story was bred by King George, who bought her dam from Mr Russell Swanwick of Cirencester.

Foxy Gal (1928): By Sir Gallahad III, out of Filante, a daughter of Sardanapale. Bred in America.

Frankly (1925): A half-sister to Blenheim, King Salmon and His Grace, by Franklin out of Malva, by Charles O'Malley from Wild Arum, by Robert le Diable. Bred by Lord Carnarvon, and sold as a yearling for 710 gns.

Frivole (1929): By Friar Marcus from Torpille, a French-bred mare who was by Negofol out of Toque II, by Rock Sand. Frivole was bred by King George.

Judith (1929): By Colorado from Judea, a Roi Herode mare who won the Irish Oaks and was out of Sacrifice, by Symington. Bred by Captain C Moore.

Kitcat (1932): By Gainsborough from Catherine. Bred by King George.

Madame Teddy (1926): By Teddy out of Peg o' My Heart, by St Frusquin from Naughty Jill, by Cyllene. Bred in France, Madame Teddy was bought by King George at the December Sales for 850 gns.

Ocean Nymph (1931): By Beresford from Ellel, a daughter of the

276

Two Thousand Guineas winner Louvois. Bred by Mr H S Gill, Ocean Nymph made 660 gns as a yearling at Doncaster.

Papilla (1926): By Papyrus out of Mitylene. Bred by Mr Hornung, and after being sold for 500 gns was sold to King George at the December Sales for 800 gns.

Picardy (1918): A half-sister to Runnymede, by Picton out of Saint's Mead, a St Simon mare who, like Mead and Chatsworth, was out of Meadow Chat, by Minting. Bred by King George.

Picquet (1930): By Knight of the Garter out of Picardy. Bred by King George.

Polish Air (1933): By Lemberg from Vain Air by Ayrshire out of Vane an own sister to Flying Fox. Bred by King George.

Sansa (1929): By Sansovino from Limelight's half-sister Aloysia, by Lemberg out of Vervaine, a daughter of Louviers from Vain Air. Bred by King George.

Sparkling Gem (1922): By Buchan out of Beautiful Star, by Tarporley from Bonnie Jessie, by Tyrant. Bred by Mrs Craddock and was bought by King George as a yearling for 540 gns.

Stained Glass (1917): By Tracery out of Saint's Mead. Bred by King George she is the dam of Mosaic; the One Thousand Guineas winner Scuttle; Glastonbury, Glass Cutter, Ashridge, Vitrics and the two-year-old Coronach filly Nenia.

Wine Press (1928): By Sansovino out of Neuve Chapelle. Bred by King George.

Wireless (1924): By Hurry On out of Vain Air the dam of Fox Earth and Marconi, bred by King George.

APPENDIX V

Her Majesty's Brood Mares at 31st December 1967

Name	Foaled	Sire	Dam
Betaway	1950	Ocean Swell	Cassia
Mulberry Harbour	1954	Sicambre	Open Warfare
Almeria	1954	Alycidon	Avila
Alesia	1955	Alycidon	Avila
Ibrox	1956	Big Game	Northern Hope
Near Miss	1957	Nearco	Beginner's Luck
Highlight	1958	Borealis	Hypericum
Arbitrate	1959	Arbar	Above Board
Amicable	1960	Doutelle	Amy Leigh
Guinea Sparrow	1960	Grey Sovereign	Parakeet
Asturia	1961	The Phoenix	Spanish Court
Eucumbene	1962	Sica Boy	Hypericum
Kitimat	1962	Preciptic	Maple Leaf
Menai	1962	Abernant	Stroma
Altruist	1963	Above Suspicion	Alesia
Daisy Chain	1963	Darius	Casual
Tortola	1965	Narrator	Avila

Bibliography

The Jockey Club and its Founders by Robert Black, Smith, Elden & Co, 1891

British Turf by J C Whyte, Henry Colburn, 1840

History of the British Turf by J Rice, Sampson, Low & Co. 1879

Mrs Fitzherbert and George IV by W H Wilkins, Longmans & Co, 1905

Henry Chaplin by Marchioness of Londonderry, Macmillan & Co, 1826

Genius Genuine by Sam Chifney, 1804

Newmarket by Frank Siltzer, Cassell, 1923

George the Fourth by Shane Leslie, Benn Limited, 1926

Royal Newmarket by R C Lyle, Putnam, 1945

Book of Sports by Pierce Egan, T T Tegg, 1832

Eclipse and O'Kelly by T A Cooke, Wm Heinemann, 1907

Anne by Neville Connell, Thornton Butterworth, 1937

Lady Sarah Lennox by E R Curtis, W H Allen

Letters of Horace Walpole ed Peter Cunningham, John Grant, 1906

Greville Diary ed P W Wilson, Wm Heinemann, 1927

Royal Ascot by Cawthorne and Herod, A Treheme, 1902

Kings of the Turf by Thormanby, Hutchinson, 1898

A History of the English Turf by T A Cooke, Virtue and Co, 1801

Queen Victoria by Sydney Lee, Smith, Elden & Co, 1902

The King's Race-horses by Edward Spencer, John Long, 1902

King Edward VII by Sir Philip Magnus, John Murray, 1964

King Edward VII as a Sportsman by A E T Watson, Longman's, 1911

The Derby Stakes by R Mortimer, Cassell, 1962

History of Steeplechasing by M Seth-Smith, P Willett, R Mortimer and J Lawrence, Michael Joseph, 1966

Edward VIII – His Life and Reign by Hector Bolitho, Eyre and Spottiswoode, 1937

My Memories by Lord Suffield, Herbert Jenkins, 1915

Things I Shouldn't Tell Anon, Everleigh, Nash, 1924

What I Know by C W Stamper, Mills and Boon, 1913

Personal Letters of King Edward VII by J P C Sewell, Hutchinson, 1931

A Trainer to Two Kings by Richard Marsh, Cassell, 1925

As We Were by E F Benson, Longman's, 1930

Epsom and The Dorlings by E E Dorling, Stanley Paul, 1938
My Racing Reminiscences by Joe Childs, Hutchinson, 1952
All That I Have Met by Beddington, Cassell, 1929
King George V by Sir George Arthur, Jonathan Cape, 1929
History of the English Turf by T H Browne, Virtue, 1931
Correspondence of George, Prince of Wales by Professor Aspinall,
    cvo, ma, d litt, Cassell
Post and Paddock by The Druid, Frederick Warne
Reminiscences and Recollections, by Gronow, J Nimmo, 1892
The Queen and the Turf by Helen Cathcart, Stanley Paul, 1959
Famous Gentlemen Riders at Home and Abroad by Voight,
    Hutchinson, 1926
History of Racing Calendar and Stud Book by C M Prior, Sporting
    Life, 1926
Bloodstock Breeders Review
Dictionary of National Biography
Sporting Life
The Times
Racing Calendar
The Sporting Magazine
Bailey's Magazine
Racing Illustrated

Index